Ex Libris

Peter Sisario

The Broadcasters

By Red Barber

THE BROADCASTERS

WALK IN THE SPIRIT

RHUBARB IN THE CATBIRD SEAT
with Robert Creamer

THE RHUBARB PATCH

THE
BROADCASTERS

Red Barber

New introduction by
Larry King

A DA CAPO PAPERBACK

Library of Congress Cataloging in Publication Data

Barber, Red, 1908–
  The broadcasters.

  (A Da Capo paperback)
  Reprint. Originally published: New York: Dial Press,
1970.
  Includes index.
  1. Barber, Red. 1908–   . 2. Sportscasters—
United States—Biography. 3. Radio broadcasting of
sports—United States—History. I. Title.
GV742.42.B34A33   1986   070.4'49796'0924 [B]   85-23261
ISBN 0-306-80260-0 (pbk.)

This Da Capo Press paperback edition of *The Broadcasters*
is an unabridged republication of the edition published in
New York in 1970, here supplemented with a new introduction by
Larry King, and a new preface by the author.

Published by Da Capo Press, Inc.
A Subsidiary of Plenum Publishing Corporation
233 Spring Street, New York, N.Y. 10013

PREFACE TO THE DA CAPO EDITION

I wrote *The Broadcasters* as a tribute to, and an informal history of, the first radio sports announcers. I didn't think then, and I don't think now, that Graham McNamee, Ted Husing, and the others should be forgotten. In this highly commercial era of television, we look and listen to an endless stream of sports events and multiple sports announcers. We don't know or care how it began in radio, who prepared the way, who paid the price. There has been pitifully little written about these pioneers. None of them got much money, and announcers today do not work the hours, days and nights, that the radio pioneers did, and did gladly.

Since 1970, when this book was first published, drastic changes have overtaken sports and sports broadcasting. Television dominates with its money and coverage. Athletes have unions and agents. There are free agents. Certain wealthy owners have egos that match their bank accounts. Strikes by players and umpires have become almost routine. Cheating threatens college athletics, drugs the professional ranks. And announcers themselves can command rich contracts.

These changes may well be another book. *The Broadcasters* takes you up to 1970, which I look back on as a much simpler time. I am grateful I came along in 1930 and stopped being a broadcasting hobo in 1966. This book contains something of broadcasting history and something of my philosophy.

— RED BARBER
Tallahassee, Florida
July, 1985

INTRODUCTION TO THE DA CAPO EDITION

In an age of high-jinx electronics and flashy hairdos and anchormen who yell at you and show wrestling highlights and pass them off as sports and former athletes who make six-figure salaries while they learn a profession at our expense, there is the constant joy of Walter Lanier "Red" Barber, a man who should be declared a national treasure.

You are about to wander through priceless pages. Written in a style as crisp as one of his broadcasts, Red has woven his own brilliant autobiography in with his thoughts about others in the profession. It makes for nonstop reading. First published in 1970, *The Broadcasters* was then—and it is more so now—the definitive book about the profession of sportscasting. I remember that the first time I read it I literally locked myself in my Miami apartment and went straight through. The second time, after being honored to write this introduction, I savored it more like good wine.

All my life I wanted to be a broadcaster, and my first memory in that regard is the voice of Red Barber. I grew up in Brooklyn, born there in 1933, left (when the Dodgers left) in 1957 to begin my own career in South Florida. For all of those 24 years Red Barber was a part of my life. He taught me the game of baseball on the radio. Hearing him broadcast a game was a daily lesson on the use of language. Red made it more than a game. I have often said that he was the only play-by-play person who could make any situation interesting. It didn't matter if the score was 11-2 in the fifth inning, Red had something to offer, something to keep you tuned in.

He was first and foremost a reporter. He was my eyes.

Through his voice, I could picture everything that was happening. In the summer of 1943 I went with my father to my first baseball game. Up until then all I knew about the game I knew from Red. I remember walking into Ebbets Field on a beautiful summer afternoon—the Dodgers were playing the Cincinnati Reds—and thinking that everything, everything was as Red had described it to me. The infield, the stadium, the uniform colors, the way the players moved, the organ music, the smell of that great ball park were familiar to me because of Red's broadcasts.

In this book you will read about Red's adventures in Cincinnati and Brooklyn and about the "big ball park" in the Bronx. You will learn about the business and art of broadcasting. You will learn about preparation and meticulous attention to detail. There can be some pettiness in Red. (He has driven some of his bosses crazy with his penchant to dot all the i's and cross all the t's.) You will quickly learn that Red is as good a writer as he was a broadcaster —no slight feat.

I've reached a degree of success in broadcasting, far beyond what I dreamed of when I lay in my bed in Brooklyn and listened to Red Barber. One of my greatest thrills was the chance to work with the legend himself. In the late 1960s Red had come to Miami as the anchor sportscaster for WTVJ-Channel 4. For six straight years it was the top-rated show in its four time slots. There would be eight minutes of news, five minutes of weather, eight minutes of sports, and seven minutes during which I would interview people from all walks of life. My segment was taped before the program aired. When Red finished his sports news he would throw it to me.

I remember watching from my living room the first night that Red joined the broadcast. He delivered the sports news with impeccable style. Naturally, there were no foul-ups. As Red neared the end of his segment my hands clenched the embroidery of the seat cover on my couch. Then he turned to his monitor and said "Now, here's Larry King." Tingles shot up my spine. I will carry that memory as long as I live, just as you will carry the memory of his wonderful book.

There are some young men around who might be called future Red Barbers: Bob Costas at NBC, Jon Miller in Baltimore. They have all the ingredients for the pie. One of Red's legacies is Vin Scully, who learned at the master's right elbow. They, and all of us associated with sports broadcasting, owe thanks to Red Barber. He is simply the best at what he did. I am proud to be in the same business.

— LARRY KING*
Arlington, VA
November, 1985

*Larry King hosts "Larry King Live" on CNN, as well as his all-night radio show on the Mutual Broadcasting Network. He writes a weekly column for *USA Today* and can be seen every week on NBC preceding NFL Football.

This is for Graham McNamee
and for those others who first went
into a new land called radio—armed
only with carbon microphones.

An appreciation:
Don Hutter of The Dial Press edited
this book. He brought it from its rough outline,
suggested chapters, improved upon its
arrangement, held me to a schedule, and often said,
"Run it through the typewriter again."
He also taught me that writing is editing,
that sometimes what isn't written is
the best writing.

CONTENTS

March 4, 1930 . . .
After forty years broadcasting it is not
for me to say how good I was—and still am.
I determined early to be the best. I will say, however,
I have done more work in preparation for
broadcasting than any other man in my field.

I am quite pleased to be rated as a professional.
. . . March 4, 1970

ONE:
LISTEN—

This is a love song. I can't sing it.
For a good many years I have tried to say it . . .
Maybe in millions of words . . .
in this place and in that.
Sometimes there was a listener.

Let me write it.

Listen—

This is about what two people learned to do many years ago. The scientists can't come close to saying how far back it was. We were all animals then, but when one of us first began to speak sounds and someone else heard them . . . to voice sounds, to repeat them, to reply with them, to remember them . . . to understand them . . . a language—that is when man started on his upward road, when he became a higher animal.

Communication through sound . . . through symbols. Man began painting and cutting some of those symbols on the stone of the caves he lived in. He wrote on the skins of other animals. When he discovered that a reed, a grass called papyrus, could be made into something he could write on, then the brain of man, the spirit of man, his soul, leaped onward and upward with the written word . . . paper . . . printing press . . . books . . . learning was preserved.

But always man in his communication through sound wanted to extend his speaking—and the hearing thereof—beyond the limits of the physical ear . . . but for eons there was no way.

Marco Polo was gone how long? He traveled how far? No one knew for years until he himself returned to tell in his own words. Columbus had to wait for the uncertain winds to blow him back to Spain to reveal to whomever would listen that the world was not flat, that it included other continents and other seas. . . .

Until the time of our grandparents, men had to wait for the news, for the word. Back 490 years before Christ was born, out on a plain named Marathon, the Greeks and the Persians fought a pivotal battle. The Persians were favored to win, and if they did, all of Greece would fall to them. But the Greeks won. Marathon was some twenty-five miles from the Greek city of Athens. The fastest runner among the Greeks was sent to Athens with the magnificent news that Greece would live.

He ran, ran hard. He ran the distance. When he reached Athens he spoke the news. Then he fell dead. Men have always paid a price for the news. Yet, to this day, we still mark this feat of human communication. We remember this man who ran so hard for twenty-five miles. The marathon is one of our track-and-field events, especially big in Boston . . . on Patriot's Day.

Man in his desire to hear the news, in his need to get the news, has always been impatient at having to wait for it. He wrote letters by hand and sent them by the hand of a courier

. . . who ran, walked, sailed, or rode horseback with the news, with the words.

Listen—

Christmas Eve of 1968 we heard from a far distance—so far away we could not comprehend it—a man named Frank Borman, then another man named James Lovell, then a third named William Anders. With our own ears we on Earth heard their voices as they spoke from alongside the moon itself. They read the words of Genesis on how the Earth began. The communication of sound . . . of men to other men.

Listen—

In the early days of our West we had the Pony Express. Our American Indians on the Great Plains were artfully communicative through smoke. Natives in dense jungles developed the sending of sounds by drums. Ships displayed flags. Semaphore systems came into use . . . France began a semaphore telegraph back in 1794. Homing pigeons were used as news-birds. An American named Samuel Morse showed our Congress in 1844 that his electric telegraph worked. It was a miracle, but it was a miracle that required a connecting wire between the sending and receiving points.

The dots and the dashes . . . the Morse Code . . . sending and receiving words. This was the telegraph. It was immediate, but it wasn't enough. The human voice waited to be sent in place of the impersonal sounds of the electrical impulses—and, somehow, the confining, restricting connecting wires needed to be severed.

Listen—

Alexander Graham Bell was born and educated in Scotland. He dedicated himself to teaching the deaf to talk. He came to this country and taught, and his methods are still, by and large, being used. He made the electrical wire of the telegraph talk. He invented the telephone, and in 1876 man's voice traveled instantly over a line . . . human speech by electric wire.

But there still remained the limiting restriction of the

connecting telephone line and the telegraph cable. Somehow there had to be a way to send speech, to communicate through the night, through the distance, over water, through the fog. But only birds went through the air . . . this air we breathed but could not even see with our eyes.

Listen—

Heinrich Hertz, in Germany, around 1886, came upon something that was soon to be called electromagnetic waves. We speak of it today as radio. A few men with nimble minds in Russia, England, France, and in this country were fascinated. Could it be? Something of human meaning could go of and by itself through the air?

About that time there was a boy in Italy who seemed a strange lad. Instead of playing with other children, he wanted to stay by himself, in his room, and experiment with odd gadgets. His name was Guglielmo Marconi. It was he who first began sending the dots and dashes of the Morse Code through the air, without lines, without connecting wires. He began "wireless."

The Italian government would not listen to Marconi, so he turned to England. The admirals of the British Navy listened. They knew the needs of their ships at sea . . . they too had dreamed that ships could communicate with the land, no matter the hour, the weather, the distance.

But this is a doubting world, and we must touch, must see, must hear for ourselves.

Listen—

There was to be a great yacht race in 1899—the Kingstown Regatta. An Irish newspaper, *The Dublin Daily Express,* decided to have immediate bulletins sent to its office by this new marvel called wireless. That did it. The result, the story of this race, was printed in the newspaper and sold upon the streets before the racing yachts had returned to port. Wireless.

In New York another newspaper, *The Herald,* brought Marconi and his equipment to this country that same fall, and had him repeat his wireless coverage of the America's

Cup Race between the victorious *Columbia* and Sir Thomas Lipton's *Shamrock*. In two months it was 1900—a new century. And a new age in sound.

Listen—

Christmas Eve of 1906 there were ships at sea . . . operators on duty with earphones on, listening to Morse Code as it crackled through the night . . . listening to the miracles of wireless . . . instant communication . . . mechanical, but instant.

Suddenly in their earphones they heard a man speak . . . then they heard a song, a woman singing the Largo by Handel . . . then they heard a violin playing "O Holy Night" . . . then they heard a man read verses from St. Luke, and then, this man wished them A Merry Christmas.

Sixty-two years. How much time is that? In my case, it is the actual span of my life on Earth. Is it possible that our three astronauts in Appollo 8 knew about Christmas Eve in 1906 when they read from Genesis on Christmas Eve of 1968? Was it sheer coincidence? Whatever . . . it was an amazing celebration of an event. Sixty-two years.

R. A. Fessenden, an early experimenter with electromagnetic waves, a colleague of Thomas A. Edison, a professor of electrical engineering at the University of Pittsburgh, this was the man who first spoke on radio that Christmas Eve of 1906, who read from St. Luke, and after playing a phonograph record of the Largo, himself played the violin. When you speak of Christmas Eve, remember the ones of 1906 and 1968.

Radio was thrust into its adolescence by World War One; in this first of our mass killings, men needed instant voice communication in order to kill faster. Television, on the other hand, was held back by World War Two. It seemed an expensive nuisance to the armed forces, they didn't see how to use it, and it was thrown into the deep freeze. But when television did get going, it raped radio. Right after World War Two if a radio man didn't get transferred to television, he quit believing in himself . . . he felt he didn't have it . . .

that the men who did were going into television. Radio quit on itself.

Let's just say that radio—this marvelous miracle of sound instantly heard around the world . . . this miracle mankind had dreamed of, waited for, and worked toward for centuries— had no more than twenty-five good years before the blight came. What is the life of a shooting star?

Listen—

On August 31, 1920, a weak little radio station called 8MK, later known as WWJ, owned and operated by the *Detroit News,* made history. It broadcast the returns of the local election, and maybe some five hundred people heard it. Maybe.

More auspicious history was made less than three months later—November 2—when KDKA in Pittsburgh broadcast the returns of the presidential election—Harding over Cox. KDKA kept right on broadcasting, and still does. And Westinghouse, which built and owned and programed the station, also pioneered making radio receiving sets, and component parts in case you wanted to build your own set . . . which a good many people did. You should have seen the lines of customers waiting to buy parts to build receiving sets.

Radio stations sprouted like mushrooms after rain. In the East—early in 1921—WJZ got on the air in Newark . . . and David Sarnoff at age thirty became the general manager and the driving force of RCA—Radio Corporation of America.

Everybody knew who David Sarnoff was. Remember the *Titanic,* the liner that hit an iceburg and sank in 1912? Sarnoff was working for Marconi that day as a wireless operator on public display at the John Wanamaker store in New York, taking part in a publicity stunt. Sarnoff picked up the fading flash of the tragedy from the far-off scene in the Atlantic. He stayed at his post, contacting other ships, for seventy-two unbroken hours.

Listen—

As I did, the afternoon of July 2, 1921. To a man with a megaphone, standing at a window in a newspaper office in Sanford, Florida. The man would be handed a bulletin, then he would bellow it out to those of us standing in the street. After he read what was handed him, he stayed silent for several minutes waiting for the next bulletin. This was how I heard Jack Dempsey beat Georges Carpentier at Boyle's Thirty Acres in Jersey City. I was thirteen, going on fourteen. I had no idea where Jersey City was. I remember that Dempsey won with a fourth-round knockout. I remember also that the manager of the local theater cursed his luck, his judgment, and his loss of revenue. He had bet heavily on Carpentier, not in cash but in booking for that night and the next two nights a motion picture called *The Orchid Man* —a silent picture in black-and-white starring Carpentier. "Now," said the theater manager, "it won't draw flies." It didn't.

Years later, I gained the facts of the history that was made that day as Dempsey methodically, pitilessly, deflowered The Orchid Man from France.

David Sarnoff had risen rapidly at RCA. The initial success of Westinghouse, with its history-making radio station KDKA in Pittsburgh, had startled RCA. It had also made possible the acceptance of some wild ideas from young Sarnoff. Such as a broadcast of the Dempsey-Carpentier fight. This fight was the biggest sports event that had come along in years. It had New York and the country excited. Everybody was talking about it. David Sarnoff wanted this fight as a big weapon in his battle with Westinghouse.

Sarnoff got permission to "broadcast" from promoter Tex Rickard. Sarnoff knew that General Electric had made a portable transmitter for the Navy, which it had not yet delivered. He borrowed it. Then he got Major J. Andrew White, the editor of *Wireless Age,* to organize the broadcast and to announce it blow-by-blow.

Major White and Sarnoff got the Lackawanna Railroad to permit a crew of two electricians to string an antenna between two of its towers . . . and to have use of an adjacent hut, constructed of galvanized tin sheets, in which to set up the equipment. The Pullman porters kicked up a fuss. That shed was where they changed from their street clothes into their uniforms. The porters were so angry about temporarily losing the use of their dressing hut that one of the technicians, a man named J. O. Smith, slept there the night before the fight to guard the precious equipment.

Time has created the tradition that Major White did the broadcast of that celebrated fight . . . that he announced it. He did and he didn't. Smith did it—but then again, he didn't.

White was at ringside. Smith stayed in the hut. White spoke into a telephone to Smith. So—White did the blow-by-blow, and Smith wrote down what White said. But it was Smith who actually spoke into the microphone, carefully repeating what Major White had told him from ringside. The voice that came over WJZ that July second afternoon, 1921, belonged to J. O. Smith.

Yet everybody at ringside said what a fine broadcaster Major White was. So he is beyond question the first radio announcer of a major sports event. However, when someone reaches back into his memory and tells you he heard Major J. Andrew White announce how Dempsey destroyed Carpentier, smile . . . say under your breath . . . "J. O. Smith" . . . and let it go. I've had a thousand people tell me what a wonderful broadcast they heard me do when Johnny Vander Meer pitched his second straight no-hit game. I used to argue with them. Now I let it go. Nobody heard me describe Vandy's second no-hitter. The three New York teams—Dodgers, Giants, Yankees—had an ironclad ban on radio. The game was not broadcast. It was played at Brooklyn. As time goes on, listeners develop amazing memories.

Thus Major White became our first genuine pioneer in radio sports announcing. He competed with Graham McNamee during the political conventions of 1924. He got involved in the beginnings of what later became the Columbia Broadcasting System. It was Major White who broke in Ted Husing. And when White fell ill once, in the fall of 1928, Husing got his mike at CBS and never let it go.

William S. Paley told me that Major White was good, but he never really got interested in the microphone, and soon after Husing spread his CBS wings, White pulled up stakes in New York and went West—leaving the radio scene to Husing, McNamee, Phil Carlin, who worked with McNamee, the Gold Dust Twins, Milton J. Cross, Norman Brokenshire, Tommy Cowan, the Clicquot Club Eskimos . . . and the gathering storm of a national depression.

Listen—

That afternoon in July of 1921 in Sanford, Florida, there were three radio receiving sets. I am pretty sure that was the total. Sanford was a small town then. Still is. And such was the excitement of a radio set then that everybody knew who had one. Dr. Stevens had one, a man who lived out from town on a celery farm had one, and Merrill Roberts had one. Merrill built his. Dr. Stevens was a day-and-night family doctor, no spare time, so he bought his. I don't know about the set on the farm.

The fall of '21 the Yankees and the Giants played in the World Series. It was "broadcast" on WJZ, with the same relay system as was used for the Dempsey-Carpentier fight. Tommy Cowan, a genuine pioneer announcer, sat in the primitive radio shack, listening to a telephone into which a reporter from the Newark *Call,* up at the Polo Grounds, reported balls-and-strikes and runs-and-outs. Cowan repeated what he heard on the phone into the microphone. WJZ soon moved to a studio in New York. Radio was on its way.

Listen—

It's hard to tell young people anything. That's all right. We all have to learn for ourselves. But I'm sorry to see kids today flip on their transistor radios without thinking, listen to the toneless beat, the mumbled voices, and the hard-sell commercials, and take it all for granted. People who weren't around in the twenties when radio exploded can't know what it meant, this milestone for mankind.

Suddenly, with radio, there was instant human communication. No longer were our houses isolated and lonely and silent. The world came into our homes for the first time. Music came pouring in. Laughter came in. News came in. The world shrank, with radio. We heard drama that we ourselves played a part in. We had to imagine what the scene looked like, what the people who owned the voices looked like.

Winston Churchill on the radio encouraged his people. He made Adolf Hitler change his mind about invading England. Franklin D. Roosevelt used radio as though it had been created for him, for his second term, then a third and fourth. No longer did you have to walk ten blocks downtown, stand outside the newspaper office, and listen to a man yell through a hand megaphone.

Listen—

There was this boy who made his own radio receiving sets, Merrill Roberts. He and I were in the same grade. We lived two blocks apart. Merrill was a quiet boy, sort of fat, wore glasses, didn't say much. He was studious, and he was always inside his house. The rest of us were playing hare-and-hounds or kicking the football. But Merrill Roberts was fooling with radio sets.

Merrill was an only child. His folks just gave him the run of the house. He had a special room with parts of radio sets, a table speaker, and a row of batteries. You ran your radio sets on batteries then, and you were always recharging them. Seems so simple today to plug a radio into the wall socket, or easier still, plug into nothing . . . transistor. He had headphones, and there were dials to be turned and tuned. You didn't just push one knob or one button to get the station you wanted. The equipment was always squealing and spitting. There was static . . . some nights less than others, the good nights. People would hear a voice in Merrill Roberts' room say it was speaking in Pittsburgh, and they just plain couldn't believe it. It was too much.

Man had never before been able to sit in his house, twist some dials, and hear another man talking in some distant city.

Most of the early sets had earphones, and this created a new group in society—"radio widows." The husband listened and listened, night after night, oblivious to where he was, lost to wherever he was listening. Men kept record books, got confirmations of out-of-town stations.

Just about when I was halfway through high school, around 1924, Merrill Roberts asked if I wouldn't like to come to his house one evening and listen to his radio. I had never heard one. When I got there, that's when I saw all this equipment in his room and understood why he hadn't been out in the street playing ball with us.

Listen—

You start looking back, sort of watching yourself go by, and you add some of it up. Forty years in radio . . . you swing over, without losing step, into television. Thirty-three years straight announcing big-league baseball . . . thirteen World Series in this country . . . another ten for the Armed Forces Radio . . . football games all over the country . . . Rose Bowl, Orange Bowl, Sugar Bowl, Army-Navy, professional championship games . . . the first World Series after Graham McNamee . . . broadcasts in Europe and from Japan . . .

One of the first books I got to know well was about King Arthur and his Knights of the Round Table. My mother used to read it to my sister and me when we were children, before we could read it for ourselves. I always felt sad for King Arthur, who tried so hard for law, for reasonableness, who had concern for his fellow men. And I came to know how each young man felt when King Arthur took Excalibur, touched his shoulder, and made him a knight. The accolade of knighthood would send the young man out into the world to do great deeds. Deeper than I was aware of, that was how I felt after hearing the radio that first night in Merrill Roberts' house . . . The accolade.

Listen—

That was the first time I ever stayed up all night. I walked the two blocks home in the dawn. I stayed up all night drinking in the sounds of a new world. I had received intimations of a new life . . . I didn't know it, couldn't know it . . . I was excited completely.

A man spoke in Pittsburgh, said it was snowing there, and I heard it instantly in Merrill Roberts' house in Sanford, Florida. Someone touched the keyboard of a piano in Kansas City . . . somebody sang in New York . . . a banjo plunked in Chicago . . . and Merrill Roberts and I heard it instantly. It was sleeting in Atlanta . . . rain in New Orleans. When I walked home in Central Florida, it wasn't even cool.

Listen—

Before we moved to Florida, back when I was beginning my boyhood in Columbus, Mississippi, World War One broke out. There was a military flying field close by at West Point. At the sound of those first airplanes in that part of the world, I would run out of the house, into the yard, and stare unblinkingly at those small, two-winged aircraft with one or two men sitting in them, their heads exposed. But as a small boy I never wished to put on a helmet and fly one of those planes.

The early automobiles in Columbus made a frightening amount of noise when they ran, if they ran. I saw horses roll their eyes, whinny, and break into wild flight. It was wonderful to see those horseless wagons rolling around town. But I didn't set my heart on driving one. I was almost thirty when I finally bought a car.

Our first telephone was something you accepted—my parents would pick up the receiver, talk into the mouthpiece, which was connected to a wire that went from the house to a tall telephone pole that had wires running from it in all directions. That wasn't mysterious—I knew the wire would keep on going to where the other person on the phone was talking from.

But this radio in Merrill Roberts' house . . . people speaking in thin air from everywhere . . . a switching and tuning of some dials—and in came other sounds from other places.

Soon my dad bought our first radio . . . an Atwater Kent table model. There wasn't much you could get then, down in Central Florida, in the daytime. The night was when you got stations, when the reception was good. The later in the night the better. Dad and I used to sit up together, listening, night after night, into the night.

Listen—

Young people today cannot understand what it was like during the depression. In Florida we got a double dose—first the collapse of the real-estate boom, then the national depression. It was the radio that gave us entertainment, unity, an escape in misdirection. In our hard times, radio took our minds off how hard the times were. And they were very hard. Maybe that is why many of us learned to do constructive work. Individual survival, family survival became basic.

There were many voices. This was the era of Gene Austin. We waited for his next record . . . "My Blue Heaven" . . . "Melancholy Baby" . . . "Marquita" . . . "Carolina Moon." The Rudy Vallee Hour was the big show on radio. The first night I walked on the campus of the University of Florida, in the fall of 1928, the phonograph record I heard playing over the radio . . . coming from the windows of the dormitories and the fraternity houses . . . was one by Helen Kane, the Boo-boop-be-doop Girl.

But of all the voices that came over the radio, out of the air, the most exciting one, the one that electrified everyone, was the full, rich baritone of Graham McNamee. When the nation heard him say, "Good evening, ladies and gentlemen of the radio audience, this is Graham McNamee speaking," the nation hugged itself happily . . . waited for something vital to come right into the living room, into life itself . . . instantly.

Listen—

. . . You finish high school, start working at odd jobs around a small town . . . listen to the radio . . . two years go by, and you bum a ride with Andrew Caraway to Gainesville where the University is . . . you might as well work your way through college as work at home as a day laborer . . . you read a ten-minute paper on the campus radio station . . . you read it as an accidental, casual, one-time thing—for the fee of a free meal that evening . . . then, as just another job to stay in school, you begin announcing on the local station, WRUF. Forty years later you are still announcing . . .

The love song is not ended . . .

TWO:
THE PIONEERS

Dean Sidney Sweet of the Episcopal Cathedral in St. Louis used to like to have me leave him a couple of box seats whenever the Brooklyn Dodgers came to town. On the last week of a road trip in August of 1953, we were in St. Louis to play the Cardinals, after which we would go on to Pittsburgh to close out the tour. As a newly licensed lay reader in the Episcopal Church, I was scheduled to preach that Sunday at the Church of the Ascension before a doubleheader with the Pirates. It would be my first sermon in a big church, and I remember asking Dean Sweet:

"Dean, what do you preach a sermon on?"

And he said, "Preach on something you know something about."

That would have been his advice also on what goes into this book, if I had had the chance to ask him. "Write on something you know about."

This, then, will be about Graham McNamee, Ted Husing, Bill Munday, Bill Slater, Harry Wismer, and Bill Stern. I didn't have to look up much material, for this is not a formal history of sports announcers and sports broadcasting. Most of what is written in this book is written out of my head. Bill Paley at CBS was helpful on the material on Husing, and McNamee and Husing both left books behind them. But what I had to write from, boiled down to what I knew of these men.

I got tangled with Graham McNamee early . . . though he didn't know it at the time. Never knew about it. In 1931 I was in my second year announcing on WRUF, the radio station on the University of Florida campus. It was a daylight-operated station . . . five thousand watts . . . educational. It wasn't much of a job on the surface, it had no future. But it was a whale of a training school. I quit college to broadcast fulltime. I had my foot in the radio door.

And I was getting married. The woman who is still Mrs. Barber set the date for March 28, 1931, at Jacksonville, Florida, in Lois and George Treisbach's house on Herschell Street. It was a Saturday, and the time was one o'clock in the afternoon. Yes, sir, I remember that. And I remember, too, when I got back to Gainesville a week later, seeing the write-up in the Gainesville Sun. The heading was—

WRUF'S GRAHAM McNAMEE GETS MARRIED.

I'm sure that Sophie Burkhim, the society editor, intended to pay me a compliment. After all, McNamee was the biggest name in radio broadcasting. But here I was, a nobody, and I wanted full credit for my own marriage; Graham McNamee had enough.

McNamee was a hearty man. When you met him and got the direct impact of his magnetism, you immediately understood the strong, vibrant personality that came surging over the radio. He was slowing down when I first met him, even as he knew that radio was accelerating. But the fire was still there, the voice was still there. I liked him. When McNamee laughed, it was genuine. He had the strength of knowing who he was. He either took you into his life, or else he would have nothing to do with you. He was direct, honest.

Ted Husing, on the other hand, was always on stage. Ted was devious, he schemed. He defied me to like him, with an arrogance he must have thought was the image he had to sustain. I tried to like him. I refused to negotiate with Edward R. Murrow at CBS in 1946 about taking Husing's newly vacant job, until Ted himself told me he had left it. When Ted went blind, was broke, became practically a vegetable in the Burke Nursing Home in White Plains, New York, I knew I should visit him. I had sent some money from time to time to help pay the bills that Bill Paley and the Krindler-21 Foundation picked up. I knew I ought to go over there. It wasn't too far in miles, but it was very distant in emotions.

But I knew him, and I was a lay reader who was supposed to call on the sick. So I went over several times and . . . I still couldn't like him. I felt desperately sorry he was so smitten, was brought so low. He had been so proud. I would sit there and let him talk about anything he wanted to talk about. Then I would take his hand and say a prayer. He said he wanted me to pray for him. Then as I would leave, he would stick a verbal needle into me—a dull needle, not the sharp one he used to work with.

Ted wound up never knowing who Ted Husing was. He didn't like his fellow men, so how could he like himself.

Bill Munday exploded on the radio scene when he shared the Rose Bowl broadcast of 1929 with McNamee. That was the Georgia Tech-California game when Roy Reigels ran the wrong way. Once the country heard Munday with his Georgia drawl, his "crap-shooters formation" for the huddle, and his "Promised Land" for the end zone, he became the most instant success story in the history of radio. I liked and respected Munday, especially after he fought back from alcoholism . . . and won.

Bill Slater and I worked hard at liking each other, but John

Royal, who was running things then at NBC, set us worlds apart. Slater told me in Baltimore one night before a Navy-Notre Dame game, that Mr. Royal had just forced him to sign a new contract at NBC by saying, "Bill, if you don't sign now and get this matter settled . . . I'll call out to Cincinnati and bring in Red Barber to take your place."

Bill Stern came to NBC in 1936. He worked across the street from NBC at the Music Hall, but he hung around the radio studios. He got battered in an automobile accident, lost a leg, was critically ill. John Royal went to see him and promised him a radio job if he'd get well. He did, and radio was never again the same. Stern didn't care what he said on the air if he thought it was provocative or controversial. He never admitted he made a mistake. When Stern would do a football game and name the wrong ball carrier, he would simply have him lateral the ball to the right man. (College football never had as many single and double and triple laterals as when Stern had the mike. Clem McCarthy in his next to last Kentucky Derby broadcast missed the winning horse at the wire. He was an old man, and not well. Afterward, Stern took great glee in telling about Clem's mistake. When Clem was informed that Stern was making much over the error, all Clem said was, "Well—you can't lateral a horse.")

There are a lot of sports announcers who've come, and gone, and remained. We regard each other much like the leading tenors at the Met . . . we sniff at each other.

Many of the early announcers have died. Radio has changed, and drastically so, especially since television came in one afternoon in August of 1939, came in at Ebbets Field in Brooklyn, where I happened to be on hand. I had a run of thirty-three straight years—Cincinnati, Brooklyn, Yankee Stadium. The first World Series Graham McNamee didn't announce, I did . . . and when Ted Husing left CBS, I was hired to replace him as Director of Sports. So I see myself as being a bridge between McNamee and, say, Curt Gowdy. Today I don't think the early men and their microphones ought to be left silent . . . forgotten. Since I stopped baseball play-by-play in the fall of 1966, I have turned increasingly to professional writing. This book is one I've wanted to write above all others. It is much more a personal book than a record book. The broadcasters themselves were very personal men . . . especially the first two—McNamee and Husing.

The day was March 23, 1775, the Virginia Convention was in session, and Patrick Henry had the floor.

"I have but one lamp by which my feet are guided," he said, "and that is the lamp of experience. I know of no way of judging of the future but by the past."

Now think about Graham McNamee. Radio had just jumped out of the laboratories. Somebody put him in front of a carbon microphone, pointed a finger at him, and said, "You're on the air."

There was no lamp of experience for the pioneer broadcasters.

They had no past by which to judge the future. This is what made McNamee and those others so great. Nobody had ever been called upon before to do such work. They had to go out and do it from scratch. If ever a man did pure, original work, it was Graham McNamee.

McNamee grew up in St. Paul, Minnesota. As a boy he had a good voice, and his mother saw to it that Graham took singing lessons. A divorcee, she brought him to New York to further his singing career. Legitimate singing—no microphones, no crooning . . . full voice. A successful concert at Aoelian Hall . . . solo in some of the big downtown churches . . . a role in a Broadway musical. Then, as happens to many of us, he got called for jury duty. This was in May of 1923. He was killing time one afternoon . . . on jury duty . . . and he was walking around the neighborhood. He wandered into the WEAF studios, spoke into a microphone, and was hired on the spot. Later that summer—in August—he was assigned to broadcast the Harry Greb-Johnny Wilson middleweight championship fight. Just like that—go broadcast a big prize fight. The World Series was coming up in October. It was decided to use Grantland Rice, an established newspaper reporter, for the play-by-play, and to put McNamee on between innings for the "color:" talk about the crowd, celebrities, weather . . . fill in between innings.

In the fourth inning of the third game, Rice decided he'd had enough of the microphone, and McNamee was handed the entire broadcast. In his book, *You're on the Air,* McNamee does not mention Grantland Rice by name, only as a "newspaperman." But elsewhere it's written that this newspaperman, this early radio baseball announcer, was indeed Grantland Rice. And years later, Rice himself confirmed it to me, that "once was enough for me for all my life," trying to announce a ball game play-by-play.

So there was the young baritone with the magnetic speaking voice, thrown in to do a championship fight, then a World Series, then football, then coverage of President Coolidge's message to Congress . . . all in 1923. How is that for breaking into radio just as radio was breaking in itself . . . without experience?

In June of the next year, Graham was sent to Cleveland to broadcast the Republican National Convention—another first in radio history. Then followed his assignment to the Democratic Convention at Madison Square Garden—day after day, bitter hour after bitter hour. Two weeks of this raging battle, with two memorable voices heard over the radio . . . McNamee's, somehow holding up under the strain, and former Governor Jim Brandon's, drawling for all the one hundred and three ballots, "Alabama casts 24 votes for Underwood."

Nobody got mail the way McNamee got it. Keep in mind that radio was just starting, that WEAF didn't cover more than a radius of one hundred miles, that there were precious few sets in existence, and that New York's population was a fraction of what it is today. Yet after his first World Series game, some seventeen hundred letters came in to him. After he did the entire Series in 1925, it was figured he had received over fifty thousand pieces of mail. When the Yankees fired me in the fall of 1966, I got some two hundred fifty letters, and I thought I was doing very well . . . fifty thousand fan letters to McNamee for just one week's work! But this is not only a tribute to McNamee's magnetism—it also reflects radio's initial impact.

Not all of McNamee's mail was fan—some of it was pan. He made mistakes. But he had eagerness and quickness, and he kept right on going. His enthusiasm for his work and for his audience was what made him outstanding. But his lack of specialized training, of experience, made him vulnerable.

And Graham was sheer honesty. Rather than try to cover up a mistake or a lack of knowledge, he would laugh, plain laugh, right on the air . . . and the nation smiled . . . knew he was human. Other, slicker announcers would stay away from certain areas they were unsure of, and the radio audience would be none the wiser.

McNamee was a sitting duck for the ridicule of the newspapermen. He was so popular. Suddenly he was the star attraction going in or out of any ball park. The police directed his car ahead of everyone else's. The writers were deeply suspicious, as well they might be, of this new medium of instant reporting, this radio.

It was at this time, this beginning time for radio and for McNamee, that Ring Lardner, who'd spent his life around ballplayers, bitterly wrote, "I don't know which game to write about—the one I saw today, or the one I heard Graham McNamee announce as I sat next to him at the Polo Grounds" . . . there were, of course, no such things then as radio booths. You sat in a box seat in the crowd, with a plank acting as a shelf for the mike.

Perhaps it was natural that McNamee, so great in his day, should be remembered by many of his competitors for his mistakes. One time he announced, "There's a high foul ball behind third base . . . and Gehrig catches it." Writer after writer over the years has quoted this silly error to me and laughed in great glee. Graham had made an unconscious slip of the tongue; certainly he knew Lou Gehrig played first base.

I've made a million such slips—but by my time radio had developed professional engineers and associate announcers who'd spot them and write me a note. I'd correct my slip of the tongue and go on with the business at hand.

Ted Husing, in his first book *Ten Years before the Mike*, positively drooled over one of Graham's major mistakes. It was during the 1929 Poughkeepsie Regatta—a four-mile race on the Hudson River, with nine crews entered.

NBC stationed Graham on a bridge three miles from the start of the race and handed him a pair of binoculars and a microphone. He broadcast the entire event alone. The weather was terrible, boat after boat swamped and only three finished.

Early in the race the M.I.T. crew—rank outsiders—led; then in the second mile, their boat sank. Graham didn't see them go under. He was looking somewhere else, and when he trained his glasses back to where he thought M.I.T. should be, there was a shell rowing away in first place—but it was Columbia.

Graham announced M.I.T. as the winner. Not a soul in the NBC party paid any attention, not an NBC voice was lifted to help him. . . . And can you imagine trying to look three miles down a river from a bridge in foul weather and telling nine college crews apart?

One man was standing close to McNamee. And he could have saved him. This was Edward J. Neil, a trained and famous reporter who later won a Pulitzer Prize. He had resented McNamee being seated next to him at a recent fight . . . had claimed Graham's broadcasting confused his newspaper assignment.

Neil knew the first-place shell was Columbia's. He later told Husing his first impulse was to scribble a corrective note, but then he shrugged his shoulders and said to himself, "It's Graham's story—let him stick to it." And he walked away.

Radio in its fiery newness, NBC in its constant need to present star talent, McNamee's own magnetic voice and enthusiasm, all combined to burn him up—in nineteen years. NBC scheduled him for everything. He had to announce opera and concert stars, political conventions, prize fights, and football and baseball. He broadcast ten different sports on NBC. I don't know how he did it, I truly don't know. He had no time to rest or think or study—he was too valuable to be wasted for one day. He was never permitted time to prepare for a sports event the way the rest of us who followed were given time.

Our paths first crossed in Detroit and Chicago during the World Series of 1935. That was the first Series I broadcast—for Mutual with Bob Elson of Chicago—and it was the first Series Graham didn't broadcast. NBC dropped him from the assignment at the last moment and used him strictly as a "guest." Soon, almost sadly, about all McNamee did on radio was the commercials, and act as a straight man for Ed Wynn on the Texaco Hour. It was on that show that Graham once said "galoon" for "gallon"—and Wynn would make many a laugh out of it at Graham's expense. McNamee, who was one of the first great stars on radio, wound up a comedian's stooge.

McNamee and I didn't get to meet each other at the 1935 Series, but we did the next year, through Tom Manning of Cleveland, one of McNamee's former broadcasting partners. I was working the 1936 Series for NBC, taking three innings a game—Ty Tyson of Detroit had three, Manning the other three.

John Royal, in charge of programs for NBC, had the three of us in his office the morning the Series began. He laid out what he wanted done, how he wanted it done, and then he told us to scat. Manning was deeply devoted to McNamee, and the great man, at the beginning of his descent, was waiting *outside* Royal's office to give Tom a ride to the Polo Grounds.

We came out and Tom introduced us. Graham was easily

friendly and asked if I wanted to ride with him. Did I? We piled into his black Cadillac, McNamee driving and talking as though he'd known me all my life.

. . . Red Barber, twenty-eight years old, riding uptown to the Polo Grounds to broadcast on NBC the World Series between Bill Terry's Giants and Joe McCarthy's Yankees . . . riding in the front seat of a big black Cadillac coupe . . . between Tom Manning and Graham McNamee . . . and every cop waving to McNamee.

There was still no radio booth at the ball park—just that plank in front of a couple of box seats in the upper deck. The boxes were separated only by a small link chain. Everybody sat shoulder to shoulder. Right against my left shoulder, in the next box—but it might as well have been a million miles away from the mike—a silent spectator, was McNamee.

Manning had the first three innings. Tyson did the middle three. I finished.

An announcer must above everything else concentrate. I had my mind on nothing but that assignment. I'd long forgotten that McNamee was next to me. I was staring down at the field. I had to see every pitch, put down every play in my scorebook, hear every word Manning and Tyson said. I was ready, trained, and coldly eager for my New York debut. This was big work. This was my business.

The seventh inning started and so did I. The balls and the strikes . . . the hits and the runs . . . the changing of the players . . . and I drew it all down into that single microphone on that temporary shelf in the upper deck at the Polo Grounds . . . *"one microphone,"* that is what it all finally boils down to. You can't think about how many stations are hooked together, how many millions are listening. You think only of that one microphone. You and it. One.

The signal came between innings to pause briefly for station identification. I gave the cue, went silent, and started to recheck the figures in my scorebook.

A hand took my elbow and turned me to the left. McNamee said the only words he spoke all during that game.

"Kid," the warm voice said, "kid, you've got it."

That day was the only time I was ever with him. He died not too long afterward—in May 1942, of an embolism of the brain, age fifty-three. He'd lived a thousand years.

I've been trying to say something about a great man, and about what he did. He shouldn't be forgotten. But how do you capture him and bring him to life for a generation nurtured on the machinelike sameness of television? On radio that is merely transistor rock-and-roll?

Heywood Broun wrote this around 1926 or 1927: "After listening to others, and then to Graham McNamee of our local WEAF, I feel terribly proud to be a New Yorker. And not to be provincial, McNamee justified the whole activity of radio broadcasting. A thing may be a marvelous invention and still dull as ditch water. It will be that unless it allows the play of personality. A machine amounts to nothing much unless a man can ride. Graham McNamee has been able to take a new medium of expression and through it transmit himself— to give out vividly a sense of movement and of feeling. Of such is the kingdom of art."

I have said for many years . . . no argument . . . no contest —the greatest sports announcer we ever had was Graham McNamee. How he did what he did when he did . . . suddenly . . . completely unprepared . . . is to me a miracle. I have always contended that seventy-five to ninety percent of a play-by-play broadcast is done before you get to the booth . . . done by deep and thorough pregame preparation.

Graham McNamee . . . the first sports announcer . . . no preparation . . . took a carbon microphone, walked into the stadium, sat down . . . told the nation what it was waiting to hear and had never heard before . . . told them about ten different sports. I concentrated on two—baseball and football— and I thought I had my hands full.

His sign-off was distinctive. "This is Graham McNamee speaking—good-night all." I don't know what's on his tombstone, but those words would read well on it, wouldn't they?

·   ·   ·

Ted Husing is a hard fellow for me to write about—he had a great career, helped build a great network, helped establish the Orange Bowl, blew his money, and had a terrible ending. And through it all, he had a way of making it difficult for you to like him.

Ted grew up around New York and never got over the fact that he hadn't gone to college. He tried a series of jobs, and nothing went well until he won an announcer's audition at WJZ, New York, in September of 1924. Graham McNamee was already famous, and Ted was to spend his life trying to outdo Graham.

This audition had been advertised, and Ted won it from a field of 619 competitors . . . radio stations in those days held talent auditions regularly. They were rough . . . experienced announcers came from all over the country, and at their own expense.

Husing began learning his trade. He worked at WRC in Washington, then WHN in New York, then up to Boston in 1927. He signed with CBS on Christmas Day of 1927 and stayed with the network until July of 1946 when he went to WHN as a disc jockey—for more money. He always needed money.

McNamee had no chance to learn or perfect a technique of announcing sports. Husing had, and he did. He broke in with Major J. Andrew White, hung around with coaches, had the time to go to practice, and got an assistant at CBS named Les Quailey who could make any announcer look and sound good. Quailey has never gotten the proper credit for being Husing's "brains." Jimmy Dolan followed Quailey, then Walter Kennedy—Ted had three good ones who covered for him and planned for him and worked for him his entire career.

Quailey left Husing in the late thirties to head the sports department for N. W. Ayer . . . supervise football and baseball for Atlantic Refinery. He retired recently. Dolan went from CBS to NBC and back to CBS as Director of Sports-Radio. He retired recently. Kennedy is today the headman of the National Basketball Association. To this day, their loyalty to Ted is one hundred percent.

Ted Husing left more information about himself than did any of the other pioneer sports announcers . . . two books. He and I were contemporary, and of all the men I'm writing about, I guess I knew Husing the best, had the most to do with him.

When you sit down to write a book, you wish to be accurate, but above that, you wish to be fair. Having mixed emotions about Ted, I wanted what I had written about him checked by an expert . . . by a third party. Bill Paley at CBS was the ideal man, so late in 1967, when I was in New York for several days, I telephoned him and made an appointment to meet in his office.

William S. Paley is one major radio-television executive who spans his network's history as the top program man. David Sarnoff early worked his way up at NBC—but years ago left its programing to other people. NBC has had an almost bewildering succession of presidents and general managers and program directors and vice-presidents. ABC was created late in the game when the government made NBC get rid of one of its two networks . . . but Bill Paley has always been on top of his programs and his programing personnel.

Mr. Paley received me pleasantly, and while I sat in his tastefully expensive office on the thirty-fifth floor of his prize-winning building, he read my first draft on Ted Husing. Then he began talking.

"You have it that Ted came to CBS on Christmas of 1927. I wouldn't recall just when he came, but he was here, already here, when I bought the network in 1928. So, I didn't hire him. He was a sort of office manager, and not a very good one.

"Major Andrew White was doing our sports, and he was excellent. He had done the Dempsey-Carpentier prize fight and was famous for it. White was scheduled to do a football game in Chicago in the fall of 1928, my first year here, and he fell suddenly ill.

"On Thursday morning, Husing came bouncing into my office and said, 'Andy is sick and can't go to Chicago. Send me.'

"So I sent him . . . and he was an instant success. Major White never tried much anymore, he was interested in other things. Husing was a sensation. He did all our sports from then on.

". . . and that's how I got around one of my first personnel problems at CBS. . . . I got a sports announcer and at the same time got rid of a poor office manager."

Husing was just right for Paley. Ted was eager, brash, didn't count the working hours and would rather get an exclusive on McNamee and NBC than go to "21"—and he made "21" more of his home than he did where he was supposed to live. It was "21" that gave Ted status, or he thought it did, and he made it his headquarters. When Ted was ill and broke, it was "21"—and Bill Paley—who paid his hospital and nursing home bills.

Husing was of immense value to Paley and to CBS. Ted made his football broadcasts sound more important than they were. He claimed the entire United States for himself and for CBS. You played ball with Husing or else—he didn't hesitate to draw a bead on you. It was Husing who said on the air that Barry Wood of Harvard—a great halfback—was "putrid," the way he was performing in a game. Harvard barred him for a while, but Paley backed up Husing to the hilt . . . and Harvard backed down.

Ted on the 1934 World Series freely criticized the work of the umpires, and the Commissioner of Baseball, Judge Landis, barred him from the 1935 Series. Paley appealed to the Commissioner, but the Judge never gave an inch, and Husing was through broadcasting baseball.

In the early formative years of CBS, Husing gave everything he had. He had much to give. He had polish, diction, command, and a smooth voice. Some people felt the voice was slick, without depth and variety, but it was a famous and a potent voice.

It was Husing who gave the Orange Bowl in Miami its national stature. McNamee was famous for his NBC broadcasts of the Rose Bowl. Graham used to love those low mountains that fringed Pasadena, and he talked about them almost as much as he did the New Years' games. But when Graham began doing the Rose Bowl game it was already a going concern of major standing. The Rose Bowl dates back to 1916.

Husing desperately wanted a New Year's Day game for himself and for CBS. The Sugar Bowl started in New Orleans in an established stadium in 1935—and NBC grabbed it. Ted was fit to be tied. Now NBC had two—CBS none.

Down in Miami, which was a small town then, a post-season game called the Palm Festival started in 1933. The stands were temporary, bleacher-type seats borrowed from the American Legion. The crowd was estimated to be 3500. It was the same setup again the next year. Then some local men formed the Orange Bowl Committee and began dreaming.

The first general manager of the Orange Bowl was Earnie Seiler. He is still in charge, still the guiding genius of one of the great success stories of our time.

But in 1936 the Orange Bowl needed help, the committee talked CBS and Husing into broadcasting their game on New Year's Day. Husing had not been to Miami, didn't know what passed for the stadium, and what wasn't in the way of the radio booth. All that fall of '36 Ted gave the Orange Bowl glowing plugs on his regular Saturday CBS football broadcasts up North and in the Midwest . . . plugs that Earnie Seiler in Miami concocted and wired him.

The Orange Bowl people even paid CBS five hundred dollars against the cost of the telephone line into Miami.

As Seiler told me the story:

"We met the train when Ted came down. He wanted to go right out and check the stadium and the radio booth. And we knew if he saw what we had, he'd have gotten on the next train back to New York.

"So we told Ted everything was in order—no hurry, no problem, we'd take him to the field. But he must be tired after his long trip on the train, and let's go on over to the

Rooney Plaza on the beach, get settled, have a drink, relax a little.

"We knew Ted was a swinger, and the Rooney was a big-league hotel. When Ted got in a cabana, got a glass in his hand, saw the girls around the place, he forgot about going to the football field. We took him around to the nightclubs and kept his glass filled, and every time he said something about going to the stadium, we said just as soon as we had another drink.

"He didn't see where he had to broadcast from until the day of the game. His booth was just a chicken coop, and he had to actually climb a ladder to get to it. But by then it was too late. He had told the country what a 'great' event it was.

"From then on he helped us make it a truly great event. He helped us get good teams. For years he rode in the parade the night before the game and broadcast to the folks on the street with a public-address system."

Ted Husing was a very big man in the growth of the Orange Bowl, and I have dwelt upon it at this length because it is THE example of *one,* the power of radio and *two,* the power of Husing. I found out how large a shadow Ted had cast in Miami—I had to follow him into town in 1946. By then the Orange Bowl was big business . . . 62,000 seats; today it is 80,000.

The first time Husing and I met was the Friday night before the Notre Dame game at Ohio State in 1935. All the Ohio State games were being broadcast exclusively on a statewide hookup by the Ohio Oil Company. However, the national pressure for this one game got so heavy, the sponsors waived their rights at the last minute and allowed the networks to broadcast it. Bill Slater came in on Friday for NBC, allowing himself some time for his preparation. Husing got in well after dark on Friday, too late for practice. Mutual hooked-in to my report.

That evening at the Deschler-Wallick Hotel there was the usual press and radio smoker. My work was done as far as I could have it done until they "set it down and kicked it off" the next day. I was listening to the talk when the Ohio State publicity man, Jim Rennick, looked me up.

"Red, I'm swamped here in this room, and I can't get away. Also, none of the Ohio State coaches are coming here tonight . . . Francis Schmidt [the head coach] has them all with the team out of town. . . . Will you do me a big favor?

"Ted Husing is upstairs [and he gave me the room number] and he is demanding that a coach or me or somebody from the school came up to his room and brief him on the squad . . . you have done all our games for two years, you know better than anybody else what Ted needs to know. . . . Will you go up to Husing's room?"

I went up. Les Quailey opened the door. I said who I was, and he thanked me for coming. Husing was sitting in a chair drinking a highball. He had a rubber band on his left hand, and every so often he would snap this band . . . then snap it again . . . then have another pull at his glass. He was mad that only a kid announcer had showed up. He barely grunted when Quailey introduced us. He didn't get out of his chair.

Quailey started to ask some questions, and I began to answer them. I knew the Ohio State squad, and I knew the Notre Dame squad. I was never so ready for a game in my life. Quailey was trying to write down the stuff, but no matter what I began answering, Husing would cut in and start answering himself . . . "Don't you tell me . . . I'll tell you."

Husing was not only rude and overbearing, he was also profane . . . dirty profane. I didn't take much of that. I got up and left.

I hadn't gone fifty feet down the corridor when along came Quailey.

"Red, don't think anything about Ted. That's the way he gets sometimes . . . listen . . . I need the dope on the squad. I've got to run the players' charts—not Ted. Be a good guy and let me come to your room, will you?"

About the time we got to my room, Bill Slater was on the

phone and he wanted to come up to complete his spotting boards . . . so the three of us worked. Husing stayed like Achilles in his hotel tent . . . while Quailey did his pregame work for him.

There wasn't any particular story about my following Husing into CBS as Director of Sports in July of 1946. In fact, I saw to it that there wasn't any story. Doug Coulter and Husing had tangled on negotiations a year before, and Husing had appealed directly to Paley over Coulter's head. Coulter had even sounded me out for the job, but I had refused to be used as leverage against Husing.

Then Edward R. Murrow was brought back from London by Paley and Coulter was out. Full of honors and achievements after World War Two, Murrow was made a vice-president and placed in charge of news and public affairs. Sports was also in his domain.

Husing was looking for spending money, as always. He was bitter over the growth of the network that had curtailed his broadcasts, his authority, and his income. CBS was now a tough corporation, no longer a small show run by a handful of people. Bert Lee over at WHN offered Ted a job with more money—a disc-jockey job with all the spot-announcement-sponsors he could corral. Ted had always hung around nightclubs and bands and musicians, anyhow, so he jumped at the chance.

I got a call to come see Murrow, and I remember telephoning Husing from Murrow's office when Murrow offered me the job.

"Ted, have you quit at CBS?" I asked.

"Yes, kiddo," he said. "The job's yours if you want it."

I wanted it, and I took it.

I don't know how a man could die more terribly than Husing died. Maybe he had some peace of mind and of soul at the end. I don't know. I hope he did.

He was making big money at WHN. He was doing some football—mainly the Army games—and some horse racing.

Then his health started to go, and it frightened him. He stumbled through a year of failing strength, of blackouts, of fear. Then a brain tumor, and he came out of the operation blind.

This man who had been so proud, so mighty, so free-wheeling, was now nothing . . . almost a vegetable. He shrank into a hole, disappeared into a nursing home. He didn't wish to live. But finally, he came back in the spirit. Finally, he thought he was well enough to do some radio that Tom Harmon and CBS carefully arranged for him at Los Angeles. He did try, that one last time, but he couldn't do it anymore.

Husing's last public appearance in New York was in 1957 when he was the guest of honor at the Tenth Annual Dinner of the Sports Broadcasters Association. Ed Murrow was the master of ceremonies. Ted had been dressed carefully, and he was brought in from the Burke Home. He looked good, and his voice was the old Husing voice when he spoke. And he said:

". . . I no longer see . . . but I hear, and I feel. . . . Tonight I don't need eyes in my head, such as those eyes that used to see all the sports. . . . Tonight, my eyes are in my heart. . . ."

That was Husing's last great moment . . . maybe his pinnacle moment. He worked with Cy Rice on his autobiography, then went to his mother's home in Pasadena, made his last effort in radio on the Coast for CBS, and died.

But he did not die alone.

Husing and Paley had worked together, and Paley helped him all the way . . . nobody knows how much money, how many personal phone calls, Paley put into that final CBS contract on the Coast.

"21," where Ted spent so much of his time and money, raised funds for him, and paid nobody knows how much to doctors and hospitals and nursing homes.

Ted's mother took him home again and cared for him his last days, as though he were a baby . . . which he was again.

All his announcing days, Ted was possessed by the greatness of McNamee. He heard Graham broadcast from the Rose Bowl. He heard Graham talk about those mountains with the shadows on them that were so close to the big game. Ted never made it to the radio booth at the Rose Bowl, but he did get to Pasadena, and to those mountains. He just did get there —to his mother's house in Pasadena—and, the name of the plaque Husing received that night in New York from Ed Murrow's hands?

The Graham McNamee Award.

Bill Munday came from Georgia's red clay hills and tall pine trees. He had the most drawling and southern of all the radio voices. It was the voice he was born with, with a speech pattern he heard all his life, and spoke all his life. He was completely natural . . . an original.

Munday was a pretty good left-handed pitcher for the University of Georgia. He started writing sports for the *Atlanta Journal* and quickly showed that he knew athletics. He had a keen mind that worked rapidly. He had rich recall.

Munday got on the radio in 1928 in Atlanta, doing some of the Georgia Tech and University of Georgia football games. He was an instant hit in his hometown. When Tech went to the Rose Bowl to play California on New Year's Day of 1929, Lambdin Kay of WSB, Atlanta, asked NBC to put Munday on the network broadcast—for a portion of the play-by-play.

This was the first time since McNamee became a national figure that he shared the broadcast of a football game. And as great as Graham was, when Bill Munday took over for the second quarter, this country shook. You were first enhanced by the novelty of the way Munday spoke and the figures of speech that came so easily to him . . . but after a while you realized this man was giving you the ball game, just the way it was being played, plus marvelous color and human characterization. I wasn't in radio, then, and wouldn't be for another year, but I still remember hearing Munday's initial broadcast, feeling that immediate impact . . . forty years later, I can still hear it.

NBC didn't hesitate. They had two networks then, the "Red" and the "Blue," but until this Georgia Cracker exploded into their own loudspeakers they had not found anyone to back up McNamee. NBC signed Munday immediately and started putting him on everything. He was as "hot as a sheriff's pistol," to borrow one of his own expressions.

Munday was a shooting star. Suddenly he was ablaze all across the country. Almost as suddenly his light went out, leaving a few flickers of flame around Atlanta. Soon even those tiny sparks burned out. All went dark. Whiskey.

NBC let him go in 1934—after only five years. He managed to work here and there down South, then silence. The paper in Atlanta wrote him off. He went all the way down, and he was down so long there wasn't a soul in Atlanta that would have bet a plugged nickel on him . . . except his wife. She stayed with him—all the way.

People would tell me they saw him in the gutter—they saw him crawl into places and beg for a drink. He was gone, stayed gone for some fifteen years—and he had been so brilliant. His was the saddest case I'd known at that time, and often the alcoholic plight of Bill Munday, the thought of it, kept me at arm's length from that extra drink. Microphones, Munday, and liquor—it was a cautionary threesome.

But I hadn't met Munday then. He was gone from the action when I hit the major leagues in the mid-thirties, and he stayed gone until one afternoon in 1948.

In the fall of my first year as Director of Sports at CBS, we tried hooking two games together, did it several times the next season, and by 1948 we had created our Football Roundup . . . many games with brief highlights, a difficult technique of high-speed broadcasting from all around the country.

Bill McCaffrey, who was then my agent, sat down in my office one afternoon. McCaffrey, once "an important drinker" himself, had not had a drop in over fifteen years. He'd won his letter . . . a big A.

"You know Bill Munday?" he began.

"No," I said, "I don't know him. That is, I've never seen

him. I know something about him, however—how he drank himself out of a great career."

"Red," said McCaffrey, "Munday hasn't had a drink in two years. He's straightened himself out. He's an AA man, works at AA helping other fellows. He's got a job in the fire prevention bureau for the state of Georgia."

McCaffrey swallowed, then said, "But, Red, he needs one more thing to know he's won his battle. . . . He needs to get a network spot again . . . not a big spot . . . but on a network. He needs that for his pride."

McCaffrey, the reformed drinker, now came straight to the point.

"The next time you're picking up a southern game, put Munday on your Roundup. . . . He needs it. . . . He's come a long way back."

When McCaffrey asked that, I nearly climbed over my desk. I never made a quicker negative decision in my life.

"William, I'm not running this football Roundup as a shelter for reformed drunks. This is a tough technique—tougher than play-by-play. Suppose I put Munday on, and the pressure of going on a network again sets him off, and we don't know it until he's actually on the air. . . . Mr. Paley would kill me, and he'd have every right. . . . No, Bill, I can't do it."

McCaffrey never said another word. He left. And I started sweating. Munday had sure burned himself out. But suppose he was on his feet, suffering and ashamed, and trying to be somebody again. Maybe all he did need was just a little spot on a big network. Maybe. Dear God, he'd gone all the way down.

John Derr and Judson Bailey worked with me. We worked together very closely. We thought together, we believed together. Derr did all the organizing and setting up for the Roundup. He was good at it . . . I called him in. (This is the same John Derr you hear today on television golf coverage.)

"John, McCaffrey says Bill Munday is in shape in Atlanta.

We've got a pickup there this next Saturday. Should we give him a chance? And if we give him the chance, how can we protect the network?"

It was Derr's turn to sweat. He came back later and said his agents in Atlanta had confirmed that Munday was AA. An announcer would be stationed outside Munday's booth during the broadcast, ready to take over in case of fire, and if all went well, Munday wouldn't know anything about this "safetyman."

Saturday afternoon. In a small studio in New York, I sat down for the three-hour broadcast. Now it was my turn to sweat again. Only Derr came in and out of the studio. I listened to the various broadcasters as they reported, kept a time-and-place chart alongside my mike, and switched back and forth around six games, all going at the same time.

I switched to "Bill Munday in Atlanta, Georgia." I sweated. He fumbled around trying to get started. I sweated some more. He hemmed and he hawed, his southern drawl making it sound worse. The big drops now rolled off me. The guy had gone off the deep end. He must have. He threw the air back to me in New York.

I called in some other reports around the country—and sweated. Should I go back to Munday again? I looked across the round table at Derr, and he looked evasive. Neither of us knew what to do. Finally, I said to John, "We've gone this far —one more time." And we sent the air again to Bill Munday at Atlanta.

Old Bill came on as smooth as silk. Just as he got on the air, somebody broke loose for a touchdown, and Munday had him every yard of the way. His voice was vibrant, sure, and alert. He was Bill Munday, broadcaster, back again. That first time on he'd just plain been overwhelmed—so much had happened to him over so many years, so very much.

He went to his grave never knowing we'd stationed a "safetyman" outside his booth. In fact, Derr hasn't to this day told me who that announcer was, the one who didn't have to announce. I guess it's just as well William S. Paley didn't know how we fooled around with the network he'd built so carefully.

After that Munday would come to New York, especially during the baseball season, and would sit in the radio booth at Brooklyn and at Yankee Stadium. Then he'd go home with me. We'd have dinner. We'd talk.

He kept his job with the state of Georgia, and he got back on the broadcasts of the University of Georgia football games. But most of his time was spent for AA. Without publicity, without fees, he toured the land. He spoke at AA meetings. Nobody knows how much work he did for AA, how much grass-roots good he did.

One evening as we sat talking in my yard, watching the sun set over the Hudson River, I asked him what he spoke about at all those AA meetings.

"I just get up," he said, "and I tell them the hell *I lived in.*"

Listen . . . Bill Munday, in my book, was the broadcaster I have the most respect for. First, he was great. Then, he threw it away. Next, he fought back. He beat himself. He died in the spring of 1965, with self-respect. He was sixty-one. At one time he drank like a fish. But he was a game fish—he swam upstream—right into the Promised Land.

That's what Bill Munday always called the end zone— the Promised Land.

McNamee, Husing, Munday—these three always had a glamor, an excitement, a dramatic impact for me. But they were my predecessors; Bill Slater was of my time. Bill was one of my peers, and any mystery he might have had for me was dispelled by working with his younger brother, Tom, at WLW in Cincinnati.

When you think about Bill Slater, you could say, "Here is the classic example of what a radio sports announcer should be." He was a fine workman, with a good education.

He graduated from the United States Military Academy in 1924, having played football as a lineman until he hurt an elbow. After West Point he went into education. He was Commandant of Cadets at Greenbrier Military School. Then he taught math and coached football at the Blake School in Minneapolis.

He came East and took a Masters Degree in Political Science at Columbia University. He joined the faculty at Adelphi Academy, in Brooklyn, where he was headmaster for some ten years, leaving to return to the Army in World War Two. He came out a Lieutenant Colonel . . . and never taught school again.

Bill had the voice—it was always well-modulated, clear, and pleasant. It was the voice of a thoroughly educated gentleman who knew his business—which he always did. He had the appearance—six foot three inches tall and two hundred pounds—with an erect carriage. His grooming was impeccable, stemming back to West Point.

When he was teaching and coaching at Minneapolis, he began broadcasting high school football games in his spare time. He was good. When he came East, he got a chance to work with Husing on an Army-Navy game, and he did extremely well. But it was NBC that hired him.

Bill came along just right for NBC, which in its early days had never thought of a "backup" man for McNamee. Bill Munday, who could have done the job, had burned himself out. NBC with its two networks—it all fitted, just as though it were ordained—NBC had a need, and here was a man tailor-made for the job.

Why didn't CBS hire Slater? After all, he had gone on for them with Husing, they certainly had first crack at him. The answer is found in one word—Husing. Ted shared nothing with anybody for any longer than he had to—and Ted and Bill Paley and CBS were one and the same in the early thirties.

NBC first put Slater on football. In 1936 the network sent him to Berlin to cover the Olympic Games. The next year he got into the business of quizmaster—he was an excellent master of ceremonies. For years, until illness took him off the air, he moderated "20 Questions." This was his real forte.

Before World War Two, when Bill was on radio, his main occupation was that of schoolmaster. He did radio on the side and seemed to do it with little effort. He had a fine mind, and he organized material quickly. He was very much a reporter. He dealt in facts and didn't care where the chips fell, just so long as he announced their fall and their final location.

As one might by now conclude, Slater, with his education, Army background, and schoolteaching, was an independent man. He didn't have bad habits. He wasn't a drinker. He wasn't a nightclub man; he was a man who went home. He did his work, and he did it very well.

He did football best. He did track well. But he found out about baseball, covering the Yankees-Giants for the regular seasons of 1944 and 1945. Football is once a week, and is organized confusion anyhow. Track is quick, infrequent, and without continuity. But baseball goes on day after day, game after game, inning after inning, batter after batter, pitch after pitch. The baseball marathon was not Bill's leather.

By 1949 he was out of sports, into moderating shows on both radio and television, which he did beautifully.

As I said, here was the man with the ideal, classic background and with the vocal equipment. He had brains. He had clear eyes. He had honesty. He did well, but that was all.

He was like a beautifully trained tenor with what they call a "white" voice—he was almost without color or warmth. His light, controlled sense of humor on his quiz shows simply didn't bite enough in sports. He carried an air of slightly amused detachment into the athletic arena, which put an invisible wall between himself and his listener.

Maybe Slater was too well-educated, his diction too precise, his reporting too mathematical, himself too disciplined.

He actually came too early. Today in television, where the demand is for a "faceless" voice that comes in with a sentence, then disappears for the "former-great-star-expert," he would be ideal.

I have strong memories of Bill Slater, the last of which goes back to a World Series in which I was deeply involved, emotionally and professionally. In the fall of 1953, just before the start of the Series, the Gillette Safety Razor Co., had announced that I would do the telecast with Mel Allen. I asked to negotiate my pay instead of taking what Gillette felt free to give me—as had been their custom since they became sponsors in 1939. They told me "to take it or leave it." I left it. I resigned the assignment, the biggest assignment in my business.

The next week my wife Lylah and I were walking into Yankee Stadium for a game, very much two civilians, and standing on the sidewalk was Slater. We hadn't seen each other in two years. Our conversation was brief.

I said, "Bill, you know my wife."

And he said, "Yes, I do." Then he took my hand, shook it firmly, quickly, warmly, and went on. "You're the only man in our business who would have walked away from the World Series for a principle."

I said, "Thanks, Bill." He moved away. Lylah and I went on into the ball park.

Not too long after this, a year or so, Bill was stricken. *The New York Times* said at his death in 1965 that he had been ill for ten years at his home in Larchmont—just north of New York City. I hadn't realized he was so long wasting away. But subconsciously I'd known where he was and what was going on, and I meant to go see him, but I hadn't gone. . . .

Listen . . . "We have left undone those things which we ought to have done. . . ."

Harry Wismer and I were at the University of Florida together. I was on the campus radio station when he came down from Michigan on a football scholarship in 1932. We didn't meet, however, until years later.

He played some freshman football, then when Head Coach Charlie Bachman left for Michigan State, Wismer went to East Lansing with him.

Harry was a hustler. But he wasn't mean about it—it was just what he was, and he was good at it. He didn't have anything in the way of material goods when he started out in life, but he meant before it was over to have some, and if he couldn't get them one way, then he'd get them another. Most people work on jobs. Harry worked on people.

He hit Florida with nothing more than himself, and he started wearing his roommate's clothes immediately—just as naturally as though they were his. He went through his year at Gainesville easily and loudly. You always knew when he was around. He was an extrovert of gem quality.

After his roommate, the next guy Wismer hustled was Coach Bachman. Harry hung around Bachman, built him up, made himself Bachman's man. When Bachman pulled up stakes for Michigan State, Wismer was in immediate stride with him. Harry didn't have to pack anything. He was always ready.

Harry went out for football at East Lansing and hurt his leg. That ended his football hopes, but it also freed him for his more outstanding talents. Bachman got him a job on the campus public-address system, then on the radio broadcasts of the Spartans. That was the last real shove Harry needed, and as he prospered with his football announcing, Coach Bachman saw less and less of him.

Harry made it "good" in nearby Detroit. He got in with a big radio station and its owner George Richards . . . who also owned the pro football team. He was soon broadcasting the games of Richard's Detroit Lions. He married into the Ford family, and he used his Ford connections to full advantage with advertising agencies and radio stations. He acquired stock in the Lions.

Harry didn't have to go to school to learn how to hustle. It was just sheer, native talent with him. He was moving around, everywhere. He was in Washington a great deal, and he was obsessed with being on a first-name basis with big shots, senators, Cabinet members, even Presidents. He had a ton of personally autographed pictures of great men—framed and hung . . . everywhere.

He had a go at radio network football. With his connections and the "deft" way he applied the pressure, he was a cinch to get a microphone. Among the coaches he was known as Hollering Harry. He bellowed.

He used to announce on the network that "there is my friend Dwight Eisenhower," or "there is my friend Bernard Baruch," or any other name that came to mind . . . and often they wouldn't be within miles of the place. But that was Harry. If he had been able to sing or dance, he would have been a natural for the role of Professor Harold Hill in *The Music Man*.

I used to enjoy watching Harry hustle. He was so open about it. He was good company. He laughed. He picked up checks. He was always rolling a big, fat cigar in his mouth. He even looked like a hustler.

He wasn't shy. The night in 1940 before the Chicago Bears beat the Redskins 73 to 0 in Washington, I was sitting in the pressroom that had been fixed up by George Preston Marshall, the owner of the Skins. I was to do the entire game for the Gillette Safety Razor people. Their advertising manager, Craig Smith, was at the table. So was Marshall. Along came Wismer. He never needed to be asked to join any crowd he wanted to join. He just sat down, ordered a highball, rolled his cigar around, and started hustling, right to my face.

"Say, Craig," as he started in on the sponsor, "I ain't doing anything tomorrow. Let me do the game. No fee. I'd just like to be on the broadcast."

Smith said, "Red is our man."

Harry said, "I know that. I don't want his game. I just want half of it . . . you know . . . two voices . . . change of pace." And he turned to Marshall. "George, don't you think I ought to have half of it?"

Marshall said, "It's not my decision. I've got enough problems without worrying about who's going to broadcast."

Then Harry turned to me "What would you say, Red— would it be all right with you if I had two quarters . . . if I had one quarter. . . . Say yes, Red, and Craig can fix it right now."

"Harry," I said, "it won't be all right with me for you to have one play tomorrow, much less two quarters."

And he laughed. "Red, if I was sitting where you are to-night, I wouldn't give away even one play either." He ordered another drink, and he never brought the matter up again . . . but he had tried.

Following George Richards' death and his own divorce, Wismer got a piece of the Washington Redskins after things dried up for him in Detroit. He bought it cheap, got into a loud rhubarb with his fellow owner George Preston Marshall, and sold out for a heavy profit. The papers said that at this time Wismer was worth two million dollars.

Harry was broadcasting in New York, looking around for a big deal, when he came upon the new American Football League. He became one of the founders, taking the New York Titans. Or I should say, the Titans took him. As *The Sporting News* wrote later: ". . . he was up to his ears in the ketchup."

Things became worse and worse. In 1963 the AFL had to pay the salaries of the players the last part of the season. The Hustler was hustled. Sonny Werblin picked up the franchise, renamed the team the Jets, and the very next year NBC started pouring television money into the AFL.

Harry's timing had gone sour. He was just one year away from having a hit on his hands when his money and his credit and his luck ran out. He wasn't seen around much anymore. The old bounce and confidence were gone.

In early December of 1967 it all ended. Harry fell in a New York restaurant, hit his head, and died within several hours. He was fifty-four.

But Bert Lahr had died earlier that same day, and Lahr made the front pages. . . . Cardinal Spellman was already lying in state at St. Patricks Cathedral.

At the finish, Wismer was completely out-hustled.

Bill Stern and I were contemporaries, at times competitors, but we didn't spend much time around each other. I guess you could say we just didn't see anything in the same light.

For many years, Bill Stern was a very famous announcer for NBC. He made a great deal of money. His weekly network radio show for Colgate drew big audiences. He voiced a newsreel. He had books on sports published under his name, as well as many articles. Everybody knew who Bill Stern was. Nobody better than Bill Stern.

Bill has had dizzy highs and sickening lows. He is still doing radio in New York for WOR and for the Mutual Broadcasting System.

He lost his left leg as a young man, and he has blamed that for much of what has happened in his life. He had a terrible time following the amputation, but often he used his plight to get his way, to evoke pity, to escape responsibilities, to slip out of trouble. It was the loss of the leg, however, that settled his radio career at NBC.

He was working as stage manager at Radio City Music Hall in 1934, under Leon Leonidoff. But Bill wanted to get on radio, particularly on sports, and he was continually going across the street to the NBC studios. John Royal was then the headman of all NBC programing, and finally, Royal told McNamee to take Stern with him to a football game . . . and let Stern do two minutes of the play-by-play. Graham waited until a score seemed imminent and gave the mike to Bill. The game-deciding touchdown happened, and Bill described it well. Royal let Bill do part of two more games and then assigned him to do an Army-Illinois game by himself.

Mr. Royal telephoned Stern the Wednesday before the game to tell him that he was putting him on it. Stern immediately called his family and his friends, asking them to send Royal telegrams saying what a great job he, Bill Stern, had done on the broadcast. They responded—and most of them didn't wait until the game was played. It was played, but the broadcaster was not Bill Stern. When Royal got those wires, two days ahead of time, he hit the ceiling. He fired Stern forthwith.

Stern drifted from the Music Hall, drifted from New York, drifted down into the Southwest, where in 1935 he did some local football broadcasts. He got into an automobile accident, smashed his left leg—which got badly infected—and by the time they got him back to New York, there wasn't anything else to do but take the leg off above the knee.

There was no way for Bill to know it as he lay in that New York hospital, but the way things were working out at NBC, the timing was just right for him to get back into radio. McNamee, who had set up Bill's two-minute debut, was increasingly valuable to NBC on the Rudy Vallee Hour and on the Ed Wynn Show, and was finding it increasingly hard to get sprung for football. Bill Slater had a run-in with Mr. Royal over his expense account on the 1936 Olympic Games—both were headstrong men, but Royal was the boss—and Slater quit, or was fired.

Stern was desperately ill, terribly tormented. He thought he was finished. He grew worse. John Royal heard about it, dropped what he was doing, and went over to the hospital. He told Bill that if he would get well, he had a job announcing sports at NBC. Bill got well. Royal kept his word.

So Stern lost a leg, but gained a wide-open shot at NBC. He moved in with a rush, soon was made Director of Sports. Mr. Royal was now being edged toward retirement. Stern ruled with an iron hand. It was all his. He told whatever tall tales on his radio show he wanted to tell—the taller the better. He kept it that way for some fifteen years, until as time passed, television came on, and Tom Gallery was hired by NBC to replace Stern as Director of Sports.

In those days, there was a constant duplication of football coverage by the two major radio networks. Ted Husing, in his abiding jealousy of and efforts to compete with Graham McNamee, started it. Where McNamee and NBC went, Husing and CBS went. And when Stern came along, the rivalry continued. He and Husing had a compulsion to keep each other in sight, do the same game, badger each other, try to embarrass each other. They had their fun and games, like cutting the other's broadcast wires, or nailing tight the doors to a booth.

At times they forgot about the audience in their hostile absorption with each other.

When I followed Husing in 1946 into the post of Director of Sports at CBS, the first thing I intended to do, and did, was put a stop to duplicate coverage of football games.

John Derr and Judson Bailey joined me at CBS. The three of us were CBS Sports. John stayed on the radio side and ran the office. Judson centered on television. We worked very smoothly together. When we did a football game, John spotted one team, Judson the other.

For two years, Derr, Bailey, and I didn't bother checking with Stern what football game he was going to do. We knew he wasn't going to beat the bushes as we did, and should one game get so important that we had to do it, then that was it, whether Stern or anyone else was going to cover it. Also, we were moving toward the multiple coverage that became the CBS Football Roundup.

The Roundup did several things: it got to the listeners—and very fast—all the scores of all the games, including live highlight pickups of six of the top games—it saved us from going down the drain with a game that got too one-sided. It was a three-hour sweep across the country—using a staff of sixty to seventy people—and it eliminated any "filling in" for time outs and half times. It competed with television.

Bill Stern had a hand in our decision to go with the Roundup. I was assigned to do the television broadcast of the 1948 World Series . . . the then Boston Braves and the Cleveland Indians. That was the first World Series on television. To follow the Saturday game, we needed a football game that was in Central Time, so that it would be unlikely to compete with the baseball game, which was played on Eastern Time. We needed a football announcer, and we got Connie Desmond, my partner over at Ebbets Field. Next, I wanted a game NBC wasn't going to do.

I called Stern the first of the week and asked him what was his game. He said he had not made up his mind. I asked him to pick one, and then I would select another one. He said "no," I should choose one. I said I was looking at Army at Illinois. He said he was not considering that one—that for sure, he wasn't going to schedule it. I said we would, and I asked Derr to book us in. We were given booth space at Champaign and were told there were no other radio requests on a network level.

I went off to the World Series, and what happened? Three networks did the game—CBS, NBC, and ABC. Derr told me later that he had no sooner checked into the hotel in Champaign than in walked Stern, with a big wolf grin, and said, "I just couldn't let you fellows have it to yourselves—I had to come out."

After that, CBS didn't have to worry anymore about duplicating a game with anybody. We went for the Roundup. I never did thank Stern for helping us decide to take the plunge . . . but wasn't that some service to the radio listeners around the country? Three networks doing one game on the first football Saturday in October?

Television tore up the entire pea patch. Radio was so big, so dominant, so powerful in 1939 that television seemed mostly talk and conjecture. NBC did the first sports event on television—a Princeton at Columbia baseball game that spring. Stern was the announcer. In August of '39, NBC did the first telecast of a big-league game—Cincinnati at Brooklyn, and I did the announcing.

Stern didn't know when he worked on that Princeton-Columbia telecast in 1939 that he was taking part in something that would shake the foundations of his professional life. The fake lateral passes that were safely invented for radio could not be employed on television.

By 1952 Stern's radio show had run its course. Television was now the Big Apple—audience, sponsors, money, glamor. Tom Gallery moved into the main office of NBC Sports and began calling the shots. Stern got a contract with Anheuser-Busch, quit NBC, and took the beer business with him to ABC.

However, something was going wrong with the fellow. He wasn't a drinker. People began guessing. It broke wide open at the Sugar Bowl, January 2, 1956. Bill was to do the broadcast with Ray Scott assisting. The engineers came to the booth. Scott came. The agency people came. But no Stern. Time got shorter and shorter, and Bill arrived just at air time, and in woeful condition. He signed-on, but couldn't continue. He wanted to hold the mike, but ABC took him off the air . . . and kept him off. Reliable Ray stepped in and broadcast the game.

Stern was on drugs.

The whole terrible story is told by Bill himself in his book *The Taste of Ashes,* written with Oscar Fraley. Bill poured it out to Oscar, word by word, page by page . . . then okayed the manuscript for publication. He had to go to the hospital.

I hope he is cured. I wish him well.

These were the network pioneers, the early giants of radio and sports broadcasting. There were others who were important, though perhaps not as well known—such as Bob Elson, Ty Tyson, Jack Graney, Clem McCarthy, Tom Manning. I worked with most of them, and I'm going to write more about them, too. But first I'd like to go back to when it all started for a broadcaster named Red Barber. . . . I know his story a little more in detail.

THREE:
FOCUS 1

WRUF

I was working as a day laborer in 1928 at any odd job I could get, down in Sanford, Florida. Things were bona fide tough. In 1927 Florida had gotten hit by a depression—two years, as it turned out, before the rest of the country—and by summer of '28 it was hard to get a job of any kind, and when you got one, it was from daylight to dark for two dollars a day . . . and back-breaking. I figured that that way I wasn't going anywhere, I might as well head up to the University at Gainesville and work my way through school. I didn't know what I'd study—but I had nothing to lose. Nothing.

Since that hot afternoon in 1921, when I had stood in the crowd listening to a man with a hand megaphone relay the blow-by-blow reports of the Dempsey-Carpentier fight, radio stations had exploded across the country like mushrooms after a spring rain.

AT&T was in the broadcasting business at the start of things, but in a pivotal settlement with RCA, AT&T agreed to cease broadcasting and just furnish the long lines—and thus the National Broadcasting Company was formed. NBC formally went on the air November 15, 1926 . . . and by January of '27, NBC had its two networks: the Red, fed by WEAF . . . the Blue, fed by WJZ. Throughout all the changes, moves, deals, dreams, plans, battles, and money that went into forming NBC, the hand of David Sarnoff was everywhere.

NBC had hardly set up shop when the foundations of the Columbia Broadcasting System were laid. This new network went on the air September 18, 1927. CBS at the start was very shaky, often being on the thin edge of going broke. The first year was one crisis after another. The turning point was reached in September of 1928 when the Samuel Paley family in Philadelphia, owners of the Congress Cigar Company, saw what local radio advertising on WCAU had done for the sales of their La Palina cigar. They had money to invest, and they had an ambitious twenty-six-year-old son named William S. Paley.

The Paleys put up the needed money and put in William S. as president of CBS. Young Paley immediately brought Paramount-Publix in as a forty-nine percent partner, which solidified the position of the fledgling network. CBS was on its way.

When I got to Gainesville in 1928, I knew nothing about the formation of CBS and NBC. I knew who Graham McNamee was, everybody did, and that was about it. I entered school with one hundred dollars, and just about the day Ted Husing took that CBS football mike from Major White, I started looking for any kind of a job that would keep me in school.

In the birth-pang days of radio, a little five thousand watt station was born on the back-campus of the University of Florida . . . WRUF . . . Radio University Florida. It was just beginning to cry out its assorted noises—mostly records—when I came to town, riding in the rumble seat of Andrew Cara-

way's Ford. As we drove into Gainesville, I saw the tower of
this radio station and thought nothing more about it. Some
of the boys in the dormitories had crystal sets with earphones
. . . they tied a fine wire to the window screen for an antenna
. . . and thus heard the local station. But a crystal set, the fundamental simplicity in a receiver, cost ten dollars at the hardware store. For ten dollars I didn't need to listen to any radio
station—much less this one that operated daylight only . . .
educational only . . . well-worn phonograph records of limited
variety . . . and a few professors droning on and on. There
was to me nothing exciting about WRUF as compared to
hunting for my next meal.

I'd worked two years before I came to college. I was used
to work; in fact, I didn't know there was anything else to do
but work. So—with this job and that job . . . and a helping
hand from two professors, Alan Burritt and Hampton Jarrell
. . . I got through my freshman year. That summer I worked
at a cash job at Sanford, lived off my dad at home, deposited
every paycheck in the bank, and two weeks before I was to go
back to school, the bank failed. The second year I got to
Gainesville with a good deal less than one hundred dollars,
and immediately I started student-working again, harder than
the first year. That fall the national depression hit—men
jumped out of skyscraper windows . . . Black Tuesday . . .
October 29, 1929.

However, I did have a big plus my second year. I had a job
waiting for me at Ma Trumper's eating house. She didn't pay
you money. She did better than that. When you waited tables
for Ma, she fed you. And, friends, when you got down to bed-
rock, as long as you can eat, you are going to be mighty hard
to discourage.

But a fellow also needs a place to sleep, and I got a free one
a month after school began. I ran into one of my profs, Wal-
lace Goebel, and asked him casually what he was doing, and
he said seriously he was hunting for a janitor for the University
Club, where he and a half-dozen other professors stayed. I

told him he had just found one. I didn't go straight back to the club with him. I detoured to where I was precariously holed up, got my belongings, and then dug in as "janitor-in-charge" in return for a free room and bath. I remember gathering my belongings—it was swiftly simple. Laid a sheet on the floor, piled the stuff in, picked up the four corners, slung the wad on my back, and walked off down the street . . . about six blocks.

McNamee was riding the crest of the radio wave. Husing was coming on, Munday was the new fair-haired child. And I was home free—meals, room, books in the library. By now I thought I wanted to be a professor, maybe in English. I was taking a full load of classes, and I had the bear by the tail on a downhill pull. I had it made. They couldn't starve me, and they couldn't freeze me out.

Christmas holiday came, and I went home for a week, then came back a few days early to catch up on some overdue homework. Nothing was open around school, especially Ma Trumper's. The University Club, which was nothing but a rooming house, was open, and I was sitting downstairs at a table one particular morning, about eleven, working on a term paper on one of the James who got to be King of England, when Ralph Fulghum walked in. A prof in the College of Agriculture, Ralph put on a forty-five minute farm program at noon on WRUF, five days a week. He bore down on me like a country hog after city slop.

"Red . . . you're just the fellow I'm looking for. A couple of the men who've written ten-minute papers for today's farm program have been called out of town. . . . Come on over to the radio station with me . . . and read one of them."

"Ralph," I said, still pushing around the notes I had in front of me, "I haven't lost a thing over at that radio station. Not a cotton-picking thing. And besides, I'm busy."

Fulghum was a skinny, tall drink-of-water. He sort of stood there for a moment, hesitating. Then he looked at his watch real sad.

"Look," he said. "I haven't got time to hunt up anybody else. There are three papers . . . I'll read the first and the third . . . c'mon with me, and read the middle one as a change of voice."

All the profs in the University Club were very nice young men. They expected me to be janitor only when I was cleaning up the house, making the beds, swabbing the toilets. The rest of the time they let me be myself—play bridge with them, drink whiskey with them, go around with them. By this time of the morning, I had the house swept and in order, and I was now dealing with Fulghum as an equal. Also, I was fast running out of patience—I'd come back to Gainesville early, I was trying to catch up with some book-and-paper work. My ox was in the ditch.

"Ralph," I said, and I meant it, "I'm busy, and I'm not going out to the radio station with you."

He didn't hesitate any longer. "Read this paper for me, and I'll buy your dinner tonight."

That did it. Ma Trumper's was closed, and whatever I ate that night I'd have to pay for.

"Ralph . . ." and I was already on my feet . . . "I'll read all three of those papers for dinner tonight."

"No," he said. "One will be enough."

Off we went, and I read the paper. So when I started in radio I got a fee. I never did believe in working for nothing.

WRUF had two studios. Actually, it had one studio and a second one that wasn't big enough to cuss a cat in without getting hair in your mouth. The big one had a grand piano and room enough to set up a ten- or twelve-piece band—which happened a half-dozen times a year—whenever a band wanted to broadcast for nothing. There were windows on three sides of the big studio. On the fourth side was a glass panel that opened into the little studio. There they did talks—you could get two or three people in at the same time if everybody stood up. This was years before air conditioning, and the station then was sitting on part of the farm grounds of the University, right amidst the Agriculture College. In the summer the windows would be open, and it was a matter of course that from time to time a cow would stick her head inside, look around the studio, and listen some. And it wasn't uncommon that she would moo right into an open microphone. This was what you'd call primitive, grass-roots radio. I remember one afternoon I was announcing a local ball game—we had the mike sitting on a wooden box in front of me—we were sitting on bleacher-type wooden seats behind first base, right out in the open—and some boys started killing a rattlesnake exactly underneath where we were sitting—a long freight train started going by outside the fence behind home plate—and then part of the stands caught fire. The director of the station told me later I hadn't missed any of it.

WRUF was a great training school.

On that day in late December 1929, as Fulghum and I drove up to the station in his Ford, Graham McNamee was staying at the plush Huntington Hotel in Pasadena, California, waiting to announce the Rose Bowl Game. Ted Husing was all dressed up to the nines, sleeking around New York, wishing he had a Bowl Game to do. I don't know where Bill Munday was—Atlanta maybe. He had done a full schedule of games for NBC that fall.

We drove up to the station over a dirt road, a sand road that ran in from the paved highway that went south to Ocala. We went in the small reception room, and nobody was there. Ralph led me into the small studio, sat me down at the table, moved the mike in front of me, handed me several sheets of paper, and said that when he pointed to me from inside the big studio, I was to start reading and keep on reading until I got to the end of the paper. Then Ralph went next door and started putting the Florida Farm Hour on the air.

The little studio had two glass panels—one was to the big studio and the other opened on the control room where the engineer sat. That was the control room for both studios and also for the transmitter, the controls of which stood exposed as naked as the day the equipment came out of its crates.

The engineer could see into both studios. He played some phonograph records, turned your mike on or off, constantly reminded you that when you talked into the mike you should try not to spit—the sound of spit particles hitting the mike was like an egg frying—and tried to keep the station on the air, which took some doing. This was before equipment was developed that automatically held your station to its assigned frequency. The engineer had to watch needles and indicators, and he was always jumping ·up and adjusting something. Stations wandered so badly in those days that the government had a staff of men going around the country just to check on how far signals got off channel.

As I waited in the little studio for Fulghum to point his finger at me, I couldn't hear what he was saying or doing in the big studio. I could see him, but that was all. This was before we had loud speakers in the studios that would let us hear what went on, and then would cut off when our studio took the air.

After I'd sat there awhile in that little room about the size of two coffins, this man came in from the place where the equipment was—I didn't know then you called him the engineer—or called it the control room. He didn't say "hello," or "kiss my foot," or anything. He just started tapping the mike with his pocketknife, then he turned, and walked out, went back to his chair, and sat down. Just like that. It was later that I learned that another of the engineer's duties was to shake loose the carbon granules in the mike by tapping it every so often with a hard object. . . . The engineer at WRUF was Banks Duncan, a man who was as sparse with words as sports announcers are free with them during a ninth-inning rally.

Finally, Fulghum waved a warning that my time was coming close. Then he pointed his thin finger at me, and I read the paper. It hadn't entered my mind to rehearse it by reading it over before air time. After all, I was performing one specific task for one specific purpose. A free meal. I read the paper. It was titled "Certain Aspects of Bovine Obstetrics." It was a thorough and frank discussion of the subject, intended to be of direct and practical help to Florida livestock people. As I read it, I got the suspicion that the prof who wrote it never intended to be in town on the day the paper was scheduled for broadcast.

It didn't bother me any. It wasn't my paper, my farm program, my radio station, my carbon microphone. After I finished the paper, I got up and walked out of that little square studio and into the empty reception room. I was headed back for the University Club. Fulghum had to stay on for a half-hour to complete his work, but mine was finished. I had done my half of the bargain—Fulghum would do his that evening.

A medium-sized man came up to me as I headed for the front door. He asked me if I had read that farm talk. I said I had and kept on walking. He asked me to wait a minute.

"I'm Major Powell, the director of the station . . . I'm new here . . . and I'm looking for a student announcer to work part time . . . thirty-five cents an hour . . . your voice registered well on the air. How about taking the job?"

I told him I did not have the time to take the job. I thanked him and again started for the door. He stopped me again—he pressed me to take the job. I explained I was carrying twenty-one hours in classes . . . all the school would allow . . . that I had a job waiting on tables . . . had a job as janitor . . . there was no way I could work at the radio station, or anywhere else. Further, I had achieved complete security, therefore, I was in no way interested in the radio station. I walked out the front door and back to the main campus—to that part of the campus where the cows didn't roam.

I don't know what McNamee had for dinner in Pasadena that night, what Husing had in New York, what Munday had in Atlanta. But I know what I had for dinner in Gainesville, Florida. A steak. At Louie the Greek's Restaurant, right on the northwest corner of the square in downtown Gainesville. Louie was a nice man. He had a wooden leg, and he wobbled when he walked. He sold you meal tickets, but if he knew you,

he'd let you have a meal ticket on credit. Nobody will ever
know how many boys he kept in school, and how many punched-
out meal tickets Louie wound up eating himself. There was a
dark-haired waitress there named Christine, who had the
smallest waist I ever saw. Christine was brunette-beautiful—
until she smiled—then there was a side tooth missing. . . . It
was a very good steak, my first fee in radio.

Classes soon resumed, there were tables to be waited on,
beds to be made, floors to be swept. Often, the professors
needed me to be a fourth at bridge. I had met Lylah, and we
spent all the time together we could find. The more I saw, the
more I liked the life of the college prof, and the more I wanted
to major in English. My mother had taught school, loved English, read to us as children. Each day was full. Life tasted
good.

But every so often Fulghum would come in and tell me that
Major Powell had sent word for me to come out to the radio
station and take that job . . . that he was holding the job for
me. And I would tell Ralph to tell the Major I wasn't about
to come.

This went on for two months—until Ralph and I got cross
with each other about it. Finally, he said, "Look—Major
Powell is making my life miserable out there at the station.
I don't care what you do. But, please, go yourself and settle it
with him, once and for all. I'm through being a messenger
boy."

I went the next day. It was midafternoon. I went because
I was sick and tired of Fulghum nagging me about it. I
wanted the whole business dead and buried. I told Major
Powell again—very carefully—that I did not have either the
time or the interest to work at the radio station.

He sat at his desk a moment, then he said, "I told you this
job was part time . . . thirty-five cents an hour . . . the hours
you work. I understand how busy you are. . . . Now—how
much money a month will I have to guarantee you for you to
drop your other jobs and come out here?"

I knew how to end it, I knew just what to do. I would ask him for all the money in the world. That would stop him. I added up in my head . . . "twenty dollars a month and I could eat" . . . "ten dollars a month and I could have a private room" . . . "another five dollars for laundry and odds and ends" . . . "thirty-five dollars" . . . "I'll ask him for so much more than he can pay that he'll throw me out of here." Remember the depression was on. It was root-hog-or-die in 1930.

"Major Powell," I said, cool as an icebox cookie, "you'll have to guarantee me *fifty dollars a month."*

"Good," he said, just as coolly. "You start tomorrow."

I could have cried. There in a flash went my complete security. There went my job at Ma Trumper's. There went my room at the University Club. No man ever walked to the death chair at Sing Sing as slowly as I did the next day to that radio station . . . March 4, 1930.

There is a lot of talk about this being the Age of Aquarius. I don't know if it had any bearing or not, but I do know that Fulghum and I were both born on February 17, 1908.

CINCINNATI

When Sidney Weil went broke and lost ownership of the Cincinnati Reds in 1933, the bank brought in Larry MacPhail, and MacPhail promptly sold Powel Crosley controlling interest in the team. Mr. Crosley already owned radio stations WLW and WSAI. For several years, the Reds' games had been done on a low-powered station, WFBE, by Harry Hartman. MacPhail wanted radio. He believed in it, in its promotional power, in its teaching of the game to women, and he especially wanted his out-of-town games done to keep the fans in touch with the ball club no matter where it went. MacPhail opened the doors to everybody, and his first year at Cincinnati he had three stations broadcasting—Crosley as president of the Reds put WSAI, his smaller station, on the games, and Hartman continued on WFBE. "Oatmeal" Brown announced on WKRC—the only year that station broadcast baseball.

In 1934 I was paid twenty-five dollars a week to come to Cincinnati as a baseball announcer—and I did other announcing chores at the station before I went to the ball park and then after the games were over. At the end of my first year, I was making fifty dollars a week, and with the depression on, to double your salary in one year was a little of all right.

It is my memory that we broadcast only about fifteen or sixteen at-home games in 1934. There was still the grave fear of radio hurting the actual gate, and even MacPhail at the start walked as warily as an old cat in a new house. On the other home games, we did a minute bulletin from the park every half-hour. The out-of-town games were done from Western Union "paragraph one" reports from a studio in Cincinnati. Nobody traveled to broadcast games in those days. The line charges plus the other costs were too much. And we could not get permission to do all the away-games—the Dodgers and Giants refused completely, and St. Louis and Pittsburgh banned Sundays and holidays. It was a far cry in 1934 from the radio-television coverages we take for granted today.

I had won an audition at WLW in 1933, and after four years on WRUF—I had quit college in 1930 to work fulltime at the station—I was hired by Crosley in 1934 to broadcast the Reds' play-by-play on WSAI, as I said, for twenty-five dollars a week.

When I got to Cincinnati, there weren't too many baseball broadcasters around. We were an in-bred group, and naturally we knew a great deal about each other. We had a proud profession in those days, we were creating something new, something exciting, each day was vibrant with vitality and freshness. We didn't make much money, but neither were we constrained, constricted, and hamstrung by commercials, advertising agencies, radio station big shots . . . and television, with a depersonalizing blanket, wasn't even a bad dream.

Harry Hartman was the pioneer baseball-sports announcer in Cincinnati. His station, WFBE, was owned by the Scripps-Howard papers (later it changed its call letters to WCPO). In 1929 Harry started doing a sports strip across the board—fifteen minutes of news and interviews. Any sports figure from Jack Dempsey on down who came to Cincinnati went on with Hartman—the studios were in the Sinton Hotel, as I remember, a completely convenient location for anybody staying in downtown Cincinnati, a compact area of a few blocks around Fountain Square. You didn't call a taxi to move around in downtown Cincinnati in those days.

Harry was basically a time-salesman for WFBE. He got his own sponsors. He was a good-natured, energetic extrovert. He had a limited education, and he used remarkably few words on the microphone. He made do with such expressions as *socko* and *whammo* and *bammo*. He worked day and night. He did fights, wrestling, anything—and in 1930 he convinced Sid Weil, at that time the owner of the Reds, to let him broadcast the team's games.

Harry also was the public-address announcer at Redlands

Field. He sat behind home plate, on the ground level, behind the foul screen, with two mikes—he would talk into the radio mike, with the public address one cut off, until he had to make a game announcement. Then he would talk into both of them . . . simple—beautifully simple. Harry was about five and a half feet tall, and must have weighed in at three hundred pounds. He was roly-poly and had a lot of dark hair. When the afternoon sun got real hot, as it did most every summer afternoon in Cincinnati, Harry simply took off his shirt. Harry was a beautifully simple man.

If ever an announcer had cold reasons for hating the guts of another announcer . . . the way it happened to work out . . . it was Hartman for Barber.

IF Harry Hartman ever said a bitter thing, a mean thing, a snide thing, a small thing, a critical thing about me . . . I never heard about it. And in as small a town as Cincinnati was then, as happy as it makes some people to carry gossip, and as cut-throat as was the radio business . . . *IF* Harry had ever said it, I would have heard about it, no later than the next day. I got to be pretty successful at Cincinnati—and I cost Harry Hartman his job, the job he had pioneered, the job he had loved with every ounce of his three hundred pounds. Harry has been dead a long time, but I would like to write for the record that I have not met any more Harry Hartman's. I soon learned in big-time radio the lesson a country boy on a farm learns—don't ever turn your back on a mule, or he'll get you in the end. Harry Hartman was a most notable exception.

With his complete and direct simplicity, Harry taught me something one afternoon that eventually saved me considerable embarrassment during a World Series. As the Reds' public-address announcer, Harry had the job of informing the people in the park of the various player changes during a game. This particular afternoon, Bill Klem, the all-time great umpire, was working behind the plate as the umpire-in-chief. It became very obvious that the Reds were about to change pitchers. The one who was in the game started to walk off the mound, and the one who was coming in started walking from the distant bullpen. Harry didn't hesitate. One pitcher was going, another was coming in. Simple. Also, it was as hot as an afternoon in Cincinnati, down in the basin of the Ohio River, could get. Harry reached for his public-address mike, turned it on, and bellowed the name of the relief pitcher . . . "Now coming in to pitch for the Reds" . . . .

Bill Klem, standing back of the plate, jumped seventeen feet up into the heat. Waving his mask, he stormed back toward Hartman . . . Klem walked all the way back to the foul screen, pushed his face against it, as close as he could get to Hartman, and bellowed, "By God . . . don't you ever again announce any player coming into game UNTIL I tell you he is coming in." I could hear Klem from up on top of the stands where I was sitting. Klem went on. "A man is not officially in a game just because you announce it on the address system . . . he is only in a game if the umpire-in-chief tells you to announce it, and THEN you announce it . . . and if an umpire tells you to announce him, he must come into the game." With that Klem officially told Hartman who was coming in, and made Harry announce him all over again.

The next day I went to Klem and had him carefully brief me about the official status of player changes over the public-address system.

Two years later the Yankees and the Giants were in the World Series—the game was at Yankee Stadium, and the Giants were going to bring in a relief pitcher from their bullpen. In those days, the visiting bullpen was in the runway behind right center field. You could not see from the broadcasting booth into the bullpen and, therefore, could not see who was or who was not warming up.

Bill Terry was the Giants' manager. Joe McCarthy was managing the Yankees. Gus Mancuso, the Giants' catcher, turned to the plate umpire . . . time was called . . . the announcement thundered throughout the triple-decked stadium: "Gumbert is now coming in to pitch for the Giants." I was announcing this portion of the game, and I routinely repeated what I had heard the public-address announcer say. I then went on, checking the runs, the hits, the errors . . . filling in time while the new man came in from away out yonder in right center. He came through the gate and routinely—a check reflex—I noted that he had his glove on his left hand. That meant he was a right-handed pitcher. Gumbert was a right-hander. Then I noted that he was tall. Gumbert was tall. BUT about the time the man was halfway to the mound, I suddenly jumped . . . it was not Harry Gumbert . . . no . . . it was Dick Coffman. I hesitated long enough to be sure to myself it was Coffman. . . . I paused to recall that the announcement had said that Gumbert was to come in. . . . Then, bless Harry Hartman's embarrassment that hot afternoon in Cincinnati, I was able to say into the microphone:

"The announcement said Gumbert . . . but this is Coffman walking in . . . and what is at point right now is the authenticity of the announcement. If the announcement was ordered by the umpire, Coffman can't pitch . . . Gumbert, wherever he is, must take the mound and face one batter before Coffman can come in the game."

Coffman walked right onto the mound . . . and here came Manager Joe McCarthy running out to the umpire. The argument didn't last long. Gumbert was sitting in the Giants' dugout all the time. He was made to go to the mound and pitch to one batter, while Coffman stood aside and waited. As I recall, Gumbert walked him. Catcher Mancuso had gotten confused, had told the umpire Gumbert, and so, Gumbert it had to be for one batter, and Gumbert it was for one batter.

This was long before we had telephones in the booth to the dugouts or to the press box. Without what happened to Hartman, without the terrible, public dressing down he got from Bill Klem, I would have been a mess at the microphone that afternoon.

In that beginning season of 1934, I was a green, unknown announcer on a small station in a small park in Cincinnati. This was long before ballplayers were paid or given anything for going on the air with you. A player then did you a favor, stopped what he was doing, to give you an interview. Charley Grimm, the manager and first baseman of the Cubs, started me off as my first guest on Opening Day in 1934—he even let me break into his meeting with his players before that game. I was so innocent I never knew they were having a meeting, so I beat on the clubhouse door and demanded that the trainer, Andy Lotshaw, produce the Cub manager. Lotshaw wanted to brain me, and only ignorance and Charley Grimm saved me . . . and maybe my job. I will always remember Cardinal manager Frank Frisch leaving infield practice—he was his own second baseman—and standing at the mike with me, drying his face and arms with a towel. Dizzy Dean was in big demand wherever he went, but he always found time to come to the mike with me.

But the player I remember as doing me the biggest favor is Waite Hoyt. When I got the job at Cincinnati, I had never seen a professional ball game, much less announced one. I had never seen a big-league ballplayer. The Cubs played the first series, then the Pirates came in. I had the job of picking some key ballplayers to come to the park at noon before the afternoon games to do a fifteen minute interview with me. I had no help from anybody. The Pirates stopped at the Sinton Hotel. I walked into the lobby and glanced around, trying to see who looked like they might be ballplayers. A big, red-faced man roughly asked me who I was, and I said I was a radio announcer looking for some Pittsburgh players to interview. He said loudly he was George Gibson—that he was the manager of the Pirates—that he wanted nothing to do with "———" "———" radio announcers. He screamed profanity at me. He dressed me down. He yelled so that everyone in the hotel lobby heard. Everyone watched. Gibson bellowed how no-good and detrimental were all radio announcers. I'd never had such a belting, and stunned, I stood there and took it. Finally, Gibson got on the elevator and left.

I was rooted to the floor. Numb. I was still scared of my brand-new job—if I failed to get any players, missed the interview on the air, I was sure I would be fired and have to slink back to Florida in complete defeat. That was the lowest moment I ever had in all my forty years of radio. No other moment comes even close.

Two men got up from a couch and walked over to me. "My name is Waite Hoyt," one of them said and pointed to the other. "He is Freddie Lindstrom. Gibson had no call to talk to you like he did. We're ballplayers, and we'll go with you to your program." You ask me, "The greatest interview I ever had?" That one.

It was after that initial baseball season in Cincinnati that I came to know Tom Manning, one of the first of the big-time network announcers. I had heard him down in Florida, announcing the World Series with Graham McNamee, and I remember straining inside to be up there with them.

That fall of 1934 I worked a split football schedule—half the time I did University of Cincinnati games on WSAI, and the rest of the time I went up to Columbus to work on the Ohio State games. The Cincinnati games I did alone—play-by-play, color, whatever it took. But the play-by-play of the Ohio State games was done by Grant Ward, who had been in the state legislature and had been doing the games over the Ohio State University station for some years. WLW in Cincinnati and WTAM in Cleveland, where Tom Manning was the regular announcer, were bought by the Ohio Oil Company that fall, but they had to take Ward's play-by-play . . . so on alternate Saturdays, Manning and I would do the color and the commercials. Manning used to come down even for the games he wasn't working, and that is how we began to know each other. Also, on one of the games, for some reason, they put both of us on the color. He was always chipper, always breezy, always pleasant. I was a green kid to him. In fact, he called me "Kid."

The next year I did the Ohio State games on WLW all by myself, and that one game in 1935 with Notre Dame was a season in itself. I still see Notre Dame scoring those two touchdowns in the final fifty-five seconds.

Tom Manning died at the age of sixty-nine, but he was

dead inside himself long before his fatal heart attack. He hated advancing age, he hated not doing the big broadcasts, he hated his deafness, which increased with his years, and he hated to part with the vibrancy of his youth.

Manning was born in the Irish section of Cleveland, near the West Side, called the Angle. His dad died when Tom was eighteen months old, and life was one battle after another, one job after another. Tom started peddling newspapers so young he couldn't remember when it was. He won a contest for the newsboy in Cleveland with the loudest voice. He hustled. Often he had to fight his way with his fists. This was a tough part of town, where the cops always walked in pairs. He went to school some, but not much. Sometimes Tom would say to himself, "Not bad for a dummy from the Angle. . . ." A dummy he was not.

Manning was a trim, smallish man with flaming red hair. His eyes were bright blue. He bounced when he walked. He exuded confidence—he had learned early the value of a sharp front, a confident appearance, and the necessity of never standing still when you could be easily hit. He was a fancy dresser. Sharp.

As a kid around town, with that hustle and drive and loud voice, he was soon yelling through a megaphone at prize fights, ball parks, anywhere they needed something announced to the crowd. He actually hardened his voice with abuse until it was raspy, but it was always strong. He used to stand on the playing field of old League Park—years before they built the present Cleveland Stadium—and announce the batteries for the games. In 1925 he began calling them on the radio, but this was sporadic until he went with WTAM in 1928 for regular coverage. However, WTAM lost the games after the 1931 season, and Tom was forced to live in Cleveland and hear Jack Graney and other men doing the play-by-play of the Indians. NBC thought well enough of him to use him on nine World Series and on several heavyweight championship fights. He knew fights and baseball—he'd been around them all his life.

Late in his career, late in his life, he came back into base-ball to announce the 1956 and '57 Cleveland games with Jimmy Dudley. I used to see him when the Yankees and the Indians played. I was no longer a kid to him, and by then we had a serious bond between us. He had become completely deaf in his right ear, and I was deaf in my left ear. We could sit along-side each other and be "eared" right. In our bond, we both suffered from being accused of rudeness—many times people who didn't know the situation would speak to us on our silent sides, and when we didn't answer, we would be marked as snooty guys who didn't have the time to be polite.

The road was too much for him, the pace of modern broad-casting was too demanding. He retired, saying his ear bothered him with all the travel in airplanes. Maybe it did. The last few times I saw him, his deafness was closing in on him, and his age was shaking him.

I rate Tom Manning as the announcer in sports who went the highest from the lowest start.

I think of Tom Manning and I recall sitting in Lois and George Treisbach's home one afternoon in Jacksonville, listen-ing to the 1933 World Series in the same living room where they gave Lylah and me our wedding. The broadcast of that particular game ended, and I said to George something I'd never said before to anybody else.

"Someday," I said, "you are going to hear me announcing the World Series, like you just heard Graham McNamee and Tom Manning."

Nobody could have told me that afternoon that "someday" was going to be 1935 . . . just two years later, and I would find myself on a sleeper to Detroit, to join the Chicago an-nouncers Quin Ryan and Bob Elson for the first World Series on the new network, the Mutual Broadcasting System.

Mutual had been formed the summer of 1935, and its first sports event was the first night game in the big leagues . . . at Cincinnati. And I announced it—just happened to be in the right place at the right time. Mutual then had three stations—WOR in New York, WGN in Chicago and CKLW in Detroit

—and baseball's Commissioner Landis said he would recognize Mutual as a network and let it broadcast the World Series if it could persuade WLW in Cincinnati to join it, rather than stay with NBC. John Clark, the general manager of WLW, said he would take Mutual—thereby making it possible for there to be a Mutual—*if* his young announcer, Red Barber, got a share of the broadcast. And what do you think Fred Webber of Mutual said to John Clark? . . . I just happened to be in the right place, at the right time, with the right boss.

That first World Series came full circle for me the next spring when I returned to Florida and ran into Joe Lang, another good friend, who had married Esther Jordan, Lylah's oldest friend. Meeting Joe, something came up that was to fester inside me for eighteen years and finally exploded in 1953 when I became the only announcer ever to walk away from broadcasting the World Series.

Joe worked for Baird Hardware, sometimes selling on the road, sometimes taking inventory in the store. He was proud of me, and I wasn't too unproud. That was a hell of a leap from Gainesville, Florida, to the World Series in two years.

"Red," Joe said, "I was telling Esther last fall—that with you announcing the World Series . . . with the Ford Motor Company sponsoring it . . . over the Mutual Broadcasting System . . . with WLW and WGN and big stations like that . . . man, man . . . I said to Esther . . . that I would be happy to have the money you made in one week announcing the World Series, for what I would make in a whole year working for Baird Hardware. . . . A whole year!"

Joe meant that. He was glad for me and for all the money I must have made for that great assignment. I said nothing. But right then it sank home, and I couldn't explain it to anyone, because they would not have believed it, that I got not an extra dollar for announcing that World Series. I got my expenses paid, and I was paid the privilege of being on the broadcast. But no extra money.

That's how it was for all of us in baseball then, in 1935.

JUDGE LANDIS

I want to stay with that first World Series a bit longer, not for anything that happened in the course of the six games it took the Detroit Tigers to beat the Chicago Cubs, but for something that occurred hours before the first ball was pitched.

If any of my early experiences could be said to be pivotal, that was it. It began with a long-distance phone call from John Clark as I was preparing to broadcast the Ohio State-Kentucky football game from Columbus.

"Red," said John, "get on the train tonight for Detroit. . . . You're on the World Series broadcast tomorrow . . . I agreed that WLW would take the broadcast from Mutual instead of NBC, provided you were one of the announcers. . . . Report to Quin Ryan and Bob Elson of WGN, Chicago—they'll be at the Statler Hotel. . . . Good luck."

I got on the train. I had no scorebook—as it worked out, I scored my first World Series on borrowed scraps of paper. I was at the Statler so early Wednesday morning I found both Ryan and Elson still in bed. They told me Judge Landis had called a meeting for all the broadcasters in his hotel suite at 9:30. They didn't have to tell me to be there on time.

I'd never met Elson before. He was an established young announcer in Chicago, who had started under Pat Flannagan. Chicago is where baseball broadcasting really began. Quin Ryan, the program manager at WGN, the *Chicago Tribune* station, was "an old-timer"—and he was to do the color for Mutual.

Elson and Ryan took me into the Judge's suite. They told the Judge who I was, and he said "hello" and went on smoking his cigarette. He wasn't impressed with me, but I sure was with him.

In 1919 baseball got into more trouble than a one-armed paperhanger in a high wind. The exposure that some Chicago White Sox players had thrown games to Cincinnati in the World Series sickened the country. The knowledge that gamblers had controlled the outcome of the event was more than anybody could stand—even the club owners, who until then had run baseball to suit themselves, using a three-man commission of owners.

The very life of baseball was seriously threatened. The most important asset the game possessed—the belief of the public in the integrity of the players and the games—had been badly damaged.

A major decision had to be made . . . and it had to be made by a group of thoroughly frightened and aroused owners: Hire *one man* . . . a commissioner . . . an absolute monarch . . . a boss . . . and turn the game over to *him*. They chose Judge Kennesaw Mountain Landis.

Judge Landis got his name because his daddy was a Union soldier in 1864 in a battle that was fought in Cobb County, Georgia, where stands Kennesaw Mountain. The name meant something to Judge Landis' father—he got a leg shot off in that battle. And the boy, given the name Kennesaw Mountain, must have had something of the blood and fighting and struggling of that place rub off on him. He never ran from a battle in his life. In 1907, in a rebate case of national attention, Judge Landis fined the mighty Standard Oil Company $29,-240,000. That's right—$29,240,000.

In 1915 K. M. Landis, as a Federal judge had a salary of $7,500 a year. Baseball then was in a serious battle, with the "outlaw" Federal League fighting the established National and American Leagues. Landis happened to draw this case, and he presided very deftly and impressively. Some of the baseball men put his name in the back of their heads . . . but they didn't dream they'd ever need him. Certainly not in four years' time.

The Black Sox scandal broke and Baseball came running to "The Judge." They offered him $50,000 a year for seven years. He was not impressed. He did not seem too interested.

The baseball men asked him for his terms, and Judge Landis said, "the authority to do anything I consider right in any matter detrimental to baseball."

That was it. That was how Judge Landis came into office

as the first Commissioner of Baseball. With absolute power. They used to call him The Czar. He cleaned up the Black Sox situation immediately—he suspended for life all the eight players involved: Shoeless Joe Jackson, Ed Cicotte, Chick Gandil, Buck Weaver, Happy Felsch, Swede Risberg, Fred McMullen and Claude Williams. The law courts failed to convict these eight players, but the Judge did. For life. At once. And for as long as he lived, the Judge guaranteed baseball's honesty.

Men were arriving in a steady stream, saying "Hello, Judge," and "Good morning, Judge" . . . men I'd heard about, but had never seen.

The Ford Motor Company was sponsoring the World Series, using all the networks. NBC had put both their nets— the Red and the Blue—together, so with MBS getting into it, that made three broadcasts for the first time. Multiple network coverage of the Series continued until Gillette bought the exclusive rights in 1939 and limited the reporting to just one network. Today, the listener takes what they give him. Then you had a three-way choice, and the competition was keen.

Paul White, the first CBS news chief, led his delegation of Franz Laux from KMOX-St. Louis, Jack Graney from WHK-Cleveland, and Truman Bradley from WBBM-Chicago.

The NBC contingent arrived . . . Ty Tyson from WWJ-Detroit, Hal Totten from WMAQ-Chicago, and the distinguished newscaster, Boake Carter, who was to do the color. Graham McNamee was with them, but this was the first time he wasn't to broadcast the Series since he'd made radio history in 1923. The newspapers then simply said, "McNamee was dropped at the last minute."

He was the one man I wanted most to see, and I saw him from across the room. I knew them all by name. I had a back-row seat, and I never opened my mouth. I just looked and thought and tried to add some of it up.

At nine thirty sharp, the Judge said:

"It's time . . . shut the door. Anybody who isn't here now, won't get in."

The room, filled with famous voices, went completely silent.

The Judge had thin, aesthetic features, with a mass of white hair. He was always proud of his hair, and he wore it full, always conscious of, always displaying that white mane.

He had force. He was boss, he knew it, and he went to his grave as boss. Baseball never stopped to thank him—it just went to work after his death to see to it that there wouldn't be another commissioner with his powers.

He stood. He kept a cigarette in his hand. He both smoked it and used it as a pointer to accentuate his words.

"Gentlemen, I'm glad to see all of you here this morning . . . Graham," and he nodded toward McNamee, who must have been having a most painful time, "I'm especially glad to see you."

He puffed on his cigarette, then he turned to another announcer, the former ballplayer, Jack Graney. Jack once played outfield for the Indians, and since 1932 he had been broadcasting their games. I didn't think anything about it then, but Graney was making history—he was the first former player to announce on World Series radio.

"Jack, I'm glad to see you here. I have kept you off the broadcasts of the Series because I didn't want the opinions of a player. I hope that by now you've forgotten you ever played baseball. I expect to get good reports on your work this afternoon."

The room seemed to get quieter. Graney was staring at the floor.

"There is one announcer, you gentlemen know him, who isn't here . . . and I don't have to go into that."

He was talking about Ted Husing, who had second-guessed some of the umpiring during the previous World Series, and the Judge had barred him. Everybody in the room knew about that.

I had heard it the summer before over the baseball grapevine—and, believe me, our State Department doesn't have one nearly as efficient—but I never really wondered about it until many years later, until that afternoon in 1967 when I went to see William S. Paley to ask him to check over what I had written about Ted Husing.

When Paley got to the part about Landis barring Ted from the 1935 Series, he said, "I don't remember this," and then simply went on with his unhurried reading.

I realized then that there was nothing in writing anywhere about Husing's World Series termination. In his own two books, Husing makes no mention of it, nothing to explain how he, one of the two great early sports announcers, suddenly stopped broadcasting America's biggest sports event after years of steady coverage.

"But no," I thought, "of course there is nothing written—Husing would wish it buried and forgotten—and very little to remember . . . a telephone call from Chicago, probably from Leslie O'Connor, the Judge's assistant, to Paul White in charge of CBS news, that 'it would be better not to submit Husing's name again'. . . ." And Paley had been so loyal to Husing. Yet my final thought on the matter that afternoon, watching one of the two most important and powerful men in radio reading my manuscript, was "Bill Paley, you've sure won a lot of battles—but you lost the one to Landis so quickly, so quietly, so completely, you don't even remember it or wish to remember it."

And Judge Landis, that morning in Detroit in 1935, said only that one sentence, not even naming Husing. We in the room knew, however, and what followed made it clear that his reference was no idle preliminary. He had called this meeting for a reason. He lit another cigarette.

"Gentlemen, I congratulate you. You are the best in your business, or you wouldn't be here in this room at this time. . . . You are the very best in your business. I am very aware of who you are.

"But, gentlemen, this afternoon on the playing field there will be two ball clubs that for this year are the best in their business. They know how to play baseball and they know it very well. They have demonstrated their abilities over the full season."

He paused to blow out smoke.

"Gentlemen, in the dugouts this afternoon will be two managers, who for this year are the best in their business . . . they are the two winning managers, and they know how to manage.

"And, gentlemen, there will be four men in blue suits on the field this afternoon . . . the umpires . . . and for this year, and for this Series, they are the best in their business."

Judge Landis, his white hair shaking, was now under a full head of steam. He wasn't stopping to choose his words or to pull on his cigarette. His voice hardened.

"Gentlemen, I wouldn't presume to tell you how to conduct your business. But I will tell you to let the ballplayers play—they don't need your help. Let the managers manage. And above everything else, you let the umpires umpire.

"When you arrive in your radio boxes today, I want you to know that the full power of the Commissioner's Office will see to it—will guarantee it—that you will not be disturbed in your prerogatives. I promise you that not a single ballplayer will interfere with you at your microphone . . . not a manager will try to tell you anything . . . and, certainly, not one of those umpires will come up there and tell you how to broadcast."

He stopped. Content that what he had just said was heard, was understood, he went on.

"Gentlemen, you report. Report everything you can see. Report what the ballplayers do, but don't feel sorry for them or rejoice for them. Report what they do. That's all the listeners want to hear—what the ballplayers do.

"Report what the managers do. Report each move each manager makes, but just report it. He knows more about what he is doing than you can know . . . and what he does—or why he does it—is none of your business.

"Report what the umpire does. Report what he calls the pitch—not what you think he should have called. In fact, you are in the stands . . . he is right behind the plate. You can't see what it is, and it isn't your business to think you can see what it is. It is his business to see what it is and to call it what it is . . . and he, gentlemen, will call it what it is. You report what he calls it.

"By report, I mean you have the right to say what is going on, no matter what is going on, or where it is going on. But don't voice your opinions. Don't editorialize. Report. . . ."

The stage lost a consummately fine actor when Judge Landis went into law. He paused again, leaned forward, and lowered his voice.

"This is what I mean by reporting. Suppose a ballplayer goes to the dugout and fills his mouth with water. Suppose he also has a chew of tobacco in his mouth. And he walks over to where I'm sitting in a rail box, he leans in to me, and he spits right in my face.

"Report each step the player makes. Report how much spit hits me in the face. If you can see it, report how much tobacco gets on my face. Report my reaction, if any. Report what happens thereafter. Report but don't feel disturbed about the Commissioner. That will be my affair after I have been spit upon. Your job is simply to report the event.

"And, gentlemen, one more thing. . . . There are a lot of motion-picture actors who show up at the World Series every year, taking bows and getting their pictures taken. They haven't been around all year, but now they're here. Gentlemen, I don't want any of those Hollywood characters named on the radio. The World Series is for baseball people.

"Gentlemen, good day."

The room emptied.

FOUR:
BASEBALL
ON THE AIR

In 1920 there was this new thing people were beginning to talk about. It was called "wireless telegraphy." The pioneer sending station was KDKA in Pittsburgh, owned by Westinghouse—and there was a young man on the payroll named Harold Arlin. A foreman during the daytime, he began announcing on the "wireless telegraphy" at night. . . .

The afternoon of August 5, 1921, Arlin went to Forbes Field in Pittsburgh, where the Phillies were to play the Pirates. He set up his equipment inside the screen behind home plate. And over this "wireless telegraphy," he announced the first baseball game. He continued part time announcing on KDKA. He reported such things as scores and news from the studios, he announced a football game, he did a tennis match. From time to time Arlin interviewed people. But after a few years of these occasional broadcasts, Arlin left the announcing field to other men, to McNamee and Husing, who went on to gain glamor and network audiences.

On August 5, 1966 . . . forty-five years later . . . the Pittsburgh Pirates did a rare, rare thing in this materialistic world . . . they remembered. Harold Arlin was brought from his home in Mansfield, Ohio, brought out of retirement, brought to home plate—and Bob Prince, who broadcasts the Pirates today, presented Arlin to the fans as the man who forty-five years before, right in the same ball park, announced the first baseball game on the radio.

Two months after Arlin's 1921 broadcast from Forbes Field, in the East, the first World Series game was put on the air—but not from the ball park . . . and not by an announcer seeing the game for himself and reporting it as best he could.

WJZ went on the air officially from Newark, New Jersey, October 1, 1921. The World Series that fall was the first one in which the Yankees played, and they were facing the New York Giants. WJZ was going to really create a splash by having the opening game broadcast. October 5, 1921.

A young man named Tommy Cowan was given the announcing job. He was told to talk into a telephone with the hook removed. The day before he had gone to Thomas A. Edison to personally borrow from the old inventor his phonograph and records, to use for music on the radio. Edison refused to speak on the microphone himself, but lent his phonograph, very grudgingly—with much suspicion.

Cowan sat in a shack on top of the Newark Westinghouse Building. The transmitter was a duplicate of the one at KDKA. A newspaper reporter was at the Polo Grounds at one end of the telephone—Cowan was at the other end with the receiver at his ear. The reporter said, "Ball one," and Cowan repeated into the mike, "Ball one." Cowan got so punch-drunk from listening and repeating that after the game was over he didn't have any idea whether the Giants or the Yankees had won. The upstart Yankees won that game, but John McGraw's Giants won the Series.

Outside of this brief swim in the stream of sports-announcing history, Tommy Cowan became justly famous as the studio announcer for many of the great entertainers and singers of the day. He began wearing a dinner jacket for his broadcasts. When New York City went on the air with WNYC, the first city-owned radio station, Cowan was the station's chief announcer. As I type this, I have before me the death notice of this announcer who "broadcast" the first World Series, who was truly the pioneer announcer in the East. Tommy Cowan died on November 3, 1969 at the age of eighty-five.

Following Harold Arlin in Pittsburgh and Tommy Cowan in Newark, there was a beginning growth of radio-and-baseball —crude, fitfull, hit-or-miss—but a growth. The next milestone of note was the dramatic impact of Graham McNamee in 1923. Things were never the same again.

But as radio became more polished, as more and more people got receiving sets of one kind or another, the men who ran baseball and football were deeply concerned. Nobody was neutral about this new medium of instant communication. In those days—long, long before the television bonanza—the only real income from sports was the sale of tickets.

Some powerful men in both baseball and football were deathly afraid radio would keep people at home and out of the parks and stadia. They said, "Who will pay for something they can get free?" A number of colleges forbade radio broadcasts of their games—when I was announcing in Florida in the early thirties, the old Southern Conference slapped a complete ban on radio reports of all its football games for two seasons.

Regular play-by-play radio broadcasting of baseball started in Chicago in 1924 with Hal Totten (a rewrite man on the *Chicago Daily News*) as the announcer. Quin Ryan of WGN, the *Chicago Tribune* station, began almost immediately thereafter. William Wrigley, Senior, who owned the Cubs, believed in radio completely. He believed it would increase fan interest, would attract more people to the parks, and he proved it with the success of Ladies' Day. Thanks in large measure to Mr. Wrigley—his son Phil is the present head of the Cubs

—Chicago became the first hotbed of radio baseball coverage. For several seasons in those early days, seven Chicago stations did the games . . . and Mr. Wrigley charged no rights fees. He figured the radio reports were good for him, for his ball club, for baseball. He installed at Wrigley Field the first glass-partitioned radio booths.

Pat Flanagan started in Chicago in 1929 at WBBM and quickly became a very big man in that city. He did several World Series on CBS and hung up his mike in 1943. Pat died in 1963. He was always a pleasant man, with a well-modulated voice. We met in Cincinnati in my first season there. The Cubs were in for the opening game, and Pat came down from Chicago to announce it. He made the round trip . . . with an engineer . . . and all expenses paid. They stayed at the Netherlands Plaza Hotel, which was brand new . . . last word. But WBBM in Chicago could afford only one such trip that year, and it did that one just to open the season and try to get the jump on all those other stations in the Windy City who were also doing baseball.

Bob Elson got on a WGN baseball mike in Chicago in 1931 with Quin Ryan—and he is still announcing. He has been the Voice of the White Sox for a long, long time. Bob has more seasons of big-league broadcasting under his belt than anyone . . . thirty-nine, interrupted by two years in the Navy during World War Two.

The pioneer Chicago baseball announcer was Hal Totten. A twenty-three-year-old reporter for the *Chicago Daily News* when he asked for that historic 1924 microphone assignment, he remained on the play-by-play Chicago scene through 1944, then worked on the Mutual Game-of-the-Day off and on through 1950. He broadcast the World Series for CBS with Major Andrew White in 1926 and '27, and he was on the World Series for NBC with Graham McNamee in 1933, '34, and finally, in '35. When Totten left Chicago in 1950, he went out to Keokuk, Iowa, to manage a radio station, then got into minor-league baseball as president of first the Three I and then the Southern Leagues. He now lives in Cedar Rapids, retired from professional baseball.

I was never fortunate enough to know Hal Totten, to be around him, to ever do a game with him. But I remember hearing him down in Florida, with his pleasant, calm voice . . . a business-type broadcaster.

Chicago spawned a lot of baseball announcers: Russ Hodges who is still calling 'em for the Giants—first in New York, now in San Francisco . . . Jimmy Dudley, who went on to Cleveland and then moved to Seattle when the Pilots got their franchise in 1969 . . . Jack Drees who came back to do White Sox television in 1969—the same Jack Drees you've heard on horse races on CBS.

There were four of the pioneer Chicago broadcasters working on the 1935 World Series that I did for Mutual—Totten, Elson, Ryan, and Truman Bradley, who came from WBBM and was on the CBS crew. It was the last World Series Totten worked on, and also the last one for Bradley. And it ended the baseball-announcing career of Quin Ryan in two games. This was my first assignment with Bob Elson, and I found him a crackajack announcer, sharp and knowledgeable, but Quin Ryan was in direct contrast—Elson kept learning and working, while Ryan was primarily a WGN executive who never bothered to improve as a broadcaster. He did not prepare himself. He thought, there in 1935, on the World Series, on a network heard in New York, Chicago, Detroit, and Cincinnati, that he was still talking to the boys in the barbershop back in 1925. Ryan did the pre- and post-game color for games one and two in Detroit. I was shocked that he never went to the dugouts or to the field—he just came to the booth and read from some newspaper stories he had torn out of the sports page. . . . In the summer of 1933, I had tried and failed to see Ryan at WGN to ask him for a job—I couldn't get past the receptionist. After the second game of the 1935 World Series, I was told to take his place, do the color, as well as split the play-by-play with Elson. Ryan and I never saw each other again.

The broadcasting of major-league games kept increasing, city by city. But at the same time, the opposition to radio was stiffening. In 1932 baseball almost legislated radio out of all the parks, so strong was the fear of this instant communication by some of the clubs. It came to a vote among the owners in 1932. Both the National and American leagues sidestepped the issue—and adopted a policy that left it up to the individual clubs. The three New York teams—the Yankees, Giants, Dodgers—entered into an agreement that none of them would allow broadcasts. And in 1934 they were so adamant about it that they signed a formal five-year agreement not to broadcast . . . not even to permit Western Union re-creations to be done from out of town. In other words, in the regular season there were no broadcasts anywhere of any games played at Yankee Stadium, Ebbets Field, or the Polo Grounds . . . until 1939, when Larry MacPhail broke the ban.

What follows will be of necessity as rough as a corncob, and as spotted as a Dalmatian puppy. The records of the beginning broadcasters are scanty—and at times are at variance. This is understandable for several reasons: one, at the beginning, nobody thought it was worth writing much about a fellow announcing balls and strikes on a local radio station; two, many newspapers of the period were hostile to radio and refused to publish much about it; and three, a great deal of what has been written in recent years has been recorded from hearsay and memory, both of which are somewhat unreliable.

But this is not intended to be an historical document. I never intended to research this book like a terrier shaking a rat. All I wish to do is recall the excitement of the early days and the impact of the early sports announcers, especially the baseball fellows, keeping in mind that all of them did football in season as a matter of course. I have enough accurate material to hit the high places until 1934 . . . then I got to Cincinnati and began to know firsthand what the detailed score was.

We have twenty-four major league baseball teams today, each with its own dog-in-the-manger radio-television franchise. In 1930 we had sixteen big-league teams, and eleven of those teams were in five cities: Chicago, St. Louis, Philadelphia, and Boston, each with two teams, and New York with three, counting Brooklyn. They paired to do home games only, making it a single broadcast per town. Today only Chicago and New York are in both leagues, and each team is broadcast separately. In 1930 not all teams broadcast, especially in New York, and usually one announcer comprised the entire broadcasting crew—working with one engineer.

The best I can dig up is that around 1930 Fred Hoey did the games in Boston, Ty Tyson in Detroit, Franz Laux in St. Louis, Harry Hartman in Cincinnati, Tom Manning in Cleveland . . . and in Chicago were Hal Totten, Johnny O'Hara, Pat Flanagan, Quin Ryan, and Bob Elson. The other fellows who did games were on most spotty schedules—like ships that passed in the night, they came and went. There are no footprints in the air.

I can be more definite, however, about who was what who was where two years later. A book was
—*Baseball* by Speed Johnson—the
through the summer
ahead of it
ball
It is
wrote
Detroit,
library
Library
Spink, th
friends. Y
this section
of them. Pr
For 1932,
of thirty-five

doing any play-by-play baseball, the same ten I mentioned above for 1930. Most of the others were included because they did sports commentaries or were with the networks, as was the case with Graham McNamee and Ted Husing. (The name of Bill Munday is missing.)

For the sake of historical memory the other men listed as announcing sports in 1932 were: Dave Parks in St. Louis, John Kolbmann in Philadelphia, Bob Hawk in Chicago, Andy Stanton in Philadelphia, Arch McDonald in Chattanooga, Ellie Vander Pyl in Cleveland, George Bischoff in Des Moines, Joe Tumelty in Philadelphia, Russ Winnie in Milwaukee, Jack Martin in La Crosse, Wisconsin, Ed Cochrane in Kansas City, Earl Harper in Cleveland, Ed Sprague—(who later worked with me a season in Cincinnati)—in Pittsburgh, Tony Wakeman in Pittsburgh, Bill Williams in Boston, George Sutherland in Detroit, Bob Newhall in Cincinnati (Bob was very nice to me when I arrived in town . . . when he retired a couple years later and moved to Sarasota, Florida, I was given his fifteen-minute program on WLW), Wes McKnight in Toronto, Tom Stull in Cincinnati, Merrill Bunnell in Ogden, Utah, Al Nagler in Detroit, Oscar Reichow in Los Angeles, Chuck Simpson in Knoxville, Bill Johnson in Fort Wayne . . . and, Walter (Red) Barber in Gainesville, Florida.

This list from *Baseball* sounds like the begats. However, is not a complete listing of sports announcers of that year, ught it covers well, as was its primary intention, those t the big-league baseball microphones. The author of had to limit his material somewhat, and he had to announcers around geographically, I would think, roader publicity and sales for the book. As I said, tion of Bill Munday, who was a firecracker in f Jack Graney, the first former ballplayer to cing booth, who was starting at Cleveland nar Wiig, who was announcing in Roch- was on the CBS World Series crew this is the best listing of sports an- d that time.

I got to Cincinnati in 1934, and I will be cheerfully responsible for what is written here from that date on.

I met several men that summer who hadn't the slightest idea of going into radio broadcasting, but eventually did—Dizzy Dean of the Gas House Gang Cardinals, his shortstop Leo Durocher, his manager Frank Frisch . . . Charley Grimm, the manager and first baseman of the Cubs . . . Waite Hoyt and Pie Traynor of the Pirates . . . Mel Ott of the Giants . . . umpires Dolly Stark and Larry Goetz, the only two umpires I know about who got into my business. (Stark retired early from umpiring because of a bad knee and worked on the games at Philadelphia for a season. Goetz, after being retired, tried to make it as a color man for Mutual on their Game-of-the-Day . . . but Larry had a lisp in his speech. I never could understand how anyone at Mutual could have asked Goetz to do something at which he had no hope of succeeding.)

It was Mutual who put Mel Ott on baseball games after he was fired by the Giants and replaced with Durocher. Ott's radio career, slow in smoothing out, ended in a fatal car crash. Durocher, after losing out with Stoneham at New York, went on the air for NBC for a couple of years on their Game-of-the-Week (there are some National League umpires today who wish Leo had continued his broadcasting career). Charley Grimm was like a monkey on a string for Mr. Wrigley at Chicago—managing his Cubs, announcing them, going back and forth between the two assignments. Pie Traynor never did play-by-play, but for years he was a respected commentator in Pittsburgh with a sports program.

Of all these player-broadcasters, Frank Frisch was asked to undertake the toughest job, one of the meanest in the history of big league play-by-play. General Mills sent him to Boston in 1939 to break off the career of Fred Hoey.

Since 1925, Fred Hoey had been announcing the Red Sox and the Braves games, whichever team was home in Boston, over the Colonial Network. He was a household word in New England. They gave him a "day" in 1931, said nice things about all the fans he had made with his broadcasts, gave him presents, a scroll, and a check for three thousand dollars. Hoey owned New England. He had a dry, rough voice, and he barked balls and strikes without elaboration—but he was the first man up that way in this new field. And anyhow New England was conservative in the matter of words, so, by and large, Fred Hoey was a most satisfactory announcer for that close-knit part of the world. He announced the Boston games for some fourteen years. Twice, the sponsors and the radio station tried to fire him, the second time they succeeded.

I never heard Hoey do an inning of a game. I never knew him. But a friend of mine, Til Ferdenzi, who is now in sports publicity for NBC, after years as a crack baseball writer for the *New York Journal American,* wrote me about Hoey, and here are some of the things he said:

"Fred Hoey was my first broadcasting hero as a kid growing up in the Boston area. Poor old Fred had a bit of a drinking problem, and eventually his love for the sauce greased the skids for him as a baseball announcer. Demon Rum pockmarked his entire career—so much so that in the moment of his greatest triumph, the first game of the 1933 World Series, he was forced to retire from the announcer's booth after a couple of innings because of 'a bad cold.'

"In 1937, right at the height of his popularity, the sponsors and the station decided to fire Fred. This news was met with a deluge of protests to the radio station, newspapers, and sponsors. The firing was front-page news, and a boycott grew and grew. The protest culminated in the picketing of the two ball parks. As far as I know, his dismissal occasioned the first pickets to march around a ball park in protest of the firing of a play-by-play announcer. In fact, the protest was so effective, Hoey was rehired and wasn't fired again until March 18, 1939, when he was replaced by Frank Frisch."

(Fred Hoey was always a lonely man, who never married, and his end came on November 17, 1949. Here is how it read in the paper that day: "Winthrop, Massachusetts, November 17 —Fred Hoey, sixty-four, retired veteran sports writer and baseball broadcaster, was found dead in his gas-filled room at 77 Triton Avenue late today. Medical Examiner Dr. Michael A. Luongo said Hoey's death was accidental due to asphyxiation. His body was found on the kitchen floor by a delivery boy. . . .")

This is the Boston background that Frisch had to buck in 1939. Frank had been a star ballplayer for both the Giants and the Cardinals. He managed the Cardinals for five and a half years . . . managed the Gas House Gang to their World Championship over Detroit in 1934 . . . and was fired in St. Louis in September 1938. General Mills was the dominant sponsor in Boston for 1939, and they had much grist in the radio mill. In addition to Boston, they were breaking the barrier in New York that same season and were just about everywhere else in baseball broadcasting. They decided no more Fred Hoey. Frisch had never broadcast, but he was a name, he had been a star, he had been a manager, he was colorful . . . and he was tough. General Mills—really it was one man, Cliff Samuelson—decided Frisch was the man to do it. Out went Hoey, in came Frisch. Frank weathered the storm of 1939. He buried the ghost, once and for all. But it was hard. Frisch told me how hard it was, trying to sleep in his hotel room while pickets were hollering down in the street. The very next year he got a chance to manage the Pittsburgh Pirates, and he told Boston and its clans a not too fond good-bye. The Pittsburgh job lasted through 1946, then Frisch did radio work at the Polo Grounds for two years until the job of managing the Cubs came along.

Dizzy Dean—who won thirty games in 1934 while his brother Paul was winning nineteen—hurt his arm and in 1938 was traded to the Cubs. The arm went from bad to worse, and in 1941 Diz signed on to broadcast baseball in St. Louis. Broadcasting has never been the same since. The Boston fans protested that Fred Hoey was *not* broadcasting—a lot of them at St. Louis, especially schoolteachers, at first protested that Dizzy *was* broadcasting.

Diz mangled the English language far more thoroughly than any other man at a mike—and over a long period of time, and always for top money. Diz said "slud" for "slid" . . . he said the runners returned to their "respectable bases" instead of "respective bases." He rarely pronounced a ball-player's name quite correctly. He didn't want to. He read personal telegrams, sent greetings across the country to friends, sang "The Wabash Cannonball" or any other hillbilly song he wanted to sing, right in the middle of a game.

Strictly speaking, Diz was not a working play-by-play announcer. He was Dizzy Dean, with enormous charm and color and appeal. He was smarter than a fox—I think he always knew what he was doing and what he was saying—and I wish I had the money he has made and saved. He has it buried in tomato cans all over Mississippi.

Dizzy first broadcast at St. Louis, then came to New York to Yankee Stadium for a year to do the pre- and post-game television shows, played golf with Dan Topping and won much of the Topping money, then for years was on the Game-of-the-Week for CBS. He worked with Buddy Blatner, then with Peewee Reese. No, that is incorrect. Dizzy never worked with anybody. They worked with him, doing whatever it was he wanted them to do. Diz was a law unto himself on the mound, and he didn't change any when he went into radio. He had great talent, but in my judgment, Dizzy never was teamed with a play-by-play man strong enough to discipline his broadcasting gifts. . . . When NBC got the exclusive Game-of-the-Week a couple of years ago, Curt Gowdy, who might have been that man, was not of a mind to let Dizzy make a shambles out of the assignment. Gowdy had given up his life-time security with the Red Sox and with Tom Yawkey, and he wanted a fair crack at being the chief announcer NBC had hired him to be. Dizzy was under a long-term contract to a brewery in St. Louis, and they put the heat on NBC and on Gowdy . . . really turned it on. For a while NBC Sales hinted to Gowdy that he ought to take Dizzy. Did I say "hinted"?

Waite Hoyt pitched into the season of 1938, winning 237 games in his career, good enough to pitch himself into the Hall of Fame. He got into radio the next year. When the Brooklyn games went on the air in 1939, Hoyt did a feature-commentary program before and after the games. He did that for two years, then got an offer to come to Cincinnati to do the play-by-play. He broadcast the Reds games for twenty-five years. He was the best of all the former athletes who went to the microphones—highly intelligent, industrious, a great story-teller. Just before he went out to Cincinnati, he told me he did not know how to score a game, that he knew he had to score when he got into the booth, and would I show him how to do it? He could have asked me for more than that . . . much more.

Hoyt had little trouble making the transition to the radio booth. He easily learned to score and to do all the other mechanical things the job required. He always was an excellent talker. Today he is the best man living to tell you about Babe Ruth and Miller Huggins and Ty Cobb. The only problem Waite had in Cincinnati as a broadcaster was the one Fred Hoey had and Bill Munday had—as well as a few others of us. Alcohol. Hoyt went into AA, worked at it, became the headman in AA out there . . . and has never let himself down. Hoyt is one of the few broadcasters who beat whiskey in time. Munday did, but so late, so terribly late.

Another fellow who beat it, who was also a ballplayer who got into announcing, and did a most able job, was Harry Heilmann in Detroit. Harry quit his drinking in time, but arthritis cut short his career as a truly great batter, and cancer closed him out entirely too young . . . fifty-seven. Heilmann won four batting championships in the days of Cobb, Ruth, Sisler, and Speaker. When Ty Tyson quit announcing the Detroit games in 1940, Heilmann got the mike. He was much like Hoyt—he was a ballplayer who knew he needed to work hard as an announcer, and work hard he did.

Let me tell you something he did for me one afternoon in

Detroit. I was out there for an evening broadcast of the Sammy Kaye Show for Old Golds. The Tigers were playing at home in the afternoon, and I went to the park to visit. Heilmann asked me to announce the second inning for him, and I said, "Sure." This is what he said when he introduced me: "I have Red Barber in the booth with me, and he is going to announce the second inning . . . then he has to leave to rehearse a network program he is in Detroit for . . . I want you people in Michigan to know something—that when you hear Red announce this next inning, you are going to hear the finest baseball announcer in the business." And you know, I almost couldn't announce it after he said that.

We used to sit around—especially during spring training—and he would drink coffee and tell me stories of Ty Cobb and Tris Speaker and Walter Johnson. Harry also used to talk about when he was a heavy drinker, and he would do such crazy things as get into an Austin car and drive it down a flight of steps, into a basement speakeasy, right up to the bar. And he would grin. He had a husky, warm voice. . . . Dizzy had a rounded, full voice. Frisch had a high tenor. Hoyt's voice was high and crisp. . . . One night, in that husky voice of his, over a half-dozen cups of coffee Heilmann said:

"Cobb was managing the Tigers, and a lot of us began missing trains. Cobb announced that the next man who missed a train he would fine five hundred dollars—no matter who he was or what excuse he had. All the writers were watching to see who got the first fine—it was going to be a big story. We were, of course, playing only afternoon games and doing all our traveling by train. We finished a series in New York and were to get a midnight train for Boston. I had some friends in New York who were getting married, and they gave a real party—a blast. I didn't come close to catching the midnight train. The stuff I drank that night!! I didn't know whether I was in New York or Boston, and I didn't care. Some friends poured me onto the early-morning train for Boston, and I was still wearing my tuxedo. When the train pulled into Boston, it was almost time for the game—so I got in a taxi and went straight to the park, tux and all. The road secretary was waiting at the gate, and he rushed me straight to the clubhouse. Cobb was waiting, pacing the floor, and cursing something awful. Ty said, 'Listen, you drunken, so-and-so, you are going to play . . . I don't care how you feel . . . you are going to play. It is time for the game to start right now . . . the clubhouse boy will get you dressed . . . I'm going out and get into an argument with the umpires and keep arguing with them until you get out there.' And that is just what Ty did—he got into a terrible argument, and he made it last . . . it must have gone on for fifteen minutes. Being the visiting team, we hit first, and I came up in the first inning. I don't know how I saw the ball, but I hit it against the fence. When I got to first base, the coach told me to go to second, and as I got to second the third-base coach was waving me to come on to third . . . then he gave me the 'slide' sign, and I slid into third . . . right on my belly. As I lay there, half-blind, all that stuff I drank suddenly came up, and I vomited all over third base. God, I was sick. And Cobb made me play the whole damn game . . . and I got three more hits. As soon as the game ended, Cobb wouldn't let me go to the clubhouse—he sent me directly to the hotel in a cab with the road secretary, while the writers were still in the press box doing their stories. All the writers had been after Cobb to know if I had missed the train . . . and if I was going to get fined. So I went to my room in the hotel still in my uniform, and Cobb told me not to answer the phone when I got in the room, not to open the door, not to do anything until he, Cobb, came. I lay on the bed, too sick to take off my uniform. The phone rang and rang. I never answered it. The knocks came on the door, and I never stirred or said a word. Finally, it got quiet. Then there was this heavy knock, and a voice said, 'Open up—it's Cobb.' So I got up and opened the door and let him in. I lay back on the bed, and he stood over me, and for half an hour he called me everything one man in this world ever called another man. He was mean. He was complete. He was good. He left nothing out. Finally, he stopped speaking. He just stood there and stared at me. He looked at me for a long time. Then he pulled a pint of whiskey out of his pocket, and as we started to drink it, he said one more thing. 'How the hell can I fine a man who is hitting .400?'"

These were some men—these first baseball men to go on mikes:—Frisch, Dean, Grimm, Traynor, Hoyt, Heilmann. Some men. Jack Graney in Cleveland in 1932 started ahead of them, was the first ballplayer to announce on a World Series. I met Jack before his World Series broadcast in 1935, but other than that I was never around him much. Graney hung up his mike in 1953, the year before I came into the American League, so I missed him. Graney lives in Bowling Green, Missouri. He had his eighty-third birthday in June of 1969, and that same week he celebrated his fifty-third wedding anniversary.

So, I got to Cincinnati in a pretty good year, 1934. Yes, as the song goes, it was a very good year.

And speaking of Cincinnati, of the broadcasters I came to know those first years up from Florida, I would be remiss if I were to leave out a certain announcer named Sol Fleischman and a notable moment he helped to contribute to broadcasting history one spring afternoon in 1935. The moment occurred, actually, not in Cincinnati but in Florida.

Larry MacPhail had managed to get WDAE in Tampa to give him free time each noon on the days the Reds were to play exhibition games there. It was up to me to get the ballplayers on those programs, interview them, point out the Reds that would be playing that afternoon. . . .

On a certain day that spring of 1935, the Reds were going to play the Yankees over in St. Petersburg. Thus there would be no broadcast of the Red players. Toronto was then a farm club in MacPhail's new Cincinnati farm system, and Toronto was also training in Tampa that year. Ike Boone was the Toronto manager.

Sol Fleischman was then the sports announcer for WDAE.

He is still on the air for the station these days, giving fishing bulletins and advice, and he is now known as Salty Sol.

Sol used to hang around and watch me interview the ball-players, and his eyes were sticking out two inches from his face, he wanted to interview some of them so badly. He came up to me the night before this game in St. Pete, and he asked me if sometime he couldn't talk to some of them on the air. I said, "Why not tomorrow? Why not do your own show, all by yourself? The Reds will be gone, I will be gone, the time is open . . . I will take you over and introduce you to Ike Boone . . . you can get Ike to get some of his Toronto players . . . and you can have your own show . . . all to yourself."

The moment we got back from St. Pete the next day, I found out what happened. Ike was as good as his word. He came to the mike on time. He brought some of his young players, Mayo Smith included. Mayo, who in 1968 managed the Detroit Tigers to a World Championship over the St. Louis Cardinals, was a kid outfielder then.

Sol interviewed Ike, then Ike took charge. Ike began interviewing his own players, and Sol was pushed off the mike and right out of the picture. Ike got Mayo on, and he said:

"Mayo, where are you from?"

Mayo said, "Lake Worth, Florida, Ike."

Ike said, "Say! They tell me Lake Worth is close to the Everglades . . . and they have a lot of big rattlesnakes over there . . . is that true, Mayo?"

"Ike," came back Mayo, "you are right. Just the day before I left home to come over here, I was chopping wood in the backyard. I laid the axe down to get another piece of wood . . . when I turned back, there was a six-foot rattlesnake coiled around the handle of my axe."

Ike was really interested.

"What did you do, Mayo?" said Ike into the microphone. "Did you pick up the axe and kill the snake?"

"No, Ike," came back Mayo into the microphone. "I hauled ass."

That one word, that one day, caused Sol Fleischman to turn

to fishing reports. On that one word, needless to say, WDAE cut the mike and ended the broadcast.

To wind up this section, I want to talk about two men who never wore a baseball uniform and who were among the best in the broadcasting business—Ty Tyson and Arch McDonald.

Tyson, who pioneered baseball announcing in Detroit, died at age eighty in 1968. Tom Manning, who began it in Cleveland died at sixty-nine. When I was on the radio in Florida, I used to hear Manning from time to time on the World Series with McNamee. I never heard Tyson except when the three of us broadcast the World Series together for NBC in 1936. I would be around Tyson during the spring, and Manning and I shared some Ohio State football broadcasts, so I got to know them fairly well. But again, I was in the National League when they were active, and both of them were in the American League.

They were exact opposites. Tyson thought and spoke deliberately. Many people said he was a "droll" man at the mike. He wasted few words. You never got a quick answer from Tyson—you asked a question, he looked at you, thought about it, then answered. His shortage of words at times bordered on being rude. I found him more sarcastic than droll. H. G. Salsinger, a veteran writer for Detroit, was also on the bitter side, and he and Tyson were always together. The younger generation never got the best of it around that pair.

Tyson started both football and baseball on the air in Detroit. He announced what is credited to be the first football broadcast in the Midwest when he did Wisconsin at Michigan in 1924. His first baseball game was Cleveland at Detroit in 1927. The Tigers won the American League pennant in 1934, and Judge Landis said Tyson could not announce the World Series because he was too partial to the Tigers. Almost overnight a petition of some 600,000 names was secured, and the Judge split the difference—Tyson stayed off the national broadcast, but was allowed to do the World Series on his Detroit station, WWJ. When I worked with him on the NBC network broadcast in 1936, he didn't sound partial to me. He didn't use enough words between pitches and plays to give you an idea how he felt.

Ty quit the play-by-play grind in 1940, but in 1951 when his friend Harry Heilmann was dying, Ty returned for that one season. Then, one night in 1965, Ernie Harwell—an announcer who came up to Brooklyn in 1948 from Atlanta, went to the Polo Grounds, on to Baltimore, and then to Detroit—did a very kind, very thoughtful, very generous thing. He declared a radio night in Tyson's honor, brought the old man out to the park, got him up to the booth, talked about him in his presence over the air, and put him back on a mike for an inning. The Yankees happened to be the visiting team, and so I was there. Tyson was then seventy-eight, he was a shrunken old man, bald, but with those sharp blue eyes watching you. He had on a beret to keep his bald head warm. He tottered when he walked. He always wore glasses. He peered at you, just like a dried-up bird. I was deeply touched by Harwell's kindness—as was all of Detroit.

Arch McDonald was known as The Old Pine Tree. He started out in Chattanooga, announcing the games there for the showman of baseball showmen, Joe Engel. Arch was a Southerner, came on with a heavy drawl, looked like a politician, and spoke like one. In fact, he once ran for Congress, but the voters kept him at the mike. Arch with his drawl didn't waste too many words, and at times he was acknowledged as the "master of the pause." Before he got onto microphones, he worked as a delivery boy for a butcher, a harvest hand, a peanut vendor in a ball park, a patent-medicine salesman, a boxing referee. All these things in his background came out in the course of his broadcasts.

Dizzy Dean used to sing hillbilly on the radio . . . Arch merely talked it, when he wanted to talk. That is how he got his nickname of The Old Pine Tree. He used to quote from the hillbilly ballad "They Cut Down the Old Pine Tree." (. . . "to make a cradle of pine for that sweetheart of mine.")

He used the title, "Cut Down . . . (sometimes he said chop down) . . . the old Pine Tree" when his ball team stopped the opposing team's rally, or when a pitcher got a batter out. Let's say, the Senators were in trouble, and then came up with a game-saving double play. Arch would boom, "Well—They Cut Down the Old Pine Tree."

He was a good phrasemaker, but his weakness was in using his few good phrases over and over. He created the title of "Yankee Clipper" for Joe DiMaggio the one year he broadcast in New York, 1939. New York heard "the ducks are on the pond" (meaning men on base) and "right down Broadway" (a pitch across the center of the plate) a few times and resisted somewhat. But Washington liked his corn-pone expressions, and didn't care how frequently he used them—or how slowly he drawled. Arch was a hometown, small-town-type announcer— and Washington in many, many ways is a small-town city.

Arch was a close friend of Happy Chandler when Chandler was in the Senate. When Chandler became Commissioner of Baseball in 1946, he put Arch on the World Series broadcast, and thereby did his friend Arch no favor. Arch's style was of the early days of radio, and by 1946 the national audience had come to expect expert, crisp, undated reporting of the World Series. There was a demand around the country to take Arch off that Series broadcast, and Commissioner Chandler went up to the booth after the first two games, came back down, and said to the press:

"I just went up to the radio booth and touched Arch Mc-Donald. I touched him to see if he was still warm and breathing. He is both. As long as he stays warm and continues to breathe, he is going to announce this World Series."

Robert Browning wrote something to the effect that a man should die at his pinnacle moment. Arch McDonald had many pinnacle moments in his nearly thirty years on Washington radio. He broadcast the Senators for twenty-two seasons. He often broadcast the football games of the Washington Redskins. He broadcast part of the game the Skins played in New

York on Sunday afternoon October 16, 1960. He got on the train with the team for the trip home, sat down to play bridge, picked up his hand, and died. The train took him on to Washington.

From the beginnings of baseball, Western Union had an exclusive in the ball parks . . . paid money for it. All the ball-parks were connected. The writers usually filed their stories from the park . . . their running stories had to be written as the game progressed, with a Western Union operator sitting alongside, sending as the writer wrote.

Western Union developed and sold a special service called "paragraph one." This was a pitch-by-pitch description of the ball game, and it was for sale to anyone who wanted to buy it, especially radio stations. An experienced operator was in each big-league park to send this "paragraph one" . . . a receiving operator would go to wherever the service was to be delivered—newspaper, radio station, private group, bar, what-have-you. I had the same receiving operator every game . . . he knew all the sending operators in the system. The game was sent by wire in Morse Code . . . dots and dashes . . . I never knew a dot from a dash. The receiving operator would sit at a typewriter, with the Western Union equipment alongside— both the sounder—the instrument that stuttered the code— and a sending key, with which he could "break-in" on the sender and ask for additional data, amplification, or a repeat of a play. Sometimes for a big game there would be a round-robin of Western Union wires from the park to hundreds of radio stations . . . and all the operators would be able to send as well as to receive.

There were many radio stations around the country that did nothing but re-creations of big-league games . . . never did an actual game. For example, WHO in Des Moines used to re-create the Chicago games . . . day after day after day. They had a good-looking, fresh-faced young announcer named Dutch Regan. Once, for some reason or other, he was in Hollywood, and somebody got him to take a routine screen test. He became Ronald Regan, the actor. Years later, when General Electric decided they wanted a host for their television program on Sunday evenings who could act as well as M.C., Ronald Regan replaced Red Barber. The last time I heard about him he was governor of California.

WSBT, the radio station in South Bend, broadcast all nine Notre Dame football games in 1929 from Western Union wire reports. That was one of Rockne's undefeated teams. They had an eager kid out of high school named Reggie Martin who did those games—they were all road games as they were building the stadium at Notre Dame. He fiddled around with sports announcing a few more years—South Bend, Toledo, Chicago. Then he got smart and went behind the desk. Right now he happens to be the general manager of WGBS in Miami—which means that right now he just happens to be my boss.

Most days there would be only a handful of stations taking a game, and it would work comfortably. On a big game with many points hooked together, the sending operator at the park would get furious if stations began breaking in on him . . . and so would I, standing in an empty studio, waiting for a play while some guy in Iowa chattered away, to be followed by a fellow in Alabama asking for a repeat, and then a man from Indiana would break in. At times the physical equipment would fail, sometimes for fifteen, twenty, thirty minutes, until the trouble could be located and repaired. When I did studio reports, or wire games, in Cincinnati, the Western Union failure was always east of Pittsburgh . . . when I was in a studio in New York, the trouble invariably was west of Pittsburgh. I never knew why Pittsburgh was always the pivotal point. . . .

Western Union sent a skeleton outline: Lombardi up . . . S1C (for strike one called) . . . B1L (for ball one low). . . . Out . . . high fly to short right. Mungo coming in to pitch for Brooklyn. . . . Frey up . . . B1W (for ball one wide) . . . DP (for double play) . . . Reese to Herman to Camilli.

The information came in dots and dashes, with long pauses as the operator waited for each play and each pitch. I always believed the audience should know the full truth. I never made any effort to conceal that a wire-report game was a wire-report game. A lot of fellows used sound effects and crowd effects and pretended they were at the game. When the wire would go out, they would have the batter foul off innumerable pitches . . . if the wire stayed out, they had egg on their faces. I didn't have to tell my audience I was doing a wire report— although I did any time I felt it was indicated that I should. I deliberately stood at the mike, looking over the shoulder of the operator, reading what he typed. The sound of the dots and dashes, as well as his typing were completely audible. I wanted those working sounds to be constantly heard . . . I didn't want to try to fool anybody . . . neither did I want to be blamed for a garbled play sent to me, when I never saw the play.

The audience always knew where I was and what I was doing. They believed what I said because they never caught me playing games with them, trying to con them, or fool them. I did the best job I could with a re-creation . . . always as a re-creation. That was good enough for the audience. And when the wire failed, and I had no information on the game still in progress, no matter how heated the situation in the game might be, I could stand on the truth and the audience accepted it. I would say, "the wire has gone out (. . . east or west of Pittsburgh, as the case might be . . .) as soon as the service is fixed, we'll bring you up-to-date. In the meantime, let's review what has already happened . . . check the scores of the other games . . ." etc. Then, after getting everybody brought up-to-the-minute . . . *if* . . . the wire was still out, I would say, "It's still out . . . let's relax and have some music from a phonograph record . . . and the second the wire comes in again, I'll be back with you."

I have heard how men who could "read" Morse Code would stand at a bar, hear my broadcast, and bet the next fellow whether the batter got a hit or went out. It never happened, couldn't happen on my games. Yes, it could and maybe did on some other announcers'—there were fellows who liked to let a half-inning or so come into the studio, and then go on the air with it and build it up to high heaven.

Let me put it this way: when you announce a live game, a game you are seeing for yourself, you announce it through your eyes. You say what your eyes see, what your brain tells you they see. When you announce a game from Western Union, you are in a blank studio hundreds of miles from the game itself. I always stood to be more alert—sitting down was too comfortable . . . and by standing I could move easily to look over the operators' shoulders, write in my scorebook, and should I begin to get drowsy, I could stretch and maybe do a few knee bends . . . that small studio got mighty monotonous at times. But in announcing a game in the studio from the Western Union skeleton of words, I always had with me a rapidly running series of mental pictures. I always saw the park in my mind . . . when the batter's name was typed . . . "Lombardi up" . . . I saw Lombardi from the many times I had studied him, and from seeing him mentally, I spoke audibly—"The next batter is Old Schnozz, Ernie Lombardi . . . a big towering, right-handed batter . . . he takes his stance with his back foot close to the catcher . . . he is the only fellow in the big leagues who uses an interlocking finger grip . . . which goes back to when the index finger on his left hand was broken, and he needed to protect it from his top hand . . . his right hand. Lom is hitting against a seven-man outfield . . . he is the slowest runner in the league, so all four infielders are playing back on the outfield grass . . . the defense is around into left . . . he always pulls the ball. How he won that batting title last year when he never gets a leg hit, I'll never know. Everything he hits has to be sharp, clean, into a hole or over the fence . . . Lombardi sets . . . pumps the big bat . . . takes the pitch . . . it's wide for ball one. . . . Lom goes down and gets a handful of dirt, rubs his hands together, throws the dirt away . . . gets in again. . . . One ball . . . no strikes . . . one out in the fourth inning . . . no score . . ."

I announced what Lombardi did from what I knew he was doing . . . and I did this for every player in the league. When a new man came in the league, I carefully, mentally photographed him. I used my eyes against the days in the studio when I would be unable to use them.

As I stood looking over the operator's shoulder, announcing from the moving stream of mental pictures, I was "in" the action . . . I wanted to know, needed to know the uncertainty that could only come from the waiting expectancy of the next pitch. Therefore, as soon as I saw it typed, I said it, and I kept announcing what my mind told me they were doing, as I waited for the next pitch . . . and the next pitch, and the next. In 1940 the Dodgers opened the season by winning their first nine games. The ninth game was in Cincinnati, and Tex Carleton of the Dodgers had a no-hitter going. New York was excited. I was in WOR's studio at 1440 Broadway. Carleton got two out in the ninth. The burning question was, "a no-hitter or not?" Western Union got the next batter up. Then came the pilot word, *OUT* . . . I didn't hesitate. I said, "It's a NO-HITTER . . . I don't know how he went out—but he's out." You couldn't get it into a mike any faster. No Morse Code readers won any bet at a bar on that game.

Today instead of sixteen major league baseball teams we have twenty-four, scattered all over the country. Each club has its own broadcasting team—most of these crews consist of three men, a few of four. That's a lot of announcers fighting for microphones. And there is also another separate crowd of broadcasters for football. It used to be that baseball announcers could move into football without much conflict, but now the two seasons overlap too drastically.

The sheer number of broadcasters today, coupled with the increasing usage of former athletes as color experts, plus the saturation of commercials, has brought about the depersonalization of sports broadcasting. Announcers are becoming faceless voices, especially on the networks. A football play-by-play announcer today has time only to name the ball handler, say what down it is . . . and the color man, the former athlete, shoulders in to gild the lily . . . then bark another play, give the score hastily . . . get out of the way for the commercial . . . another play . . . in comes the color man . . . and so on.

The greatest danger with sports announcing today—and this comes from the top, from Commissioner Rozelle, Commissioner Kuhn, Commissioner Kennedy, from the network directors of sports, from the sponsors, from the agencies—is the Gee-Whiz-Jack Armstrong-All-American-Boy School of Microphone Mouthings. Not every pitch is a "great" pitch . . . not every effort on a two-yard gain is a "great" effort. Aesop had a bitter fable about the shepherd boy who kept calling "Wolf" until nobody believed him, so when the wolf finally came, he had an undisturbed picnic. The danger to the Commissioners, to the network directors, to the sponsors, to the agencies is the wearing down of the audience by the constant overselling of routine plays until there is nothing left but a vocal sameness that is not worth listening to. When a truly great play occurs, it is an anticlimax. With too many of our modern broadcasters, there are no longer any peaks or valleys—the land is flat. Flat land is monotonous.

When Sandy Koufax quit pitching, NBC put him on its Game of the Week, and if ever a man was mismatched, it was Sandy. He was a great left-handed pitcher, and when he was on, which was often, nobody could beat him. But Koufax was just as ineffective on camera with a microphone as he had been airtight throwing a baseball. After "setting up" everything possible to help him, NBC finally moved him off the Game of the Week to the backup, or secondary game. But that name, Sandy Koufax . . . Mickey Mantle retired in the spring of 1969, and NBC grabbed him for key spot assignments. This moved out Peewee Reese, the old Dodger shortstop, but Reese caught on in Cincinnati in the job vacated by Frank McCormick, the former Redleg first baseman.

And that's how it's come to be in baseball broadcasting—ballplayers bumping ballplayers. Reese originally got his job at NBC when Curt Gowdy decided he wouldn't even try to share a mike with Dizzy Dean . . . and only after Gowdy failed to get Ted Williams to be his broadcasting partner. That is a mess of big-name ballplayers for just one job.

This is not intended to be a book of records, but I do wish to mention the other former players who broadcast in the big leagues in 1969—there were eighteen of them all told.

In the American League: Johnny Pesky was at Boston—when Ted Williams got the managing job at Washington, he wanted Pesky to be a coach for him, but Pesky was held to his broadcasting contract; there were none at California after Buddy Blattner quit at Anaheim to work the games at Kansas City; Mel Parnell came to the Chicago White Sox after being at Boston; Herb Score was again at Cleveland; George Kell was held over at Detroit; there were no former players at Minnesota, Baltimore, Seattle, Washington, and Oakland, but the Yankees had two in Phil Rizzuto and Jerry Coleman.

The National League breaks down this way: five clubs had all-civilian broadcasters—Los Angeles, Houston, St. Louis, San Francisco, and Montreal . . . the job at Montreal requires fluent French, so a reputation as a pitcher or batter isn't quite enough there. Eight former players had jobs on the other seven teams: Ernie Johnson at Atlanta, Lou Boudreau at Chicago, Joe Nuxhall along with Peewee Reese at Cincinnati, Richie Ashburn at Philadelphia, Nellie King at Pittsburgh, Duke Snider at San Diego, and Ralph Kiner at New York.

NBC has the Game of the Week, the All-Star Game, and the World Series—these broadcasts are the big plums, the big showcase, and should be the big money. In 1969, there were four regular NBC jobs with Mantle appearing upon occasions like the World Series. That made it three former players with Sandy Koufax and Tony Kubek. Curt Gowdy and Jim Simpson were the only two civilians in that set-up.

To go back a few years, a rather interesting case in point about ballplayers and broadcasters happened at Yankee Sta-

dium. I arrived there in 1954. At that time, Mel Allen and
Jim Woods were the play-by-play men . . . both professional
broadcasters. Along came Phil Rizzuto, away went Jim Woods.
Jerry Coleman, the former second baseman, was added to
create a four-man team. Then away went Mel Allen, hello
Joe Garagiola. Bang, Barber hit the dirt, and for the season of
1967 the three former ballplayers comprised the entire radio-
television team. A few years later, Garagiola went to the NBC
Today Show on a full-time basis, and Frank Messer was
brought from Baltimore. This made news inasmuch as Messer
had not been a player, and the replacement for him at Baltimore, Jim Karellas, had not been a player, either. A small ray
of hope for the professional announcers . . . small, but a ray.

In 1954, Mel Allen was at the top of his career, an excellent
announcer. The only criticism anyone ever heard of Mel in
those days was his deep devotion to the Yankees and their
well being—but I always thought he had that under control.
After all, the woods were full of Yankee-haters, and their
wrath fell mainly on Allen. There was no fault to be found
with Mel's mike ability or his voice or his reliability.

Jim Woods was a very sound announcer. He went on to
the Giants—then to Pittsburgh . . . now is at St. Louis. Good,
clear voice . . . nose for the news story—when I ran the Football Roundup for CBS I always assigned Jim to an important
game. Jim knew his business, and most important for an associate announcer, he got along well with the principal man.
Jim fitted in, and when I arrived at the stadium his willing-
ness to accommodate himself was valuable. Mel and I never
had a coolness between us, and Jim helped what could have
been a sticky situation. After all, I had been top man five years
at Cincinnati, fifteen more at Brooklyn, and here I was suddenly stuck under Allen's nose in the ball park where he had
been unchallenged top man since he got out of the Army after
World War Two.

I was very blessed in my associates. Twice I was a member
of a professional threesome that could cover a ball game. At

Brooklyn, there were Connie Desmond and Vince Scully. When I first went to the Stadium, a lot of the Yankees . . . Gene Woodling, Joe Collins, Jerry Coleman . . . used to tell me they would hurry home after their game just to hear us three fellows broadcast from Brooklyn. That is high praise. Then, at Yankee Stadium for three years, there were Mel and Jim and me. We handled radio and television, plus the before- and after-game interviews. Adding it all up, I would have to say that Allen, Woods, and Barber were the best baseball broadcasting trio in history. Unless it was Desmond, Scully, and Barber—anyhow both teams worked together, we knew how to do it, we did it.

The sponsor for the games at Yankee Stadium was Ballentine Beer. Carl Badenhausen was the headman at Ballantine. Mr. Badenhausen liked to hang around his country club in New Jersey, liked to play golf . . . and he loved hanging around with the Yankee shortstop, Phil Rizzuto . . . and dearly loved playing golf with Phil. Rizzuto was a fine shortstop, a very talented man on the field who could manipulate a bat with consummate skill. But in 1956, the end of the line came for Rizzuto the ballplayer. Late in the season the Yankees were driving for a pennant, had a chance to pick up Country Slaughter, and to make room for Slaughter, they let Rizzuto go. It was August 25—the day of the Old-Timers' Day. Rizzuto came to the park to play ball, and found out he was an old-timer.

One evening that fall, I walked into Toots Shors Restaurant. Standing at the bar was Jim Woods. He said, if I had a minute, there was something he wanted to tell me.

"Red," he said, "I'm all shook up. George Weiss called me this morning, asked me to drop by the office this afternoon. I thought it was the routine renewal of my contract for next year with you and Mel.

"When I went in, George was fussing around at his desk, looking unhappy, uncertain, which as you know isn't like George. He said for me to sit down. 'Jim,' he began, like he was fishing for words, 'Jim, you have done nothing but good work for the Yankees . . . you've made a great team with Mel and Red . . . I appreciate it, Jim, I really appreciate it. . . . But, Jim, I've got to do something I've never had to do before in my life . . . I've got to fire a man without cause, a man who has done good work. . . . Jim, Ballentine has ordered Rizzuto into the broadcast. You are out.' "

Rizzuto had never done one inning of play-by-play.

Of the three former players I worked with at the stadium— Phil Rizzuto, Joe Garagiola, and Jerry Coleman—only Rizzuto remains, and that figures . . . if he fell in a ditch at midnight, it would have hot and cold running water. Phil has the quickest reflexes, next to Jackie Robinson, I ever saw. He has a sparkling charm when he wishes to turn it on, and no matter the jam he gets in, he gets out of it by assuming a childlike innocence he can call upon instantly. But Phil has not become the professional broadcaster he should be because he won't do the professional preparation.

Jerry Coleman went very far without many microphone talents. Jerry was the man you would expect he'd be, after learning of his two combat assignments in the Marine Air Corps. Jerry had baseball knowledge, he worked assiduously, was sensitive, but his voice and temperament didn't blend into the mike. Rizzuto's voice was no sharper, but Phil somehow had the airwaves instinct.

Joe Garagiola is a star these days on The Today Show on NBC. He has many talents, and he fits into this show—he is under control there. Garagiola had a limited education in St. Louis, he was not a great ballplayer—in fact, he was a fringe catcher and light hitter. But he always had the gall of a brass monkey, and once he started into radio with Harry Carey in St. Louis, he made up his mind to pay the price . . . and he paid it by work, study, practicing his speech, listening to himself on tapes, driving to improve himself.

Somebody at NBC liked him—despite his singsong voice —and sprung him on the World Series. He was a quick sensation as a funnyman, but he was a strongly disruptive influence on the announcer he was paired with. Or paired against, as it sounded. Joe just kept on driving, no matter who was on the air. He was rude in his treatment of his colleage, but maybe it never entered Joe's head that he was rude. Joe was so self-centered I don't think he ever once paused to consider anybody else.

Joe has always had a biting, bitter sense of humor, and it caught on. Make no mistake, he can be funny for that type of humor. I admire the laughs he gets as an after-dinner speaker, although he and I differ about how play-by-play should be conducted. But when you think where he started from, and where he is today—fame, money, NBC—he is the former athlete who has gone the highest, made the most of himself on television. About Joe's grammar—Will Rogers often said, "There's lots of folks who don't say ain't . . . who ain't eating."

Of all the baseball players who got to the microphone, I should say that the best one was Waite Hoyt. Hoyt worked at it, brought a keen mind to the mike, and always possessed great natural ability to tell stories. When I was working in New York, I had opportunities to hear Ralph Kiner on the Mets—a good man, steadily improving. In my judgment he anchors that three-man crew of Lindsey Nelson, Bob Murphy, and himself at Shea Stadium. Peewee Reese surprised me with his easy facility at the mike after he laid down his glove at shortstop . . . Buddy Blattner has made a good professional career in the booth since he quit infielding.

In my measured opinion, the greatest television sports announcer of today is Curt Gowdy. He is the best man on football, baseball, basketball, track, winter or summer Olympics, or fishing. He has amazing versatility and authority. He knows his business. Gowdy received in 1970 a well-earned Peabody Award—the only sports announcer ever to get one. He was born at the right time, just as McNamee was for his time.

Gowdy is from the high country of Wyoming. He grew up in Cheyenne, and as a boy he was either playing sports, fishing, or listening to sports on the radio—Ted Husing, Notre Dame, Southern Cal. Curt's mother made him take some speech lessons as a boy, and she finally sent him down to the local radio station in the fall of 1943.

Curt then was having a bad time. He had gone into the Air Force from college in 1942 and hurt his back. The back got worse, he got discharged, then had the first of two operations. He was learning to live with pain—he has never since been free of back pain—and one season at Boston, doing the Red Sox games, it looked like he was finished, through, a cripple.

In 1943, his mother suggested he go down to KFBC in Cheyenne and see if they had a job for him. They did, odds and ends, high school football—and he was off.

Gowdy steadily developed, grew, worked, took advantage of his chances—on to Oklahoma City, then to New York to assist Mel Allen at Yankee Stadium, to events at Madison Square Garden, to Boston in 1951 to do the Red Sox . . . and when NBC got baseball, plus AFL football, Gowdy was their man. With Al Hirshberg, he did a book, *Cowboy at the Mike*. His background is all in his book, even to remembering I gave him his first network broadcast of a football game when I was at CBS. Gowdy was instantly good—after he did that game down in the Southwest, my boss at CBS, Edward R. Murrow, sent me a telegram that said, "Well, you finally did something right around here—you put Gowdy on the air."

Read Gowdy's book—study his career—and you are convinced he was born at the right time, had the right chances. He has certainly made the most of them. And to this day, Curt remains the quietest, nicest fellow you'd wish to be around. Except—he will cut your throat for the location of a good fishing hole.

I rate Gowdy the top man in *television* sports. The best *radio* announcer for baseball—baseball only, as that is all he does—is Vince Scully of the Dodgers. He has done television, but Walter O'Malley in Los Angeles has, by and large, kept local television out of his park. I have to be careful writing about Scully, as he is my boy—he was my choice at Brooklyn to join Connie Desmond and me when Ernie Harwell went over to the Giants to join Russ Hodges. Connie and I brought Vince along, and when I left Brooklyn, Vince became head-man in the booth—and is still with the Dodgers. They call him the Transistor Kid out in southern California. He merely owns the place.

Scully has a quick mind, incisive voice. He works. He stays up-to-date on the ball club. He has news balance, and he re-spects confidences. He is in command of his booth, of the ball game, and of his integrity. He is a reporter first. Scully tells you what happens to the ball. As does Gowdy.

Both Gowdy and Scully can stand the pressure.

Ray Scott based at Minneapolis and Jack Buck at St. Louis both do very good jobs. They have my fullest confidence, and in recent years, I have heard many of their games, both foot-ball and baseball, although Scott has stopped doing balls and strikes. Buck got the top spot at St. Louis when Harry Carey lost it, and in 1970 he brought in the best associate broad-caster in the trade, Jim Woods. To be the number two man requires entirely different emotional traits than to be number one. To be number two means that you are good enough to do the number-one spot when you have to, but have enough humility to step back when number one is on the job—and not be envious. Woods is excellent—on and off the mike.

Among the former football players who have moved into television, I think Pat Summerall has done the best job. Pat really went to work at CBS—he studied, he researched, he labored like he had never kicked a football for points in the NFL. He worked in the studios until he became a rounded broadcaster. His voice is pleasant, and in recent years, he has adapted himself to the requirements of the work, rather than remaining a former big-name player who is ill at ease in a booth. The late Paul Christman blossomed when he was teamed with Gowdy, and he continued doing very well in the Midwest with Ray Scott until his fatal heart attack. Kyle Rote is an able partner now with Gowdy. Frank Gifford at CBS in New York has made himself a most attractive sports announcer, and, presenter of news on television. Bud Wilkinson, the former Oklahoma coach, has always done a distinguished commentary on the college games—so much so that he stands out above his play-by-play men on ABC. Tom Harmon, the former Michigan halfback, for years has been a staple radio-television commodity—commentaries, interviews, commercials, but no particular play-by-play. He is very definitely today a professional network sports announcer.

When I did the first telecast of a big-league ball game at Brooklyn in 1939, there were two black-and-white cameras, no monitor, no real communication with the director in the truck outside the park, no assistant director with me, and I sat in the open—right out among, shoulder-to-shoulder with, the third base fans in the upper deck. Today, Gowdy sits in a tightly policed booth (try to get in, or even get close), surrounded by as much complex equipment as an astronaut confronts—monitors, earplug phones, playback devices, stop-action-cameras, color cameras, slow-speed reruns, taped commercials, skilled assistant commentators, statisticians, spotters, overhead blimps, assistant directors and assistant assistant directors as numerous as the begats, even to a man down on the field who tells the officials when to call a time out. And the referee calls it.

Gowdy's job today is harder than the job of broadcasting sports has ever been. It is too complicated. Complicated not only by equipment but by the egos and demands of the myriad men involved. I wonder how Gowdy stands it. When he does an event today, particularly in baseball, he had better not even pause to catch his breath—if he does somebody like Tony Kubek will have grabbed the air and gone with it.

Eddie Arcaro told me once, "I rode beyond my time." As far as I am concerned, I broadcast play-by-play beyond mine. I understand why I no longer am invited to broadcast network television sports—I came up in a simpler era, and the one thing I did was control my booth absolutely. I was the boss, I ran it, I took the rap for all the mistakes, I permitted no horseplay during a game, I made it strictly a working area. I allowed nobody in but those actually at work, and this went for my wife, the club owner, anybody. I made an exception one afternoon at Brooklyn—I let my dad sit in the booth during a game, which was merely returning a favor. . . . When I was a boy, he let me ride the locomotive he ran.

But today I can't control the booth I work in, and neither can Gowdy or anyone else. There are too many people, too much complicated paraphernalia, too many network men with assignments, too many cameras and mikes, too many associate broadcasters, too much money, too many commercials. The in-fighting and the behind-the-scenes disembowling that reaches all the way to the top of the network reduce the announcer to being the "fall guy" for the public. I hope Gowdy gets a great deal more money than I ever got—whatever he gets, he sure earns. After all—despite all the mechanics and the array of personnel, Gowdy finally must present it to the audience.

Graham McNamee did an incredible job in his time, without experience, and without precedent. He had the voice with its excitement, he came at a time when people were hungry to hear anything, and he had the temperament to undergo what he did. Maybe Gowdy could not have done what McNamee did—certainly Gowdy hasn't that magnetic voice and bursting enthusiasm. And by the same token, if McNamee had been trapped in Gowdy's modern booth for a few minutes, gotten tangled with instant replays, and his mike snatched away by his colleague a few times, been told in his ear-plug by the director when to speak and when to shut up . . . knowing Graham as I did, he probably would have gone right back to Carnegie Hall and resumed singing . . . stayed on the concert stage the rest of his life and to hell with microphones.

FIVE:
FOCUS 2

MacPHAIL

Larry MacPhail's impact on modern baseball, on radio and then on television, was enormous . . . and I happened to be around and involved in a great part of it. Why MacPhail wasn't elected long ago to the Hall of Fame at Cooperstown, I don't know, unless it's because he stepped on too many toes— baseball is infested with pouter pigeons. MacPhail and Branch Rickey between them brought big-league baseball out of the horse-and-buggy days and into modern times. Take away the achievements of these two men and there wouldn't be any baseball as we know it.

In his three years at Cincinnati, MacPhail became convinced that radio was his best friend. At the start, in 1934, he insisted that WSAI give him fifteen minutes of air time from the ball park at noon when the team was at home. I was to interview players from both the Reds and the visiting teams . . . talk about the starting pitchers for that afternoon . . . about any-thing else I could find to talk about. This was to call attention to the game to be played that day.

In 1932 Franklin Delano Roosevelt flew to Chicago to accept his first presidential nomination. In the summer of 1934, Larry MacPhail flew his entire ball club to Chicago, making it the first big-league team to use an airline. Most of the Redlegs were scared silly, but MacPhail was adamant. He had the pub-licity drums beating, and everybody was afraid to stay off the plane. Except for Bob Newhall. Newhall had the choice fif-teen-minute sports strip on the big station . . . WLW . . . at 6:30 Monday through Friday . . . just ahead of Lowell Thomas . . . who was just ahead of Amos 'n Andy. Newhall had been a sports writer and sports editor in Cincinnati for years . . . then joined WLW as sports commentator. He was top dog. MacPhail wanted all the publicity on this flight he could get. WLW arranged for a shortwave transmitter to go aboard the plane—a Ford Tri-Motor. The airline people scheduled the flight's takeoff for just before Newhall's air time. The idea was for Newhall to broadcast his program from in-side the plane as it flew the Redlegs toward Chicago. It was a great idea, and Newhall never hesitated. He said two words, "Hell no." I was young, expendable, making thirty dollars a week, so I went up in a plane for my first time and broadcast back to Newhall in the studios . . . Bob O'Farrell was the manager, and he went on the mike to say how it looked from up there in the air . . . Dazzy Vance spoke, and the old devil saw a graveyard and told about that—some of the players al-most jumped out then and there . . . Paul Derringer went on the mike . . . and before I could get frightened, we landed at Indianapolis to let the engineer, the equipment, and me get off. The plane went on to Chicago . . . the engineer and I drove sedately back to Cincinnati, unaware of what had been set in motion.

MacPhail used his time in Cincinnati to learn about the

effect of radio. He became sold on its power, especially in teaching baseball to women. He grasped immediately that radio turned a game played by two teams into a contest involving interesting personalities who had hopes, fears, families, troubles, blue or brown eyes. And he grasped radio's value in keeping the fans posted on everything the team did when it was out of town . . . and informing them that the team would return to town on such-and-such a day with such-and-such a team, and at such-and-such a time.

MacPhail installed the first lights in a big-league park the summer of 1935. The year before he had created the first season ticket plan in baseball. He laid the groundwork for those Cincinnati pennants of 1939 and '40. But—he and Mr. Crosley had a difference of opinion in 1936, and MacPhail was out of baseball in '37. It just happened that Mr. Crosley owned the ball club that MacPhail had sold him.

The affairs of the Brooklyn Dodgers had gone sour. The team was owned fifty-fifty by the heirs of Charley Ebbets and Stephen McKeever. They were on hostile terms with each other, and things went from bad to worse, not only with the club's completely divided authority, but with money. The real owner, in effect, was the Brooklyn Trust Co. It had the ball club in its vault, and it didn't want it there—it wanted its money back.

The headman of the Brooklyn Trust Co. was George V. McLaughlin. The president of the National League was Ford C. Frick. They agreed they would have to force the heirs to accept a man of their choice to run the Dodgers . . . really run the club. Be the boss. Pay back the bank. Straighten out what should be a valuable franchise. George V. and Ford C. selected Larry MacPhail.

MacPhail took over in 1938, the last year of that five-year radio ban among the three New York clubs. But there were things to do before tackling the radio situation. MacPhail painted the ball park, cleaned the rest rooms, put new uniforms on the ushers, started a farm system for young players, and called upon George V. McLaughlin at the bank. "George," said Larry, "I need fifty thousand dollars to buy Dolf Camilli from Gerry Nugent of the Phillies." As he tucked the check into his pocket, Larry said to McLaughlin, "Put it on the tab, George." Then he installed lights—had them put on the tab— and in the first night game at Brooklyn, which was the first night game in New York, Johnny Vander Meer pitched his second straight no-hit game. At times I believe MacPhail planned it.

As firmly as MacPhail believed in radio, just as firmly did Ed Barrow and Charles Stoneham fear it. Jacob Ruppert owned the Yankees, but Barrow was his general manager . . . he had built the Yankees, built Yankee Stadium. Barrow ran the Yankees, and what he said went. A man of enormous force and stubbornness, he was utterly opposed to radio. Charles Stoneham, the father of Horace,, the present owner, had the Giants. He was also a man of strong opinions, and he also had abiding misgivings about radio. The Dodgers, before Mac-Phail's arrival, were so divided by their fifty-fifty ownership that they did anything Barrow and Stoneham wanted. Thus, the five-year radio ban by the three New York teams. When MacPhail came to Brooklyn in 1938, that agreement had one more year to run.

Also, it should be noted, a lot of smart fellows in radio and in advertising agencies believed that radio play-by-play could not succeed in a city as large and complex as New York. They said that radio reports of ball games—while popular in small towns—would not be accepted in the metropolis of New York. Further, they said that the afternoon soap operas had such a hold on the listeners, nobody would tune in to a ball game.

In the mid-thirties, General Mills came out with a break-fast food called Wheaties, and somebody came up with the idea of advertising Wheaties as The Breakfast of Champions. This theme lent itself to play-by-play baseball, and General Mills decided to go for the business. Meanwhile, over at Socony-Vacuum, there were other people who thought that radio baseball might be an excellent vehicle for selling Mobil gas and oil.

Cliff Samuelson became the chief negotiator for baseball at General Mills. He also dealt with the ball clubs on behalf of Mobil, and when it came to cracking New York, which took big money for those days, he acted for Proctor & Gamble's Ivory Soap. Samuelson knew that when MacPhail went to Brooklyn if anybody could or would break the radio ban in New York, it would be MacPhail. Samuelson wanted New York like David wanted Bathsheeba.

MacPhail thirsted, too. Finally, he told Samuelson he would refuse to renew the agreement with the Yankees and Giants . . . that he would go on the air in 1939 . . . Brooklyn by itself, home and away . . . for three considerations: seventy thousand dollars for the rights, any fifty thousand-watt radio station in New York, and Red Barber to announce. Samuelson agreed, got WOR, but swore MacPhail to secrecy about me, claiming that if I were to know about the deal, I would bleed him to death for money . . . that I would bankrupt General Mills. MacPhail kept his word. Samuelson spent months telling me how many crack announcers were dying to come to New York and do the job . . . that maybe I had a chance to get the job . . . that he personally would put in a good word for me. Finally, he offered me an announcing job in New York, but he said he didn't know whether I'd be assigned to the New York broadcasts—the Yankees and the Giants had by then been forced to follow MacPhail on the air—or perhaps it might even be Brooklyn. I was offered eight thousand dollars for the year. I took it . . . I jumped at it. Bill Corum and some others wrote in the New York papers that I came for twenty-five thousand dollars . . . and Corum wrote it so often he finally said I had told him that that was the correct figure. Mr. Crosley offered me sixteen thousand dollars to stay in Cincinnati, but I wanted New York, even if it cost me. That first year in New York I didn't see too many Broadway shows. MacPhail told me later he was sure sorry, but what could he do? . . . Anyhow, he paid it back in 1945.

Once MacPhail was going to broadcast from Brooklyn, the other two New York clubs had to go along. Had to. Hated to, but they did, and they arranged a schedule with Samuelson for the same three sponsors. When the Giants were in town, they would be aired . . . and the same for the Yankees. Neither team played in town when the other was home. The New York broadcast did no out-of-town games . . . MacPhail had Brooklyn on the air every time they played, no matter where.

I signed my contract with General Mills in December of 1938 and started for my job at Brooklyn in late February of 1939, via the Dodgers' spring-training camp at Clearwater, Florida. I was to report to MacPhail and to my new ball club down there, get familiar with the players, then drive up to New York and begin announcing the exhibition games from Western Union wire reports.

A few days before I was to start north, I asked MacPhail about where I should live. I didn't know there was such a thing as a borough, much less that New York was comprised of five of them. He spoke about Manhattan, and about Brooklyn, and about Queens, and about Staten Island, and about the Bronx. Then he got into Westchester County, Connecticut, and across the river to New Jersey. It was all Greek to me.

Then I asked him if he had any instructions about the broadcast—as long as this was completely foreign country I was going to, I thought I'd just ask him that.

He said, "No . . . I never gave you any instructions in Cincinnati. I always felt you were closer to the job than anybody else." He turned and walked away.

That is, he started to walk away. He suddenly whirled around. His face was livid. The veins were standing out on his neck like small ropes. He was raging. MacPhail in a rage is a glorious sight, but not for ribbon clerks.

"Yes I do have some instructions for you," he shouted. All the ballplayers dropped their bats and gloves and fastened their attention on him. There was only that one voice and it sounded.

"When I told the Giants and the Yankees I was not going to renew that antiradio pact . . . that I was going to broadcast

. . . Brannick [Eddie Brannick, long-time road secretary of the Giants and bosom pal of young Horace Stoneham, who by then had the team] threatened me. *He* threatened *me!* That Brannick told me that if I dared to broadcast . . . if I *dared* to broadcast . . . that the Giants would get the *best* baseball announcer in the country . . . would get a fifty thousand-watt radio station . . . and that they would *blast me* into the river."

MacPhail was now a wild man, redder than a bleeding beet. He paused just long enough to refill his lungs, and he bellowed again . . . and by now he was jabbing me with his right index finger.

"By God . . . he threatened me . . . threatened to blast me into the river. . . . Listen—I don't know what announcer they've got, or what fifty thousand-watt radio station . . . but I've got WOR, and *that* is a fifty thousand-watt radio station." He jabbed me so deep I've still got the hole in my chest. "And . . . I've got *you.* . . . Now, young man, here are my instructions—*I-don't-want-to-be-blasted-into-the-river."*

He turned away. This time he kept on walking. That was the first of two times MacPhail ever said anything to me about broadcasting.

The two New York clubs selected as their announcer Arch McDonald from Washington. Washington replaced Arch with the great right-hander, Walter Johnson, but after one year, Arch went back to Washington, much to his and Johnson's relief. The Dodger broadcast caught on . . . that home-and-away continuity helped . . . the three million Brooklynites helped . . . Leo Durocher in his first season as a manager helped . . . MacPhail was buying and trading ballplayers, and that helped . . . MacPhail was roaring at the Giants and at the Yankees, and, in Brooklyn, that helped. And—I think, looking back, it is safe to report that MacPhail was not blasted into the river.

New York was the last big-league town to have radio baseball. But it was the first to have television, and again, it was due to MacPhail. That same first year of radio the first televised game was done: August 26, 1939, the first game of a double-header, Cincinnati at Brooklyn.

The manifold influence of television is today the single most important element in sports—money, fan interest, new fans, public acceptance. Today, football games are moved around to get them on television. The play-off games in baseball, as well as the World Series, are scheduled in order to be on television on weekends.

What television means to sports is so obvious—just light the tube and see for yourself—that I am now going to turn off my 1970 television set and go back to Ebbets Field for the first telecast of a pro game of any kind . . . back to when there was an Ebbets Field . . . back to when there were hardly a hundred television receivers in existence, and those that were had a top that was on a hinge . . . you lifted the top to an angle of about forty-five degrees . . . it had a mirror that reflected what was on the tube, which in those days pointed straight up.

Long before television, when I was in Cincinnati, I went to Philadelphia for NBC to do an Army-Navy game—the last one they played at Franklin Field before switching to Municipal Stadium. I had been on three World Series for NBC. I flew into New York by invitation for an interview with John Royal about going to work for him, and when I asked how much he would pay me and what work he would give me, he hit the ceiling. That ended that. He was a tough bird in those days—he gave you what he wanted to give you, and you were supposed to say, "Thank you, Boss." He told me I could stay in Cincinnati until I rotted alongside Fountain Square. Alfred H. "Doc" Morton then became my contact at NBC, we met several times, but couldn't work out a deal— I was doing baseball and was not of a mind to give it up just for a network berth, NBC or no NBC.

I had another friend at NBC. Bill Hedges had come out to Cincinnati to run WLW-WSAI for a year, had come out on a loan from NBC. He was my boss that year, and after he returned to New York, I used to stop in and see him and

Doc Morton, who had been put in charge of programing, wet-nursing, hand-raising television. In the late spring of 1939, NBC televised that Princeton at Columbia baseball game with Bill Stern at the mike.

Doc called shortly afterwards and asked me to come by his office the next time I was in the neighborhood. He said he wanted to televise a *big-league* ball game worse than fire—he wanted Brooklyn, figuring MacPhail might go for it better than Barrow at the Yankees or Stoneham at the Giants. But, Doc said, he didn't know MacPhail, except by hearsay, and that from all he had heard MacPhail was a man who had to be handled just right . . . or no dice. Would I go to Mac-Phail, as a personal favor to my dear friend Doc Morton, and see if I could get MacPhail's permission to allow the cables to be installed? the truck parked outside the field? two cameras to be stationed? Would I do this . . . as a favor?

It was like shooting fish in a barrel with a shotgun.

"Larry," I asked, "would you like another first?"

"Yes," he said. "What is it?"

"Be first to televise a major league ball game."

"Yes," he said again, "but I want something for it . . . you tell NBC that for the game they do, they will have to install a receiving set in the pressroom so I can see it, the writers can see it, and the directors of the ball club can see it."

Doc and NBC agreed quickly to pay the fee—the *first* television fee, sports or otherwise. One receiving set, for one day only.

Burke Crotty was the director, and he worked in the truck. There were two cameras—one on the ground level on the third-base side of home plate, where the foul screen stopped, the other on the third-base side up in the second deck, mixed right in with the fans. That's where I sat, alongside that upstairs camera. I had a set of earphones connected to Crotty in the truck, but they often didn't work, he often didn't think to speak to me, and I often didn't remember to wear them. There was no such thing as a monitor for me to see what the two cameras were showing . . . nobody then was even talking about such a thing. I had to guess what was being shown by the red light on each of the two cameras—when the light was on that camera was on the air, and I noticed which general direction the camera was pointing. Harold Parrott wrote of this event for *The Sporting News*: "The players were clearly distinguishable, but it was not possible to pick out the ball." All of the stories about the reception agreed with Parrott's . . . but also these same writers knew something was coming . . . they didn't know when or how, but it was something very powerful. They had seen the beginning. And nothing about that afternoon was lost on L. S. MacPhail.

There was no haggling with NBC and the three sponsors of the Dodgers' radio broadcasts. NBC offered each sponsor one commercial—one time between a selected half-inning—to do with as they pleased. So that first ball game also was the first commercial programming on television . . . three "live" commercials . . . one each by Ivory Soap, Wheaties, and Mobil Gas. There was no script, no idiot cards, no rehearsal. In the middle of the agreed inning, I held up a bar of Ivory Soap and said something about it being a great soap . . . a few innings later I put on a Mobil Gas service-station cap, held up a can of oil, and said what a great oil it was . . . and for Wheaties? This was the big production number. Right on the camera, right among the fans, I opened a box of Wheaties, shook out a bowlful, sliced a banana, added a spoon of sugar, poured on some milk—and said, "That's a Breakfast of Champions."

The date again was August 26, 1939. First game of a Saturday afternoon doubleheader, Cincinnati Reds at Ebbets Field, Brooklyn. Another first that day was a series of interviews on the ground-level camera after the first game. Everybody waited for me to walk downstairs—they just panned a camera around the ball park. Bill McKechnie and Bucky Walters of the Reds . . . Leo Durocher, Dolf Camilli, Dixie Walker, Whitlow Wyatt of the Dodgers answered a few quick questions. It was all set in motion that August afternoon—the play-by-play, the commercials, and the on-the-spot-in-uniform interviews.

Doc Morton had asked me to get MacPhail's permission to do that first telecast from a big-league park . . . had asked me to announce it. I wanted a memento of the event. I asked for a small engraved silver cigarette box. NBC sent it to me with this inscription:

To
Red Barber
Pioneer Television Sports Announcer
in grateful appreciation
National Broadcasting Company
August 26, 1939

Accompanying the box was a bill for thirty-five dollars, which I paid. I wanted the box, I still have it, and it sure is worth more to me than the thirty-five dollars it cost me in 1939 . . . and not just because the price of silver has gone up.

When Japan took us on at Pearl Harbor, television was put out of the picture. Television went into the deep freeze for the duration. After the Second World War it came on and came on and came on until it gave us two men walking around on the moon.

Japan also took MacPhail out of baseball. He left Brooklyn after the end of the 1942 season and went into the Army as a bird colonel on the staff of General George C. Marshall. Branch Rickey came into Brooklyn after MacPhail left, and that began the bitter, shattering trouble between these two men who had once worked so well together, been such close friends.

Colonel Ruppert, who owned the Yankees, died in 1939, and in a few years, his heirs wanted to sell the club. MacPhail, still in the Army, got Dan Topping interested (Dan was in the Marines), along with Del Webb, a contractor-speculator. The three bought the Yankees in time for the 1945 season for

$2,800,000. (You could write an entire book on the money those three men took out of the Yankees—especially Topping and Webb, what with operating profits, selling the land under the stadium, selling the stadium, and finally selling the franchise and the players to CBS.)

MacPhail engineered the purchase by the trio, and he was to run the Yankees. He brought a new broom with him and swept out Ed Barrow, who had built the Yankees, built Yankee Stadium, hired and fired, and had directed the club for the Ruppert estate. MacPhail and Manager Joe McCarthy didn't see eye to eye, and McCarthy quit in late May of 1946. MacPhail put in lights, he created the plush Stadium Club, he changed the players' dressing rooms, he installed new seats, and he painted the ball park from stem to stern. He dared the wrath of the press and the public by trading second baseman Joe Gordan to Cleveland for pitcher Allie Reynolds—and he wound up laughing.

And he turned his attention to radio and television. The year of 1945 was already contracted for in radio—station, sponsors, and announcers. So he began setting up for 1946. He telephoned me and asked if I would come to see him in the Yankees' office. At that time my dad was dying in North Carolina, and I was going down there every weekend. I told MacPhail that with my work at Brooklyn and the weekend trips, I just couldn't take the extra time. But MacPhail kept after me, and when my father died later that summer, I went to see him at the Yankee offices.

That was the summer—almost twenty years after baseball play-by-play began—when broadcasting got to be serious stuff . . . and marked the high-water mark of play-by-play income from radio alone. The announcing fees and the rights fees went still higher when television got going full blast.

MacPhail didn't waste any time.

"I know you must be wondering what I want to see you about."

I nodded. He was sitting behind his desk.

"I want you to come over to Yankee Stadium next year and announce our games. I offer you a three-year contract, guaranteed, no strings or loopholes . . . I'll take the gamble on lining up sponsors . . . one hundred thousand dollars for the three years. You will name your assistant. You will run it for us as you did for me at Brooklyn.

"This is important. You know how strongly I believe in home-and-away continuity . . . to me it is more important to have my out-of-town games broadcast than it is my home games. The way this is now set up the Yankee home games are being broadcast but their out-of-town games are forgotten because the Giants' home games are on the air. This makes no sense and is one big reason the Brooklyn broadcasts always have had the big audience—and you at the mike over there hasn't hurt any.

"I have told Stoneham that this is the last year we will share the broadcast package with him. We are going strictly on our own next year, and what he does will be his business.

"Also, I am going to find sponsors who will pay the extra costs—I am going to travel the Yankee broadcasts next year . . . every game the Yankees play will be on the air, *live* from wherever they are. No longer will my announcer have to take a Western Union description—he is to see for himself, the audience is to know he is seeing it, the audience will hear the crowds, and there will be no more Western Union wire failures . . . not on the Yankee broadcasts.

"I am telling you . . . whether you come over here or not . . . the Brooklyn broadcasts are not going to run this town much longer."

This is the way MacPhail went at a deal, once he had his mind made up. He never stopped in his presentation.

"Now you know why I didn't want to talk to you about this over the phone . . . I wanted to have you in the office. Further," and he answered the question that had jumped into my mind, "there is no secrecy about my offer to you—knowing you, I expect you to discuss it with your people at Brooklyn

. . . I do not expect your answer now. Tell Rickey . . . tell anybody you are involved with . . . naturally, this should not get into the papers."

That was the meeting. I thanked him, said I would have to think about it, and I left.

When I walked out of MacPhail's office, my steps were so light I could have walked on eggs and not cracked one: A hundred thousand guaranteed dollars for three years . . . the great Yankee Stadium . . . travel with the ball club . . . no more wire reports . . . use my own eyes, make my own judgments . . . the most successful team in baseball . . . one hundred thousand dollars. That was a lot of money in 1945—no baseball announcer had been paid that to my knowledge. And when I wasn't doing the ball games, I'd be free to do what other work I could latch onto. Future unlimited.

At that time, I had a pretty good difference going with the advertising agency that held my contract (the details of this difference are set down later on), a contract that would run out that year. . . . There was no doubt in my mind about what my decision would be.

The next morning at breakfast, Lylah and I got to talking about Branch Rickey—how much we liked him . . . and Mrs. Rickey . . . that Rickey was the only sad thing about leaving . . . he and, of course, Brooklyn itself. The people in Brooklyn had been so kind to me it hurt my throat when I thought about it. Lylah and I agreed I had to give Mr. Rickey the courtesy of a face-to-face report. Not that I really had to, not that there was the slightest commitment to tell him. Legally, I had only the men at the agency to deal with.

I went straight to see Mr. Rickey. Now, Branch Rickey was about the most persuasive man ever in baseball. I left his office with a promise to withhold my decision for three days, and then see him again.

I wasn't prepared for the workings of those three days. The Dodgers were playing at home, so I spent them in that little old band-box-and-so-human a ball park. I was keenly aware of the friendship everywhere I went—clubhouse, dugout, through the stands, along the streets as I walked to the subway station . . . guys hollering "hello" from trucks. The radio booth was mine, completely mine, and I hadn't realized it before. I had been the first announcer in Ebbets Field—I had done the first broadcasts of ball games in New York . . . here in this booth I had done the first radio appeals anywhere for blood donors, in the early days of World War Two, and the Brooklyn people had responded with a steady supply. I kept seeing the veins that said, "Put your needles in here . . . take out what you need." The blood of Brooklyn, in this broadcasting booth, washed over me when I sat down.

Yet it was MacPhail who sanctioned those blood-donor appeals the very first game in Brooklyn after Pearl Harbor . . . opening day. It was MacPhail who not only allowed me to be a reporter in the full sense of reporting, he demanded that I be. He told me once, "You know your business better than anybody . . . you are closer to it . . . you study it harder . . . you have to say what you have to say into a microphone immediately . . . you have no eraser on your mike . . . there is no rewrite man behind you to pretty you up . . . your words must be now, and your words are your complete work. I want the truth about my ball club told to the public . . . and I want the public to know it is getting the truth. I don't want a wishy-washy propagandist announcing my games. What I mean is this—when you see one of my players dogging it . . . when you see that my team needs to be burned . . . then, by God, burn it."

This is how MacPhail stood behind you. One night the Cardinals were playing at Brooklyn. Right at the start of the game a Cardinal got on first. The next batter singled to right, and the runner on first tried for third. (I heard about this later—I didn't know then, couldn't know about it as it happened.) The runner slid into third just as the ball arrived. Bang—the tag was made, and the umpire waved *out*. I announced the runner was *out*. Boom—the ball rolled out of the third baseman's glove, and the umpire waved *safe*. I announced that the runner was *safe*. Hymie Green was the bartender in the pressroom. MacPhail was standing at the bar. They had turned on a small radio set. Hymie said, "Listen to that Barber —he don't know out from safe." MacPhail said, "Let Barber broadcast—you tend bar." Hymie said, "You can't talk like that to me." MacPhail said, "I never will again—go get your money. You're fired." Tom Meany, the writer, was also standing there, and he told me about it. MacPhail never mentioned it to me.

MacPhail gave you a job to do, and if you did it, he went to the river to see that you were let alone to do it. I knew this was how it would be at Yankee Stadium with MacPhail— it had been so at Cincinnati as well as at Brooklyn.

I knew my answer—it would be "Yes" for MacPhail.

But first on Monday I had to see Rickey. I had promised to keep my mind open as much as I could.

He went straight to the point.

"I have thought about this, and more important, I have talked it through with Mrs. Rickey. Whenever I have something that is close to me, that I need guidance on, it is to Jane that I turn. We talked about this well into last night.

"Until now it was not the business of the Brooklyn club what and where your contract was, as long as you were satisfied and remained in the radio booth here. Now that you are not satisfied and are contemplating leaving here . . . now it is the business—the proper business—of both the Brooklyn club and myself. I do not intend to waste your time by saying how much your remaining here means to me, to the club, to the community. You have built quite a following since you came in 1939 . . . when Larry MacPhail brought you to Brooklyn.

"I am not going to tell you the positives and the negatives of your work here—you know them far better than any man can know them. You know what the Brooklyn job is. It may well be that the challenge of the unknown with MacPhail at Yankee Stadium will be irresistible to you. I know you are most adventuresome. I will not be surprised if going over there is a logical sequence—you and MacPhail at Cincinnati, you and MacPhail here. He is a very talented man. I know of no more resourceful, inventive man than MacPhail. I respect his judgment in making you this offer . . . and I would have been deeply surprised had he made it to you in any other fashion than the open way he did.

"Now that he has made you an offer, I will make you one. I offer you for three years a guarantee of one hundred and five thousand dollars—guaranteed by the Brooklyn club. Your contract will be with the club . . . no longer with the advertisers or their agencies. And, I hasten to say, I make this offer freely and without the pressure of MacPhail's offer. You are worth it."

In the three days Rickey had asked me to wait, my anger at the agency had died. The Yankee job still held its attractiveness, but the better than six years at Brooklyn kept coming back and coming back: the small park . . . the people . . . the players . . . the patient building, the losing, the winning . . . War Bond appeals . . . the blood donor response that never failed for so much as one day during the war . . . Manhattan having so much with its tall buildings and trains and theaters and restaurants . . . and Brooklyn, by and large, having three million people and needing a voice . . . and the fates had made me that voice. When I went into Rickey's office, I was going to Yankee Stadium, but I knew I would not only be building a following at the Stadium, but also I would be competing with Brooklyn and with what I had built there. I knew this.

However, as he talked in that sure, warm, full voice, I understood I didn't have to leave Brooklyn and Ebbets Field and the Dodgers. I didn't have to walk away from something I had been a part of since its creation. Rickey was wiping away with each word everything else except the two jobs in their basic sense . . . he was making it (1) broadcasting the Dodgers and holding that continuity, or (2) broadcasting the Yankees

and starting a new cycle . . . the money was no longer a factor
. . . it was now (1) the productive field I was already at work
in, or (2) the greener grass of the distant stadium in the
Bronx.

Except—and this was suddenly it—I could stay in Brooklyn
only if the climate remained pleasant. If Rickey made his offer
under the holdup pistol of MacPhail's offer . . . and came to
resent having had to make it . . . then I'd be better off, by far,
over at the Stadium, traveling around the American League
where I had never traveled . . . pioneering live, regular season
games wherever they were played.

This was more to me than a job at Brooklyn. But how
could I know how Rickey really felt? I blurted out:

"Branch . . . your offer means much to me. However, let
me tell you what happened two weeks ago down in North
Carolina. The funeral for my dad was going to be the next
day . . . and they have a custom down there of not placing
too much store on coming to the funeral itself—but from
seven or eight nearby counties the kinfolks came to my dad's
sister's house the evening before. They brought covered dishes
. . . cakes . . . fried chicken. There must have been a hundred
cousins and uncles and aunts and family friends. Nobody was
doing any mourning or talking sad-mouth. They weren't even
talking about my dad. What they did was assemble together—
eat picnic-style—stay around together a couple of hours—
show a solidarity—and then they scattered. Out in the front
yard a group of men were talking, and one of them said to
another, 'Jim, what did you ever do with that piece of land
you had down on the South Carolina line?' And Jim said,
'Bill . . . I found me a willing buyer.' "

As soon as I said that, Rickey got up, came around his
desk, grabbed my hand, and yelled, "I'm a willing buyer."

Now I had to go back to MacPhail, tell him I would not
accept his tremendous offer, and tell him why. I told him the
blunt truth—that as much as I appreciated it, how wonderful
it was, I couldn't see, now that Rickey had met the money,

coming over to the Stadium to compete against what Mac-Phail and I had begun building, and what Rickey and I were still building.

Larry sat at his desk, listened quietly, then said:

"I am glad for you that you have things the way you want them. You have every right to decide which way to go. I told you that when I made you the offer. Now—I'll tell you something about Rickey . . . he and I don't see eye to eye anymore . . . but when he makes up his mind to do something, he'll walk through a ten-foot thick brick wall."

We both got up, and as I left, he walked me to the door. We shook hands. He grinned.

"That offer I made you . . . it didn't hurt you, did it?"

I said, "No, sir." I got on the elevator and went back to Brooklyn.

MacPhail was as good as his word the season of 1946. He broke away from the Giants . . . broadcast all the Yankee games, home and away, and he traveled his broadcast. All his games were live, for the first time in baseball broadcasting. Also that season, MacPhail sold the Yankees' television rights to Dumont for some seventy-five thousand dollars, which was another first—the first commercial rights fee for sports on television. Mel Allen came back from the Army and was given the key job at the mike . . . but Mel was more Toppings' choice than MacPhail's, a fact that was to add to Mel's confusion when Topping fired him in 1964.

It was a good thing I didn't take MacPhail's offer to come over to the Yankees. He sold out to his partners, Dan Topping and Del Webb, after the season of 1947—which would have been after only two of the three years my contract would have called for. MacPhail's departure was full of sound and fury; Topping and I had a serious run-in at Brooklyn when he owned the Brooklyn Football Dodgers, and as MacPhail's boy I might have been a sitting duck for Topping. When Topping eventually hired me in 1954 he happened to need me, which made it a different ball game. . . .

About MacPhail's departure—he wanted to sell his share on a peak market, take his capital gains, be a millionaire, and turn his talents and attentions to raising and racing thoroughbred horses. Further, he had developed frictions with both Topping and Webb. Topping had an eye on the top Yankee spot anyhow. George Weiss was another irritant in the equation. Weiss had been Ed Barrow's assistant in charge of the farm system. Under MacPhail, Weiss was reduced to being a high-salaried office boy. There is only one boss in a Larry MacPhail setup. And—this is my observation—once Larry MacPhail has built something, he is no longer interested in it. His Yankees in 1947 won the pennant. In the most exciting World Series ever played, they beat the Dodgers for the championship. No more worlds to conquer.

The seventh and decisive game was played at Yankee Stadium. No sooner had the Yankees gotten into the clubhouse to start their celebrating, than in walked MacPhail and announced to the press that he was through—that he was selling out to Topping and Webb. That night as the wine ran red, MacPhail fired George Weiss, and the angry noise from that Yankee victory party is still echoing around mid-Manhattan. Topping hired Weiss back the next morning. MacPhail pocketed his check and went to his horse farm in Maryland, never to return to baseball.

February 3, 1970 MacPhail was eighty years old. To celebrate it he sold his swank apartment in Island House on Key Biscayne, bought a lot on an island in the Bahamas, and began building a house.

It was July of 1946. Before I could become Director of Sports for CBS, succeeding Ted Husing, Mr. William S. Paley himself had to talk to 'me. I was told no one in a fairly high position came to CBS without a personal interview with Mr. Paley. I went to the CBS offices, then at 485 Madison Avenue, and Mr. Paley received me warmly.

He smiled and said, "I listen to Bill Stern and Harry Wismer do football games . . . and they make even a two-yard gain exciting."

My heart sank. I knew I wouldn't get the job if this was what he wanted in his announcer. But there was only one thing I could say, and I blurted it out: "No, sir—I can't announce that way."

And he smiled again and said, "Good, I wouldn't want you to."

The interview was over.

In my years at CBS, I did what amounted to two jobs— the play-by-play of baseball and football, and the network requirements. It meant more work for myself, organizing an office staff at CBS and a tighter-knit crew at Brooklyn, and finding more time in the day. We had lived in Scarsdale since we came East. Immediately after CBS hired me I sold our house in the suburbs, took an apartment in Manhattan, and eliminated the commuting time.

Stanley Woodward was the sports editor of the *New York Herald Tribune.* As soon as CBS announced I was its new Director of Sports, but would continue announcing the games at Brooklyn, Stanley gave me a paragraph in his column. He wrote to the effect that I could not do both jobs . . . and that should I do them, then he, Stanley Woodward, would commit hara-kiri on the sidewalk at 485 Madison Avenue. I used to look for his body, day after day.

My immediate boss at CBS was Ed Murrow, and my main concern was the coverage of college football games.

In the fall of that first year, the Big Ten and the Pacific
Coast conferences made their deal on the Rose Bowl, which
has endured ever since. Coming into the last Saturday of the
season the Big Ten had two possible candidates—Illinois, which
was playing at Northwestern, and Michigan, which was at
Ohio State. If Illinois won, it would go to Pasadena—but if
Illinois lost or was tied, and Michigan won impressively over
the Buckeyes, the Wolverines could get the nod. Which game
to do? I kicked it around with my assistants, John Derr and
Judson Bailey. We couldn't decide. I went down to Ed Murrow's office, and he asked, "Which one would you like to do?"
I blurted out, "I'd like to do them both." Ed said, "How would
you?" And that set off, in a flash, the basic concept of multiple
coverage: the game at Columbus, Ohio, started thirty minutes
ahead of the game at Evanston, Illinois. We would use two
broadcast crews . . . have an open telephone line between the
two booths . . . instant communications. The broadcast would
begin at Columbus, which would take care of the first quarter,
then switch back and forth during the first quarter at Evanston while the second quarter was played at Columbus. When
either announcer had a hot situation, the air could be switched
within a second's time. During the half time at Columbus,
we'd do the play-by-play of the second quarter at Evanston,
and so on to the conclusion—back and forth. One way or the
other, we'd have the story of the first Big Ten team to go to
the Rose Bowl . . . we wouldn't have to guess which one of
the two games to do . . . we'd have them both. Murrow
grinned and said, "Do it." Until then the unwritten rule was
never to leave the game you were doing. We proved you could
interrupt to great advantage, eliminate the flat time outs, and
the dull booming of the bass drums at half time. Whoever
heard a good half-time show on radio?

The fall of 1947 we did two more of what we called "duals"
—two games with staggering starting times. They were all
right, but left John, Judson, and me with an empty feeling.
We were close, but it wasn't right. We knew doing a single

game was an awful gamble—the game could go lopsided early, and you were stuck with it. Early in 1948, we went down to Atlanta to do Florida at Georgia Tech. The night before, Bobby Dodd, the Tech coach, had a few of us out to Aunt Fannie's Cabin for dinner. Bear Wolf was the Gator coach. The talk got around to the game the next day, and Dodd leaned across the table and said, "Bear, I'm awfully sorry to tell you this—but we are going to beat you tomorrow by fifty points." Dodd was wrong. The score was Tech 42, Florida 7. We soon began the CBS Football Roundup—a three-hour sweep of six of the top games of the day.

Until television got going full blast, the Director of Sports for a radio network was also the principal announcer. Once we got the Football Roundup working smoothly, the job didn't require much time in negotiations of events. You scheduled a game, notified the engineering department, they ordered the lines from the telephone company, and you and your spotters and the engineer showed up. There were a few staff meetings for purposes of inner-office communication. You had a certain amount of routine correspondence to do and, by and large, that was radio. The most I had to do in off-the-field duties as Director of Sports was have dinner with the Orange Bowl and the Rose Bowl people from time to time. CBS had the Orange Bowl, and in 1948 got the Rose Bowl away from NBC for three years.

I remember fairly well about CBS getting the Rose Bowl, and for how much. Davidson Taylor was then boss of news and special events—Ed Murrow had gone back to the mike. I had had a violent hemorrhage in Pittsburgh, nearly died. They flew me back to New York. I was having no visitors, no telephone calls, when one night about nine o'clock, Lylah said I had to talk to Taylor. Dave said, "Red, I know I shouldn't call you—but I have no choice. The Rose Bowl people are in their meeting out on the Coast—they are waiting for our bid—I can't authorize our paying them fifty thousand dollars for the radio rights for three years without your okay."

I said, "Okay." So did the Rose Bowl people that same evening. NBC was determined to get it back, no matter what it cost, and they did . . . three years later. I heard that General David Sarnoff himself said to get it back . . . no matter what.

At the turn of the nineteen fifties the television tide was coming in relentlessly. Everything about television was time-consuming. We reset our sports staff at CBS—Derr became the radio man, Bailey the television man, and I was trying to carry water on both shoulders and still be a full-time mike man. Early in 1955, after nine years at CBS, after broadcasting seven Orange Bowls and two Rose Bowls, I asked to see Dr. Frank Stanton, the president of the network, Mr. Paley having become chairman of the board.

I said, "Frank, I have had nine wonderful years here, but the time has come for a decision. You and CBS need a full-time executive—a desk man who doesn't go on the air—as Director of Sports. Television alone demands a skilled negotiator. I'm a broadcaster, not an office man. In fairness to both of us, I have to resign. I intend to go back to broadcasting . . . and do nothing else."

It was a warm, pleasant meeting. He thanked me. This had to be the decision. Television had done it. NBC had already made its move, installing Tom Gallery as Director of Sports—over the bitter screams of Stern. In the years since I left Stanton's office, no working announcer has been in active charge of sports for a major network. Larry MacPhail telephoned and asked me to say a good word for his son Bill, which I did. I guess it didn't hurt. He got the job, and he still has it.

I was the first man Ed Murrow hired on his CBS staff in New York. Had he stayed as my boss, if he would have had me, I think I'd still be his Director of Sports . . . no matter how it would have made me change my life. Murrow was some man.

But the desk and the interoffice gut-fighting were for smaller men, not for Murrow. He went back to where the talent and action were, the microphone and the camera. Then to Washington, then cancer, then "thirty." His funeral nearly broke my heart.

Murrow had great talent, a great voice. He had great courage. He was the first to report who Senator Joseph McCarthy was. He had a great soul, and all his life and strength and mind were devoted to reporting what was the news . . . what was the truth. That was Ed Murrow's greatness—his respect for, his search for, his broadcasting of the truth. Always.

Murrow used to close his across-the-board radio news broadcasts with a feature called The Word for the Day. The announcer used to say, "And now here is Edward R. Murrow, with The Word for the Day." Somehow, program after program, Ed would find an apt saying or a current quote or sometimes he would have to write something that summed up all the news he had been broadcasting during the program.

Prescott Robinson was a crack radio newsman for many years in New York. He finally left WOR and went over to work at CBS. Prescott lives down in Miami now, and he does the news on WTVJ, a top television station in South Florida. When he went to work at CBS, he went to work for Ed Murrow. Prescott was telling me the other night over at his house:

"As soon as I got to CBS, Murrow sent for me. He didn't say much. All he said was, 'Be careful of the adjectives . . . when you say something was a great riot, be damned sure it was a great riot . . . not a minor scuffle or a mere commotion or a handful of people milling around. It's the adjectives you have to watch to report the news properly. . . . Be careful of the adjectives.' "

For my colleagues on the air, and there are now so many of them, may I offer what Murrow said to Robinson, not only as The Word for the Day . . . but also as The Word for every time you face a mike—

"Be careful of the adjectives."

It takes time to put some things into proper focus, and looking back over a fairly full career as a sports announcer, I can see now that if there was any one point where I achieved maturity in my work, it was in the season of 1947. Two big events occurred that year . . . one of them was the most important saving grace given modern baseball . . . and I had the microphone at Ebbets Field, Brooklyn, for both of them. Each presented a different kind of critical pressure, but I found my guidance for both in the one word so vigorously spoken in Detroit by Commissioner K. M. Landis before the opening game of the 1935 World Series.

Baseball had had no Negro player until Branch Rickey forced Jackie Robinson upon it. Forced is the precise word. There had been nothing written down in the laws or rules of baseball prohibiting a Negro, but there was an unwritten code, which was even stronger. Add it up for yourself: not one Negro in organized baseball until 1946. Something must have been going on. Something was.

Early in this year of 1970 *Time* magazine came out with a special issue, Black America. The magazine said,

> Twenty-five years ago, there were no blacks on any pro (baseball, football, basketball) team roster. The percentage of blacks in the pro leagues today:
>
> Baseball—25% (150 out of 600)
> Football—32% (330 out of 1040)
> Basketball—55% (153 out of 280)

These are the rough figures *Time* gave. They do not break down how many "stars" are black. Teams rise and fall on "star" talent. Without trying to enumerate the stars, let me simply ask:

Where would baseball be in 1970 without Willie Mays, Bob Gibson, Willie McCovey, Hank Aaron, Maury Willis, Billy Williams, Ernie Banks, Juan Marichal, Lou Brock, Roberto Clemente, Tommy Agee, Reggie Jackson, Willie Horton, Tony Oliva, Bert Campaneris, Frank Robinson, Vada Pinson, Roy White? . . . to name only a few who are now playing twenty-three years after Rickey and Robinson forced open the door. Let's look at it from another angle, that of sheer numbers. Since 1960, despite the drying-up of the minor leagues, the major leagues have expanded one third, going from sixteen teams to the present total of twenty-four. This means that a third more big-league players have been needed in the past ten years while the total of pro players has diminished. It is fair to say that had Rickey not brought in Robinson, and had Jackie not been highly successful, the big leagues could not have added eight new franchises. Without the black players there simply would not have been enough available manpower to put on the field.

Baseball, after being force-fed the Negro player, soon began to feed on him eagerly wherever and whenever he could be found. The Negro player, especially the "star," has brought in much money. But to this day baseball holds a hidden hostility to Branch Rickey. He made it change. He broke its code. Still today I hear baseball men say that Rickey should have been run out of the game. One of the current bitter jokes in baseball (and it is my contention that all humor springs from pain) says that when a Bob Gibson—a black pitcher—beats you, then blame it on two men—Abraham Lincoln and Branch Rickey.

Rickey was always a man of deep principle, always had the courage to execute his principles, had imagination, had a retentive memory. When he was a young baseball coach at the Ohio Wesleyan, he had as a catcher a fine boy, a fine player, who happened to be a Negro. The team went to South Bend, Indiana, to play Notre Dame. The clerk at the Oliver Hotel publicly rejected the Negro boy, saying loudly, "We don't register Negroes here." Rickey finally prevailed—if the boy didn't register formally, then he would be allowed to share Rickey's room.

Rickey told me in March of 1945 about this incident, how

he came to his room to find this Negro boy pulling and tearing at the skin on his hands, and crying, "It's my skin . . . Mr. Rickey . . . if I could just tear it off . . . I'd be like everybody else." Rickey told me this months before he even had a scouting report on Jackie Robinson. He told me that before he died he was going to silence the bitter cry of that boy in the Oliver Hotel. And that even his wife and his children were against him . . . saying that he was too old.

In December he signed Jackie Robinson to a Montreal contract. Montreal was then a Brooklyn farm club in the old International League. . . . Just as Larry MacPhail said he would, Rickey started to walk through that ten-foot brick wall.

From the first game with Montreal in 1946 Robinson nearly broke up the league. Almost tore it apart. Batting championship. Running the bases.

Nineteen forty-seven was an incredible year. The more I look back on it the more in awe I am of that season. During the spring Rickey and MacPhail got into their bitter fight over whether MacPhail had two known gamblers in his box at a Yankee-Dodger game in Havana, Cuba . . . whether there was one set of rules for Leo Durocher, then the manager of the Dodgers, and another set for MacPhail. Commissioner Happy Chandler held extended hearings. There was blood all over the moon.

Robinson trained during that spring with Montreal, but we all knew he was coming to the big club. There were fearsome rumblings and threats and curses all over the National League, especially in St. Louis. There were white players on the Dodgers who went to Rickey and said they wanted to be traded if the Negro came. In time they got their wish.

Out of the blue, Commissioner Chandler telephoned Rickey in his Brooklyn office. A morning meeting was in progress and Durocher was at the meeting. The day was Friday, April 9, 1947. The season was to open on Tuesday. An exhibition game was scheduled between Montreal and the Dodgers at Ebbets Field that afternoon. Rickey listened, hung up the phone, and among other things said to Durocher, "You, Leo, have been suspended from baseball for one year."

The game that day was rained out. The two teams played the next day, April 10. During the sixth inning of the game an announcement was handed the press. It read, "The Brooklyn Dodgers today purchased the contract of Jackie Roosevelt Robinson from the Montreal Royals. He will report immediately."

Should you wish to pinpoint exactly the coming of the Negro into the big leagues, that is it.

On Friday Rickey lost his manager. On Saturday he signed Robinson onto the Dodgers. The season opened Tuesday and he had no manager. Joe McCarthy, who had left MacPhail and the Yankees the summer before and gone to his farm outside Buffalo, refused to take the job. The Dodgers played their first series vs. Boston with a coach, Clyde Sukeforth, in temporary charge. Rickey had a life-long friend, Burt Shotton, who had been in retirement for several years. Shotton lived in Bartow, Florida. Rickey telephoned him to fly to New York for a meeting. Shotton didn't bring even a change of clothes, he thought so little of the trip. Rickey asked him to take over the ball club, and Shotton agreed. His first game was that same afternoon at the old Polo Grounds.

All Shotton did was calm down the most troubled team in the history of the big leagues. . . . All Shotton did was win the pennant with that team. He was in his sixty-third year. He was sixty-four the week after he lost the seven-game World Series to the Yankees—still, to me, the most dramatic World Series ever played.

That was a red-hot microphone in 1947. There were more listeners to the Brooklyn games that season than there were readers of all the New York newspapers combined. It was a highly sensitive microphone. What went into it had direct bearing on the Dodgers, on Robinson, on Rickey, on the grave problem of integration. There was not a minute, not a word, not a silence, that could be taken for granted. Everything counted. What was said, and what was left unsaid.

Mr. Rickey had selected his key player. He knew the first Negro could not fail. That he had to do it. Rickey was very wise with his choice of Robinson.

But he had inherited his key broadcaster at that pivotal mike; he was stuck with the man. The announcer was well-rooted in Brooklyn, popular, possessed a considerable following. He had been Brooklyn's first announcer, starting in 1939. He had pioneered the Blood Donor appeals, led in Red Cross Fund Raising two years. He had been born white, born in Mississippi, raised in Central Florida.

When Rickey took me into his extreme confidence that afternoon in Joe's Restaurant in Brooklyn in March of 1945 it didn't enter my mind *why* he had told me something only the directors of the ball club knew. I was stunned as he outlined what he was about to do—had in fact already set in motion. I heard routinely his story of a catcher he coached, who was a Negro and who got refused at the Oliver Hotel. That sort of procedure wasn't news to me. I was born in the Deep South, of Southern parents, whose parents were Southern.

I didn't for a moment doubt that Mr. Rickey would do exactly what he said he would. In fact, I was so convinced he would I went straight home and told my wife I was quitting at Brooklyn. I wanted no part of that.

But I didn't tell anyone else, and I began to do some inner searching. I had to face squarely the fact that my job in Brooklyn in 1945 was the best baseball announcing job in all of creation. Economics has a relentless way of being the hidden persuader. I valued the job at Brooklyn. I had fought for it, suffered for it, helped create it. But—what next?

Rickey's story about the Negro boy pulling at the skin on his hands, and crying out about the color of his skin, drove me into admitting I myself had not selected my parents, that I had no more to do with being born white than that boy in the Oliver Hotel had to do with being born black. This was the first step toward gaining my balance. Next, I realized that I was not Mr. Rickey. It was his move, not mine. Then

I soon made myself understand I was not a sociologist. Who was I then?

How would I announce Jackie Robinson? Would I say he was a Negro, and if so, how many times during a game would I say it? Would I announce things he said or would I ignore them? Would I wish him well or would I hope in my heart he failed? You can't count the millions of ad lib words you say during a baseball season, pitch after pitch, play after play, inning after inning, game after game. There is no way. But no matter how many millions of words, just two words—Jackie Robinson—would overshadow the entire season. There would be no escape from Jackie Robinson.

Now as I look back twenty-five years I think I know why Rickey took me into his confidence months before he even knew there was a Negro player of superior physical ability, and instant reflexes, and great spiritual strength named Jackie Robinson. He had told me then to give me time to think, time to get ready—or else to make me quit.

Months go by and you carry a multitude of worries in your mind. I knew Jackie was coming, the way he was playing at Montreal in 1946. I knew that with him at Brooklyn there would be listeners who had never heard a ballgame before. I knew there would be listeners weighing every word I spoke, trying to detect what I was saying, what I meant, what I felt. The ear of the black listener would not be the ear of the white listener. People hear what they want to hear, or what they are afraid to hear.

Rickey never said so, but I knew all he wanted was for Robinson to have his fair chance and to sink or swim with it. Rickey begged the Negro leaders of New York to help Robinson by leaving him alone and not softening him with lavish attention.

Robinson was a strong, proud man. He too wanted nothing more than his chance. He wanted no begging of favors.

Suddenly it was decided for me. Over the years came the word Commissioner Landis spoke in Detroit. He told us all

that morning in 1935 before we went to our three booths in
Detroit . . . "Don't manage, don't play, don't umpire . . .
REPORT."

I began that season reporting what Jackie Robinson did.
That was all. I pulled neither for him nor against him. He
was to me a ballplayer who hit a ball or missed it, who
picked up a ground ball or missed it, who caught a pop fly or
missed it. On the base he was the most exciting ballplayer I have
ever seen. On any base. There were rhubarbs at times, and
I reported them. I saw to it that Jackie Robinson got his fair
chance in the radio booth. Judge Landis helped do that. That
was all the equation needed for its satisfaction—a report.
Robinson and Rickey took care of the rest.

But looking back to when it happened, to how it happened,
and to what is going on today, that was some closed door
Branch Rickey forced open and Jackie Robinson kept open.

The Yankees and the Dodgers met in the World Series.
Rickey and MacPhail, adversaries in the spring, met again
through their teams in the fall.

Larry MacPhail, running the Yankees, had as his manager
Bucky Harris. He had as players Joe DiMaggio, Yogi Berra,
Phil Rizzuto, Tommy Henrich, Charley Keller, Snuffy Stirn-
weiss, Billy Johnson, Allie Reynolds, Vic Raschi, Spud Chandler, Joe Page, Frank Shea, and fellows like that.

Branch Rickey had the Dodgers, and he had Burt Shotton
fresh out of retirement and full of years as his manager. Jackie
Robinson was Rookie of the Year. There was a kid catcher
named Gil Hodges, who managed the 1969 Mets to a World
Championship. Peewee Reese, Arky Vaughan, Cookie Lavagetto, Eddie Stanky, Carl Furillo, Al Gionfriddo, Dixie
Walker, Pete Reiser, Gene Hermanski, Rex Barney, Ralph
Branca, Hugh Casey, Clyde King, who managed San Francisco,
and Hal Gregg were some of the other Dodgers.

The Yankees won the first two games. The Dodgers won
the next two. The Yankees took game five. In game six at
the Stadium the Dodgers won again—that was the game in

which Al Gionfriddo caught the home run off DiMaggio against the gate of the left centerfield bullpen. An excerpt of that broadcast was done on a giveaway record and has been played often over the years—when Gionfriddo caught the ball I said, "Oh, doctor." People still use that phrase in times of complete surprise. In game seven Joe Page walked out of the bullpen and saved the game for the Yankees, winning the Series for them. And into their clubhouse celebration immediately afterward walked President MacPhail to announce he was selling out his Yankee stock and leaving baseball. Oh, doctor.

Judge Landis gave me the guidance I needed for the challenging assignment of the breaking of the color line. I heard his voice a second time that year—during the broadcast of the World Series. It happened in the sixth inning of the fourth game, played at Brooklyn.

Mel Allen and I had the announcing assignment. We didn't know it then, but 1947 was the high-water mark for radio. The next year television had a partial but respectable network of stations, and soon became the dominant medium.

Mel had the first four and a half innings of the game. Bill Bevens was pitching for the Yankees. He was wild all afternoon, and eventually walked ten men, but as the innings passed he was giving up no hits. The game was a squeaker all the way, and in the late innings Bevens and the Yankees led 2–1.

The Dodgers came to bat in the last of the fifth as I took over the broadcast. Bevens got them out, still no hits, and I was confronted by The Hoodoo: "One doesn't mention out loud that a pitcher has a no-hitter going after the fifth inning. You might jinx him." This hoodoo business started in the dugouts with a fairly reasonable premise—a teammate would not mention a possible no-hitter for fear of putting undue pressure on his pitcher, who just might be pitching away blissfully unaware of what he was doing. Then, before radio came along, this hoodoo, or jinx, got up to the pressbox, and the writers turned silent whenever the occasion presented itself. When radio got going, the hoodoo spread into most of the broadcasting booths. Not mine. The first big league game I ever did was Opening Day at Cincinnati in 1934, when Lon Warneke of the Cubs went until one Redleg was out in the ninth inning before he gave up a hit—Adam Comorosky scratched a single through Warneke's feet. From that very first game on I always reported the number of hits as well as runs and errors and innings. However, it was one thing what you did on a local station and quite another in a big World Series with nearly every radio station in the known world taking the broadcast. World Series pressure is brutal.

Now, almost before I knew it, the Dodgers were at bat in the sixth inning. I had to decide then and there whether I would duck-and-dodge-and-hint that something important might be happening, or would I just plain out with the fact that Bevens had given up not one hit. Allen was of the hoodoo school, one of its staunch members. There would have been no question at all had he had the mike. Allen would have cut his throat before he'd state that Bevens had given no hits.

As the Dodgers started batting in the sixth I thought, "What am I? A dealer in superstition, or a broadcaster? People all around the world are tuning in and don't know what has happened in earlier innings."

I remembered Judge Landis saying, "Report—report everything you see. Keep your opinions to yourself. But report . . . report it all."

I said to myself, "I am a reporter."

When I leaned into the mike in the sixth inning and said that Bevens had given one run, so many walks, and no hits, the breath gurgled in Allen's throat like a country boy trying to swallow a chinaberry seed. I continued to detail, inning by inning, that Bevens had given no hits. That soon became The Story, until Harry Lavagetto exploded it when he got a double with two out in the ninth inning. He broke the no-hitter with that line drive off the concrete wall high above the frantically leaping figure of Tommy Henrich . . . and he knocked in two runs and won the ball game. The radio audience knew very well what the game was all about. Pitch by pitch— inning by inning. I like to think that my reporting that afternoon helped make Bevens and Lavagetto properly famous for their encounter.

But there was much nastiness that night in New York about what I had done, especially from so-called Yankee fans. I was even criticized on the radio by a couple of local announcers. I was held up that night as the man who had done the most unsportsmanlike thing ever in the history of sports announcing.

The next day, I went to face two men: Manager Bucky Harris and pitcher Bill Bevens. I went to them, told them what I had done, and both were instantly great about it. Harris said, "Red, if you can control hits by what you say or do not say, I want you to sit in the dugout with me during the games. I will pay you far more down here than you can make up there." Bevens smiled sadly and said, "It wasn't anything you said . . . it was those bases-on-balls that killed me."

Nineteen forty-seven was the last big year for radio. I had serious work to do that season. The Jackie Robinson assignment lasted all year, the Bill Bevens one for part of an afternoon. I'll take that as my most satisfactory year. It was good work, based on one word. Report. I think I became a professional.

Nineteen forty-seven. . . . Oh, doctor!

SPONSORS AND CONTRACTS

When Hal Totten, Pat Flanagan, and Quin Ryan began pioneering ball games in Chicago, they worked for and were paid by their radio stations. For years and years, it was the general rule that announcers were paid and controlled by their stations, and they did the commercials—when there were commercials. The radio stations found the sponsors, sold them, took their messages, and routinely handed them on to the announcers to read. When I was brought to Cincinnati by the Crosley Radio Corporation, I came as a staff man. I worked for the station twelve months a year—baseball, football, news, music . . . anything the station ordered. I had nothing officially to do with the ball club, with sponsors, the advertising agencies. In fact, WLW-WSAI forbade its talent to traffic with anybody but itself.

But when I signed with General Mills to go East and announce the Brooklyn games in 1939, I began a new working arrangement, and it was new, by and large, for the entire industry. I went East, came to New York, as a free lance. I was now under contract to the advertising agency representing the baseball sponsors, and I was paid by the agency. Again, I had no commitment with the baseball team. General Mills and MacPhail parted ways after two stormy years at Brooklyn—Cliff Samuelson held MacPhail at arm's length in a delaying effort to get the deal he, Samuelson, tried to force—MacPhail went out and got Old Gold cigarettes as a new sponsor. Good-bye. The ad agency for Old Golds was first J. Walter Thompson, then it was Lennen & Mitchell, and the man that I dealt with there was Ray Vir Din—a cold clam . . . ice water in a deep freeze.

Until 1945 I never talked with MacPhail or Rickey about the terms of my broadcasting—I reported to the advertising agency, was paid by it, negotiated my deals annually with the agency. J. Walter Thompson was pleasant—but Vir Din, at Lennen & Mitchell, was a tough man. He warned me the first time I was in his office. He didn't mean to tip his hand, but he did. He had a beautiful old pine table that he used instead of a desk, and I admired it. It was beautiful. He immediately rubbed his hands together, widened his eyes, and related how he saw it up in New England in an old lady's house—realized it was a museum piece—and got it from her for a ridiculously cheap price—something like thirty or thirty-five dollars . . . and he told me with gusto he wouldn't sell it for a thousand dollars, if that . . . that it was valuable . . . genuine American antique. I sat there and watched him and thought about the old woman . . . and I thought about old Red, too. Across that pine table was the man who would negotiate my income from baseball.

As soon as Old Gold got the broadcasts, I got to know Bert Kent, the president of P. Lorrilard—only living man they named a cigarette for, but that was years later when both Old Gold and Barber were long gone from Brooklyn. Kent, it turned out, lived in Bronxville. I lived up the road in Scarsdale. It soon happened that there was an interchange of golf, cocktail parties, dinner, and neighborly telephoning. Bert had me assigned for the commercials and the general master-of-ceremonies on the weekly half-hour network show Old Gold had on CBS . . . Sammy Kaye, Frankie Carle, Woody Herman, Alan Jones, Alec Templeton. A comedian who appeared once or twice on the show—fairly unknown—was named Jackie Gleason. In those days nothing, absolutely nothing, went on either CBS or NBC that wasn't live . . . no records, transcriptions, tapes. What killed you was the three-hour wait to do a repeat of the show for the Pacific Coast. Gleason went to the poolroom. A few of the stars must have gone where liquor was served . . . sometimes the late show was somewhat different.

Every regular on the show worked under a thirteen-week contract. You were either renewed for another thirteen weeks or you were dropped. Sammy Kaye taught me in a hurry who had the most to say about whether you got renewed or not . . . Mrs. Bert Kent. If she liked you, you could call her Lily.

If she liked you enough, you stayed on the show. There was a glass booth called the sponsor's booth, and show after show the Kents and some of their friends would be bowed into the booth. There were advertising agency men swarming around them like bees on a busted sugar barrel. Sammy always knew when Lily Kent arrived. She said, "Sammy is such a sweet boy." Anytime the Kents wanted any of us to go to dinner after the first show, we fell in line behind old Swing-and-Sway. Sammy could grouse during rehearsal all afternoon, as cross as a bear with a boil in his nose, but once Lily got in the theater his disposition improved amazingly. He got to be a "sweet boy" . . . immediately.

That summer afternoon in 1945 when MacPhail made me his offer, I walked straight from the Yankee office on Fifth Avenue to Vir Din's office on Madison. My last bargaining with the agency festered deep in my craw. My mind was set . . . I was just delivering the news in person. He and Bert Kent were well entitled to the courtesy of hearing it from me . . . especially Bert Kent, who was a very nice man. He had started as a tobacco salesman and worked himself all the way up. During the war, when you couldn't get the cigarette brand you wanted, he always had a carton or two for me whenever I saw him.

My meeting with Vir Din was cold and brief. I told him what MacPhail had just offered, a half-hour before. He said, "I told you last fall you were getting all you were worth at Brooklyn . . . all I was going to pay you . . . and that I had so recommended to Bert Kent." I said I was now going over to see Bert Kent, to tell him myself. I did.

"Red," said Mr. Kent, "I went over this situation with Vir Din last year . . . we examined what the broadcast cost . . . what returns we were getting. I am telling you that you have gone as far with us in the matter of money as you are ever going to go. All you are getting now is all you are ever going to get. . . . If you decide to go over to the Yankees, that is up to you."

This time he didn't offer me a carton of Old Golds as I left.

I had my answer, not once, but twice. I was thirty-seven years old. I was just coming into my career. I had done very good work. The Brooklyn broadcast was *the* baseball broadcast in town—in fact, twice the New York broadcast couldn't find sponsors and skipped being on the air those seasons, leaving it all to the Dodgers. There had been a succession of announcers at the Stadium and at the Polo Grounds. Here was MacPhail offering me my first real money—and within the same hour, Bert Kent told me, and I knew he meant it, that I was frozen at far less money . . . just when I thought I should be going through the ceiling. I went home and told Lylah I was going to Yankee Stadium next year, at almost double the money. We rejoiced in the only way two people can who have worked . . . waited . . . budgeted . . . done without . . . averaging less than one hundred fifty dollars a month my first five years in radio. We had even waited five years before we thought we should have a baby.

But then the next day I went to see Branch Rickey. After I said I was going to take MacPhail's offer, go to Yankee Stadium the next season under a firm contract for three years, Rickey said:

"Are you finished?"

I said, "Yes."

"Well," he said, "I'm not. I'm just beginning. Let me say quickly several things—quickly, because I must go to the airport immediately. First, I don't blame you at all for planning to accept the Yankee job. If I were in your position at this moment, I would react precisely the way you have.

"Ray Vir Din said some hard things to you. Mr. Kent, who is a fine gentleman, spoke harshly to you. But have you realized they did not, do not, and cannot speak for the Brooklyn club and for me, Branch Rickey?

"It was the policy in St. Louis, when I was there, that the announcers not be under contract to the baseball club. This was the policy I found here when I came. Up until now I have respected this policy—it has worked satisfactorily for all parties concerned. However, as of this moment, it is no longer a policy the Brooklyn club finds satisfactory in the slightest degree. As of this moment, the Brooklyn club finds that it must take serious steps to guarantee to itself the announcer of its choice . . . and I say this in full awareness that now the Brooklyn club must select the announcer of its choice, and the sponsors in turn must accept him . . . which is in contradiction to the present policy of risking what announcer the sponsor will provide.

"I will make no effort to minimize your value to the Brooklyn club, to Brooklyn itself, and to me personally. Your civic value alone is sufficient to cause this change in club-sponsor policy."

I started to speak, but he raised his hand, held me in silence. He intended to round out his point of view.

"I know without consulting them that the directors of the Brooklyn club will agree with me, that I should step in and make you a counteroffer."

Now I did speak. I had to speak.

"Branch"—he had asked me to call him by his first name after I kept calling him Mr. Rickey—he said all the writers called him Branch, so he wished I would also—"I told you my mind is made up . . . that I am taking the Yankee offer. I did not come here for a deal, for a proposition from you. I came here because I felt you were entitled to hear this from me and not from Ray Vir Din or Bert Kent."

He smiled. "Yes, yes, I know this . . . I count upon this. I have been involved in making trades all my life, and I think I know when a man comes into my office with a trade in mind. If you were interested in a deal with me, you wouldn't even be here this morning . . . you would let the word come to me from Vir Din or Kent. I value . . . I accept without reservation . . . the personality of your presence.

"However," and he leaned across the desk, "if you value my friendship, and you will consider kindly your associations here in Brooklyn, I ask you to give me three days. I must go away within a few minutes . . . I must keep an appointment that is of long-standing and of some importance. Will you do your best to keep an open mind until I return? Will you see me here at ten o'clock Monday morning? Three days from now? Is it too much to ask that you not advise MacPhail of your answer to him until you see me . . . in three days?"

I told him I would come back Monday, and I would do the best I could to have an open mind on the decision . . . but I could not promise anything more.

You know what happened after that.

When MacPhail was running the baseball Dodgers, Dan Topping owned and ran the football Dodgers, then members of the National Football League. I was MacPhail's boy and saw little of Topping. I didn't move in his set . . . nightclubs, inherited wealth, hotels, yachts, cafe society, private airplanes. However, in 1939 I did do the home games of the Dodgers on NBC television, the first televised football anywhere and I announced on radio the championship game of the Giants at Green Bay. The next year I did the radio accounts of the football Dodgers.

I was scheduled to do Brooklyn Dodger football games again in 1941—or I thought I was. The broadcasts were over WOR on Sundays, and I had reserved in my agreement with Pete Maddox, a WOR executive, the right to do Saturday football games at Princeton for Les Quailey and Atlantic Refining. There was one Dodger game out in Green Bay that I would have to skip (plane service was not elaborate in those days). After that I would be clear to do all the remaining Dodger games—and Princeton games, too—without a conflict. Topping was dealing with Gene Thomas, who was in charge of sales for WOR, and Thomas glibly promised Topping that I would be in Green Bay. I never told Thomas I would or could be in Green Bay—never talked to Thomas. I was going to Princeton on Saturday, and nowhere else. Topping heard something about this, called Thomas, and said that if "Barber is not on the train with us for Green Bay . . . he is off the broadcasts."

The train left while I was at Princeton. There it was: Topping had been promised my services by Thomas, who had never talked with me . . . my arrangement was with Pete Maddox, who I thought had cleared it with his boss, Thomas.

Monday morning I was notified by phone that Topping had signed Bill Slater to do the Dodgers' schedule, and that I was dead. I demanded a meeting later that morning with Topping and Thomas in Topping's office—and I made Thomas admit he had never had any word from me that I would do the game at Green Bay. Topping shrugged and said, "Too late—Slater does the games." That was all.

It was too late to do anything about the rest of Topping's schedule, but it wasn't too late to make WOR tear up its management contract with me—that very afternoon. I was raging, Topping was cold, Thomas took a Uriah Heep powder, but not until we had it out before Ted Streibert, the general manager, and Alfred H. McCosker, the president.

It seemed there was no way for Bill Slater and Red Barber to be on easy terms with each other. When I got dropped by Gillette on the World Series of 1944, who went on? Bill Slater.

The next five years I announced on radio the games of the New York football Giants . . . Topping was away with the Marines during World War Two and brought Tom Gallery in from the Pacific Coast to run the Dodgers for him. As the war ended, Topping and MacPhail and Del Webb bought the Yankees, and I saw Dan then for the first time since the blow up over his football broadcasts. We hadn't missed each other.

Branch Rickey and Walter O'Malley got into the doggonedest battle for control of the Dodgers and for personal survival you can imagine. John Smith would have been involved too, but he died. Dearie Mulvey was a participant, but not actively—she owned a fourth of the club, wouldn't sell to anybody—and was constantly courted by both sides—both Dearie and her husband Jim, who sat for her on the board of the Dodgers. Very quickly:

Branch Rickey was brought in when MacPhail entered the

war after the 1942 season. Several years later, the various heirs holding seventy-five percent of the Dodgers' stock were willing to sell . . . except for Judge McKeever's daughter, Dearie, who had twenty-five percent. (She died with it.) Rickey and John L. Smith and Walter O'Malley formed a partnership to buy the available seventy-five percent, each man having twenty-fice percent. Further, the three partners signed a contract stating that no one of them could sell his quarter ownership until he had legally given his other partners the right to match the offer, and if matching it, buy it. The years went by, with Rickey running the Dodgers, using his superb baseball know-how and experience. Gradually, O'Malley was learning the business, taking an increasingly active part, especially in the broadcasting rights. John Smith, the headman of Charles Pfizer Company, fell ill and died. O'Malley was the lawyer and trusted friend of Mrs. Smith. Rickey had a contract that not only paid him for and spelled out his executive authority, but also gave him a fixed percentage of all the sales he made of ballplayers—the same type contract he had had at St. Louis. O'Malley thought Rickey was getting too much money and had too much say in the ball club. Now that he, Walter O'Malley, was controlling the Smith quarter, his quarter, and, further, was on excellent terms with Jim and Dearie Mulvie and their quarter . . . he thought that he could put Rickey where he, O'Malley, wanted him. He wanted to keep Rickey's baseball brains and player evaluations, but he wanted to cut down on Rickey's authority and end his profiting from player sales . . . in effect, O'Malley would take over and Rickey would work for him on O'Malley's terms. Rickey seemed to be trapped. He couldn't find anybody foolish enough to buy his twenty-five percent, not in the obvious prospect of O'Malley taking control. Rickey was desperate. He told me so several times. He told me he had placed all his life insurance in hock to buy his twenty-five percent. Now he was caught with it, and worse, he was about to have to accept O'Malley's sharply reduced . . . humiliating, if you please . . . terms. Or do what?

All his life Rickey had nurtured friendships. He placed great store in certain of his college fraternity brothers, one of whom was the wealthy owner of the Pittsburgh Pirates, John Galbreath. In his deep despair, Rickey talked to Galbreath. Galbreath knew William Zeckendorf, then riding high in New York and other places with his fabulous real-estate transactions. Zeckendorf was a free-wheeling dealer. He agreed to buy Rickey's stock for $1,050,000, Rickey to get the million and Zeckendorf to get the fifty thousand—for his trouble—IF O'Malley met this offer, which he had the right to do. O'Malley met it, but nearly blew out seventeen hundred ulcers. It infuriated him to pay Zeckendorf the fifty thousand!

When Bill Zeckendorf made his firm offer, O'Malley faced: Rickey getting out of the trap completely . . . with a million dollars—almost three times what he had paid for his stock . . . the placing of that high an evaluation on that much stock, which the income and inheritance tax people would now use in the settlement of the Smith estate . . . the new price that O'Malley would have to later pay for the Smith twenty-five percent . . . the loss of Rickey's baseball knowledge . . . and the damage to the O'Malley *machismo,* which is male Irish ego, in Spanish.

This battle was fought in the closing days of the 1950 season. The private club box was immediately adjacent to the radio booth—six inches away, with both booths open in front— the foul screen protecting the area. I remember the last game of that season when the Dodgers failed to beat the Whiz Kids from Philadelphia in the ninth inning and force a play-off for the pennant . . . Dick Sisler of the Phillies hit a home run into the left-field stands off Don Newcombe in the tenth and the Phillies won the game and the pennant. But more than the game itself and all the high stakes it was being played for, I remember how hard it was to broadcast it. Not because of things that occurred on the playing field, but because of Rickey and O'Malley in the club box, screaming and yelling at each other . . . two strong men using strong language. I thought they would come to blows. I never heard anything like it. I kept very close to the mike so nothing they said would be picked up. There was blood on the moon.

After the decisive double play by Rickey to Galbreath to Zeckendorf, I knew I had to be through as the Brooklyn announcer. I had not gotten into the battle. It was not my fight. But I was well aware of the abiding bitterness O'Malley had to have for Rickey, and for all his works and people. As it was, Walter had more realistic forgiveness than you could expect a human to have. He did not rehire Rickey's manager and longtime friend, Burt Shotton—that figured. But he kept all of Rickey's staff who wished to remain, building around Buzzi Bavasi and Fresco Thompson, both Rickey men. To stay, however, you didn't mention Rickey anymore. It was now "The Walter O'Malley Show." He had fought for it, paid for it. Walter was now *The* O'Malley.

My contract had another year to go. Just about as soon as O'Malley was officially seated in the big office at 215 Montague Street, Borough of Brooklyn, I knew where I had to go. To Walter's office. I went expecting to be allowed to quit.

In the years of the partnership of Rickey, O'Malley, and Smith, I'd had nothing but the most pleasant relations with all three. Whenever we chanced to be together, it was always good. Smith used to take the writers and officials and broadcasters on his boat every spring, and nothing but goodwill spilled around. In that crew, nobody lost a drink. When John Smith lay dying, I used to stop in and see him on my way to the ball park. And when the final battle raged with Rickey and O'Malley, I stayed where I should—on the sidelines . . . in my booth or at home.

I walked into the office where Rickey used to sit behind the desk, and now O'Malley was sitting there. We always called each other by our given names. I said, "Hello, Walter." He said, "Hello, Walter . . . sit down."

"Walter," I began . . . I had asked for the meeting. "As you know, my contract runs through next year. You are the new headman of the ball club, and you didn't negotiate the contract—Rickey did. As the new head of the Dodgers, you are entitled next year to have the announcer of your choice. I've come to release you from my contract."

He was fixing a cigar to stick a holder on it. He smiled slightly, and he said:

"Thank you . . . but I want you here next year."

"Look, Walter," I went on. "I didn't have anything to do with your trouble with Rickey. But I know it went deep. I know how angry you were and probably will be all your life. While I didn't have a part in it, I am Rickey's friend . . . strong friend . . . and I intend to remain his friend. He made me the announcer under contract to the ball club . . . so, in effect, I was his announcer. I don't see how I can stay here . . . and everytime you see me, or hear me, think, 'There is Rickey's man.' This is asking too much of both of us, you especially."

He retained his smile.

"It is healthy," he replied, "that we talk about these things. I know you didn't have anything to do with our differences. You have great value to the Brooklyn club. You are established in the Brooklyn community. I see no reason why you can't do your work here next year, and in the years to come. Your contract is set for next year . . . let's leave it at that."

But I couldn't leave it at that.

"Walter, let me go back to Rickey. You remember when MacPhail made me the Yankee offer . . . you remember Rickey and MacPhail were by then bitter enemies. I chose to take Rickey's counteroffer . . . but he understood that in taking it, I did not give up my friendship with MacPhail. Rickey always let me keep my personal relationship with MacPhail. He never brought it up, he never made it uncomfortable for me. Thanks to Rickey I still have that friendship with MacPhail. I stopped by his farm in Maryland this spring on my way back from Vero Beach . . . and Rickey knew about it.

"I must ask you to allow me the same thing with Rickey as he allowed me with MacPhail."

He did not hesitate.

"Yes, of course. In fact," Walter said, "I respect you for standing up for a man who has been and is your friend."

"Walter," and I smiled with considerable relief, "I'll announce your ball games for you as best I can . . . without any reservation. It is now your ball club. I'll try to do for you what I did for Rickey after MacPhail left."

But it didn't work. It couldn't. I was by then well set in my working habits, in my thinking, and I had been placed on the highest peak of all, first by MacPhail and then by Rickey. I was stubborn. I wanted to do it my way. I resisted change. What a man thinks, and what he feels, are two different things at times—and they cut and bruise when they get at cross-purposes. Walter O'Malley and Walter Barber met years, and two men, too late. Had we started together, I like to think we'd have been a finely functioning combination. Walter learned baseball faster than any man who got into the business. He is the most able baseball man we have today. He should have been the Commissioner when Ford Frick retired . . . that is, he should have been for the good of baseball. He stands by his word. His mind is faster than the draw of a Texas sheriff on television.

We struggled along for three years, but you could tell he was trying to get along with me, yet watching me . . . and I was trying to get along with him, yet I was watching him. I started watching him during that first meeting in his office, when he said he didn't want me to quit. We had no sooner talked over Branch Rickey, and settled that, when he turned to something else. He asked me who would make a good manager for him the next year. I said I didn't think in those terms . . . that I only reported the play-by-play. He asked me to help him, if I would, by giving my opinions for his private estimation. I refused for a while, then told him he already had a good manager, Burt Shotton. He grunted and asked me to name some other possibilities. I said Eddie Dyer who had managed the Cardinals until Fred Saigh fired him. He said that Fred Saigh didn't like Dyer, and I said I thought he wanted to know from me and not from Fred Saigh. He asked me for another name, and I said Dixie Walker, who had managed well that summer at Atlanta and had recently been "The People's Choice" in Brooklyn. He smiled, thanked me, and said:

"I've been talking with Harold Parrott and the boys in the front office—we are naming Charlie Dressen as the manager tomorrow."

I left shaking my head . . . I know now that Walter must amuse himself by playing games. He plays people like they were markers in a checker game. He enjoys maneuvering. He works and thinks as though life was a poker game. He is a graduate lawyer, and it is a constant challenge to him to get you to think he said this when legally he said that.

We never had an open argument. In fact, Walter did me a tremendous service. I was building a house and asked Rickey for a very large advance on my salary. Rickey told me to talk to O'Malley. Walter took me to the Brooklyn Trust Company and got me a loan, a big loan. That's how I went ahead with the house. Then some time after Walter got the club, the bank suddenly wanted its money. So Walter gave me the money and let me pay it back to the ball club, month-by-month. He didn't want to have the ball club in the loan business, but he stood with me. I got my house, and he got his money back in two years, without exacting any interest.

But—it was just one little thing after another. Like one day when the attendance figures were sent to me . . . and the piece of paper had to pass through the club box . . . Walter wrote on the paper, "Don't give the paid attendance—turn the camera on the empty seats, and tell the people to see for themselves how many empty seats there are." I gave the paid, and I told him after the game it was the wrong psychology to try to force or shame the people into coming to the park. We differed. We were always guardedly pleasant, there was never a hard word, but we differed. I had dug in, and he was digging in.

Like the little cap: Lylah and I went to Spain and Italy late in the early winter of 1953, and I picked up a *boina*, a Spanish beret-type headpiece. It was fun, everybody over there wore one, and the wind didn't bother it. I wasn't a hat man, but I got fond of this thing. I could roll it up and stick it in my pocket. It was light. I got to wearing it. When I went down to Vero Beach for spring training with the Dodgers, I wore it to the park the first day as a gag. Left to my own devices, I would have laid the thing away and gone bareheaded the rest of the spring and all summer. It just happened that Barney Stein, the Dodger photographer, wanted to take a picture that day of the two Walters—O'Malley and me—for the Yearbook. Walter and I sat down together, and Stein said, "Are you going to take that beret off?" Suddenly a buzzer inside me went off. I hadn't thought anything about the *boina* . . . O'Malley looked funny as he looked at it . . . and I blurted out, "Barney, I'm not going to take it off. Take the picture with it on . . . if you want the picture." He took it. That was all there was to that. I started going bareheaded at training camp, but had a hat on when I got to Ebbets Field to announce the Opening Day game. It was cold.

I was handed a copy of the Dodger Yearbook and asked to give it liberal plugs on the air. "Mail in your fifty cents for each copy" . . . "to this address" . . . "but hurry" . . . "the edition is limited." I started looking through the Yearbook, and there it was, the picture of O'Malley and me at Vero Beach—me wearing the *boina*. That was okay. It was what was written under the picture . . . words to the effect that I was wearing the cap only down in Florida, that I wouldn't dare wear it in Brooklyn.

I started wearing it the next day, and every day, at Brooklyn and around the entire National League. One day in the elevator, O'Malley said something about the sponsor, Schaefer Beer, being unhappy about my wearing a beret that supposedly went with wine. I said to Walter, "Why do you have to tell me? Why don't you let the sponsor do it?" A while later we were all getting on the team plane at Milwaukee to fly home, and O'Malley said, "I see you are still wearing that cap." I said, "Yes."

I came in the house one afternoon and Lylah was raging. She said my agent had called—that he had been notified by Schaefer's advertising agency (BBD&O) that I was not to wear the *boina* . . . that the agency had even had a contest to see who could think of the best way to get me to take the cap off and keep it off—you know, bell the cat—and the only solu-. tion was simply to order me not to wear it. My wife said if I took that *boina* off, she would divorce me. I knew the sponsor owned the commercial time between innings, had the right to "dress the set and the cast"—so the rest of the season I took it off and did their commercials bareheaded, then put it back again for the play-by-play. I wore it. And every time I ran into O'Malley, his eyes went straight to the *boina*.

After I signed with the Yankees, I saw John Royal walking down Fifth Avenue. He laughed and said, "The Yankees, Red, don't give a damn about what you wear on your head . . . all they care about is what you put into the mike.

The last World Series I worked on was the seven-game Dodgers-Yankees Series in 1952. That was my thirteenth. It was announced to the press by Gillette that I was to do the television of the series of 1953 with Mel Allen—but both that assignment and the job at Brooklyn blew up at the same time. Let me give a little background:

Two men were responsible for baseball announcers being paid very poorly—Cliff Samuelson of General Mills in the earlier years, and Craig Smith of Gillette starting in 1939, when he bought the exclusive rights to the World Series.

Samuelson was a hard bargainer. He bought close, and he tried with all his ability to hold down what he paid in rights fees to the various teams. He used to threaten that if the rights went up, Wheaties would have to pull out of the entire picture. He got the regular season play-by-play announcers to accept modest money under the premise that announcing the local games would give them such a buildup that they would get extra local shows and thereby gain extra revenue. He got away with it. Play-by-play was new, the announcers worked for their radio stations, there had never been big money in radio, the job was still fun and prestige, and Samuelson skillfully played us against each other, saying he had a dozen good men waiting to take our jobs. He established an underlying low scale of payment for play-by-play that has never been corrected. The effects live on. With all the money in sports broadcasting . . . millions and millions . . . the men at the mike, who must make it pay off, are the lowest paid of the lot. An umpire in the World Series has always made far more than an announcer . . . and this is not meant to belittle the man in blue. As I said, all of us in the early days were on staff to our stations—I did not get an extra dollar from WLW in Cincinnati for being on my first four World Series; 1935, '36, '37, and '38—two of these series were sponsored by the Ford Motor Company. I got expenses— and an argument about them when I got home.

But I wanted to be on the World Series. That was the top job. That was what I worked for, waited for, gambled for. I had set my stubborn head in Florida when I listened to Graham McNamee and Tom Manning and Hal Totten . . . I didn't know when . . . I didn't count the cost . . . but someday I was going to be on *"The World Series."*

I was in radio seven years before we bought our first automobile. In Florida we walked or rode with friends. In Cincinnati we rode streetcars. Two winters I "signed-on" WLW, had to be at the station before the streetcars were running. I got up at four-thirty in the morning, shaved, dressed, had breakfast, and walked the two miles from Clifton—over the hill—to the Crosley Building. Do you know it gets cold in Cincinnati in the winter, before daylight?

Sometimes I would have to return to the station in the afternoon, or in the evening, for anything the station wanted— audition, rehearsal, an actual program to be announced. Once, when Charley Godwin got the chicken pox—he got married at noon Christmas day, came down with the pox before dinner —I announced two full WLW announce shifts for ten days, the early morning trick from six to noon, and the evening one from six to midnight or one A.M. I used to pray, "If God is willing, and Godwin will get well . . . I'll make it." I did not get a nickel extra for the double duty. . . . There was no union then for announcers.

Nineteen thirty-nine was the pivotal year. MacPhail took the seventy thousand dollars from Samuelson and broadcast the Dodger games, forcing the Yankees and the Giants into radio. That was the *first* season that *all* the major league teams were on the air . . . all sixteen of them.

Nineteen thirty-nine was also the year play-by-play announcers began to be placed under contracts to advertising agencies, and no longer to radio stations. Arch McDonald and I, and most of the assisting announcers in New York, were signed by Knox Reeves, the agency for General Mills.

And 1939 was the year Craig Smith first bought the exclusive rights for the World Series, rights Gillette would renew annually until the enormous growth of television expenses forced them into co-sponsorships.

Bob Elson and I were the first Gillette announcers. We were "tapped" . . . informed we would announce . . . and we both happily accepted the assignment. We would have cut somebody's throat to get it. Smith and his colleagues from the Maxon Agency kept Bob and me constantly informed how many announcers would even pay for our assignment. And I'm sure some of them would have. This was a big job. The biggest announcing job in sports in history. What an audience! Exclusive . . . no longer multiple network coverage. What prestige! This was THE assignment. We did not know what we would be paid. We were told after the World Series was over that someone had asked a labor union man in New York what should the fee be for a game, and he said, "Thirty-five dollars." Craig Smith sent me a check—it was a four-game

Series, with the Yankees playing the Reds—for two hundred eighty dollars. He wrote that while the union had scaled a game at thirty-five dollars, he was doubling the amount because we had done such a good job. Thanks to his doubling fee, we got . . . or I got . . . seventy dollars a game for an all-out commercial exclusive of the biggest job in my profession. To this day, I wonder who that union man was.

I started some serious thinking. The biggest job in my business . . . the World Series . . . exclusive to one sponsor, on one network. After doing four World Series for no extra pay—just as another one of the many jobs covered by my basic salary at WLW—now to do my fifth, and my first all-out commercial Series—and to get two hundred eighty dollars. I began to wonder what was going on. What did it mean to reach the top—the very top where there was no higher place to go? Why all the pressure and worry and preparation and concentration and risk? I could hardly eat several days before the Series started. You were doing ad-lib work . . . sticking your neck out every time you took the mike. I don't know what it is to be a headline actor on opening night on Broadway, to be a star singer at the Metropolitan Opera . . . but I know I got as many butterflies in my guts before the World Series as Broadway or the Met could deal out. You can't escape heavy pressure when announcing events like the World Series and big football games and key games in the regular baseball season. I finally built an ulcer that blew out in 1948, then kept creating more little ones, until they cut out two-thirds of my stomach in 1960.

But I kept on doing the World Series for Gillette. Always I would be telephoned by Ed Wilhelm of the Maxon Agency. "You have been selected by Craig Smith to be on the World Series." That was all. Never a discussion about how much you'd be paid. Nothing. You were telephoned, given the accolade, and you were to be grateful. You were to attend commercial-reading sessions beforehand, and be grateful. You were also to do promotional programs before the Series . . .

and for nothing. You were to be grateful. Always, just before the signal to take the air for the opening game of each World Series, Wilhelm would say, "Remember, boys, Craig Smith will be listening."

By the end of 1943, I had done five World Series for Gillette, each year from the time they began in 1939. Also, I had announced three National Football League Championships for Gillette. In midwinter, before the start of the '44 season, I was asked to come down to the old Ritz Hotel to see Craig Smith and some of the fellows of the Maxon Agency.

Craig said, "Red, I want your advice. How good a buy would the Giants-Yankees ball games be next summer?"

I gave Craig my best advice. Why shouldn't I? I said I didn't think it would be too competitive . . . the Brooklyn broadcasts were one thing . . . New York had been off the air the previous summer, which I thought was a sound indication. I could not recommend to him the New York broadcast and I said so. I said if he was interested in New York baseball, he should try to get into the picture at Brooklyn—get a piece of that. He sat there and let me give him the advice he had asked for.

Then he said, "I have bought the New York games for next year . . . I want you to announce them for us."

"Craig," I said, "I can't. I'm under contract to do the Brooklyn games."

"Look," he said, "you are our boy. You have done the World Series for us, all five of them. You have done three football championships for us. You have done everything in sports we have had. It never entered my mind you wouldn't do our games in New York next summer. Contract or no contract . . . will you do your games at New York?"

"No," I said and left. Right there in the Ritz Hotel is where the Craig Smith-Gillette-Barber milk started curdling. They put Bill Slater and Don Dunphy on their New York broadcasts, but they didn't run the Brooklyn broadcast out of town. Gillette only stayed a year. But—that fall I missed my first

World Series assignment since 1935, and I worked no more football championships. I would never have gotten back on another World Series broadcast, except that the Commissioner of Baseball made a stipulation: the principal announcer for each team playing in each World Series must be included. So when the Dodgers won, I got telephoned.

The only non-Dodger Series I was asked to announce after that was in 1948—it was the first Series on television, and I did it at the strong personal request of Smith himself.

The Series was Cleveland versus the Boston Braves, and it was the first World Series with extensive network television coverage. It was not yet coast-to-coast, but it was an impressive network. Craig Smith called and asked me to announce it, and I told him I did not feel up to it . . . that I was just getting back on my feet, and slowly, from a hemorrhaged ulcer . . . and would he get somebody else. He put it on a personal basis—wouldn't I please do it . . . I was the one man with the know-how . . . this was a big gamble for him . . . we had been associates many times in the past. He conveniently forgot the vicious curve-ball he had thrown me in the Ritz Hotel in New York. But I did it, on nerve and milk. That was my diet then. Milk. And every hour I was afraid I would hemorrhage again. Mel Allen had the radio assignment and had a bad cold, and we were roommates on the train—he was up spraying and gargling all night . . . I was up drinking milk . . . we were quite a combination.

There was one World Series where the broadcasting assignment hung on one pitched ball—with one of the two announcers hanging on that same pitch. Or I could say, it all hung on one swing of Bobby Thomson's bat . . . the Giants, led by Leo Durocher, caught up to the Dodgers, under Charlie Dressen, the next-to-the-last day of the 1951 season, and threw the National League pennant race into a tie and a three-game play-off . . . the Giants won the first game, the Dodgers the second. At the Polo Grounds, in the ninth inning of the decisive game—the game for the play-off, for the pennant, for the World Series against the waiting Yankees—the Dodgers were leading 4–1. The Giants started hitting Don Newcombe. Alvin Dark singled . . . Don Mueller singled . . . Whitey Lockman doubled, and it was 4–2, with two on. Charlie Dressen went to the mound, took Newcombe out of the game, and waved to his bullpen. He had two pitchers warming up away out there in left center-field . . . Clem Labine and Ralph Branca. Dressen waved his hand . . . pointed for the pitcher he wanted.

Shortly before the game began, I had been sitting in the visiting team's radio box at the Polo Grounds, going over the commercial copy, putting the batting orders in my scorebook, getting ready. Ed Wilhelm of the Maxon Agency walked in. "Red," he said without preamble, "I'm telling both you boys the same thing. [The other "boy" was Russ Hodges, number one announcer for the Giants—and still is at San Francisco.] If your team wins today—you are on the Series broadcast tomorrow." Then he walked out.

Ralph Branca was the pitcher Manager Dressen ordered into the game. The batter for the Giants was Bobby Thomson. On Branca's second pitch, Thomson hit the ball into the left-field stands. Hodges went on the broadcast the next day with Mel Allen.

The World Series pay scale stayed down. No negotiations were permitted. You got tapped to go on . . . you went on . . . you stood the gaff and the pressure . . . and a week or two afterward you got a check from Gillette in Boston. I was increasingly ashamed of myself. My self-respect was going down. I was being dishonest. I bargained with everybody else I came in contact with . . . freely, openly, fairly. But with Gillette and the World Series, I took what they gave me. I ate it. But I wasn't digesting it very well.

After the World Series of 1952, which lasted for seven games, Yankees and Dodgers, on ALL-OUT commercial television, coast-to-coast, I got a check from Smith for fourteen hundred dollars. That was two hundred dollars a game for the biggest sports event on coast-to-coast television, my thirteenth World Series. This was the pay-off for nineteen years of big-league announcing. I was as high in my profession as I could be. I had done more World Series than any man who ever lived. This was by far the lowest money anybody was paying me for doing anything. And worst of all was not being able to ask or know what I would be paid for my next chance to do the supreme assignment in my field.

I can recall the decision plainly—I was sitting at my desk in our house in Scarborough, New York. The view was across the Hudson River, across Haverstraw Bay. It was early fall. Clear air, painted leaves. The mail had come. I looked at the check . . . fourteen hundred dollars. I looked at the panoramic view. I looked at myself. I swore to myself I would never take this again. Before I did another World Series, I would be allowed to discuss what terms I would work under . . . how much money I would get. And I would get more money than what I was holding in my hand. I never, even in my mind, set a figure on how much . . . the amount, the exact amount, I would try to work it out. I would be given the right to negotiate with Craig Smith, or I'd never do a World Series again. I called to my wife and told her. Then I telephoned Bill McCaffrey, who was my agent at the time, and notified him what to expect a year later, if the Dodgers won again, as they figured to do. And as they did.

All during the 1953 season, the climate at Ebbets Field got colder. There was a strain in the relationship between BBD&O and me, and the lesson of that story is that you must be very careful who you do a favor for in this world.

The ball clubs kept raising their rights fees year by year. They really raised them when television came in. Just as Samuelson had predicted, Wheaties got frozen out. I guess, in all fairness to Samuelson, he did not have the money for his product—certainly not the kind of money the beer breweries, or the cigarette people, or the gasoline people had. Wheaties dropped out of it, and, by and large, beer took over.

When I first came to New York, I was master of ceremonies for a three-times-a-week fifteen-minute radio show on WEAF (now WNBC) sponsored by Schaefer Beer. There were three writers on the show—one of them was Alan Jay Lerner, who later wrote something called *My Fair Lady*. I got to know Rudy Schaefer and his family very well, and I liked and respected Rudy. I still do. He had a college friend—Princeton—Johnny Johns, who was account executive at BBD&O for Schaefer Beer.

Johns asked me to come to see him, told me that Rudy Schaefer wanted terribly to get into the sponsorship of the Dodgers—that it fitted: the brewery was in Brooklyn, Schaefer was a class guy, the beer was a quality product, Schaefer was deeply interested in civic projects, and so on. I knew why Johns had sent for me. Branch Rickey, who was running the Dodgers, never had a drink of alcohol in his life, and although Rickey was now having trouble finding sponsors, he would never accept a beer. He would not even listen to the idea. And I knew that Johnny Johns knew that I had some influence with Rickey. Johns told me how much Rudy himself would appreciate anything I could do to get Mr. Rickey just to meet Rudy, to consider a working relationship. Johns said that Rudy was ill in the hospital or that he himself would have discussed this with me. And several days later, Rudy called me from his hospital room to say he would personally appreciate whatever I could do . . . that it would mean a great deal to him.

This is how it added up to me: the rights fees and the station fees had mounted to such an extent that fewer and fewer sponsors with that kind of money were available . . . beer sponsors had the money, the baseball season coincided with the beer season . . . beer sponsors were steadily coming into baseball . . . Rickey was in complete charge of selling the broadcast rights . . . he did not have sound prospects for the needed new sponsor . . . Rudy Schaefer was a fine man, a gentleman . . . his brewery was a Brooklyn institution . . . I was convinced Rudy Schaefer would be more civic-minded on

the Brooklyn broadcasts than any other sponsor I knew about
. . . Walter O'Malley thought Schaefer was the answer, but
O'Malley could not get Rickey to change his mind.

Rickey was obligated to pay me a great deal of money,
sponsor or no sponsor. I knew that Rickey at the last minute
had produced a new sponsor the season just past by telephoning an old friend, Clarence Eldridge of General Foods. But
now Eldridge was out. No new sponsor was waiting. I owed
Rudy Schaefer and Johnny Johns and BBD&O nothing. True,
I was friendly with Bruce Barton of Batten, Barton, Durstine
& Osborne—left him box-seat tickets for games and even drove
him back and forth to Ebbets Field. But I owed Barton
nothing. Liked him, yes indeed, but that was all. The only
man I owed something was Rickey. I did not want my friend,
Branch Rickey, to be losing money and face on the broadcast
operation. Further, I saw that beer sponsorship was the answer to much of baseball's broadcast future . . . and I saw
nothing wrong with it. I liked beer. Further, I had a personal
bet on Rudy Schaefer as a man and as a Brooklyn business-
man.

There was only one person in all the world who could get
Branch Rickey to change his mind. Mrs. Rickey. She and I
had talked about music from time to time. And when this
came up, Lylah and I had a pair of tickets for a performance
by the New York Philharmonic, but Lylah got sick and
couldn't go. Rickey was away on a business trip. I asked Mrs.
Rickey if she would have dinner and go to the concert with
me. We went to "21," and during dinner I flatly outlined the
Schaefer situation. I told her my personal appraisal of Rudy
Schaefer. I told her how beer sponsorships were increasing all
over baseball—that it was an inevitable future. I didn't ask her
to do anything about it, or say anything to her husband. I just
gave her the facts of the situation.

Rickey went away again a short while afterward. Before he
left, he told Walter O'Malley he did not know how long he
would have to be out of town . . . that something might come

up concerning the broadcasts . . . and he, Rickey, would appreciate it if he, O'Malley, would act for the club should something come up. When Rickey returned, O'Malley had committed the Dodgers to Schaefer Beer.

From then on, the attitude at BBD&O was one of careful watchfulness. It seemed they expected me to be demanding something from them—something they were not about to give me. Johnny Johns never referred to his asking me for help. Schaefer said thanks once and never referred to it again. There were other people in the agency who had romanced O'Malley, and they took full credit—Wick Crider and O'Malley became inseparable. Bruce Barton cooled from his former warmth and did not permit me to escort him to Ebbets Field anymore. My agent, schooled in the Madison Avenue jungle, said flatly, "Red, BBD&O is trying to cut you down to size."

Nineteen fifty-three was the last year of my contract at Brooklyn. Toward the close of the season, at my request, McCaffrey asked BBD&O what they had in mind for me the next year. They said, "Nothing." I knew then that I was free when I announced the last game of the season down at Philadelphia. There were no options, no promises, no understandings. The end of a contract of employment, with all parties concerned, relieved me of any obligations. And I knew any new negotiations would be hard.

The Dodgers clinched the 1953 pennant at St. Louis. They had an afternoon game there on September 17, flew home after the game, played a series at Brooklyn, and ended the season at Philadelphia. I remember the date of that last game in St. Louis very well—it was my daughter's sixteenth birthday, and I was to join Sarah and Lylah that evening in New York.

On this last day in St. Louis, I was eating breakfast with Tommy Holmes, one of the regular writers traveling with the club. We were at the Chase Hotel. I was called to the phone . . . long distance . . . Ed Wilhelm . . . from the Maxon Agency in New York.

"Red," said Wilhelm, "I meant to call you yesterday, but I

didn't get around to it. We announced to the papers yesterday that you and Mel Allen are to do the television on the World Series."

I had waited a year for this.

"Ed, you know Bill McCaffrey?"

"Sure I know him," Ed said, and he sounded odd. "Why?"

"Bill is my agent . . . will you please call him and work out the arrangements?" I hung up and went to my room to wait. I didn't wait very long.

When the phone rang, it was McCaffrey. "Red, Wilhelm just called, and he is furious." McCaffrey's voice was grim. "Are you dead sure you want to go through with this?"

"Bill, I told you a year ago I intended to go through with this. I must have the right to negotiate . . . yes—I am dead sure."

It wasn't long before the phone rang again . . . maybe ten minutes. It was McCaffrey.

"Wilhelm called Craig Smith in Boston, and Smith is raging. Smith says you'll get what you got last year and no more. Smith says for you 'To take it—or leave it.' "

I remember I took a breath.

"Tell him," I said, "I'll leave it."

It was that quick.

Late that evening, as our little family was driving home, I told Sarah that on her sixteenth birthday I had given her the best present I could give her . . . I had given her the return of her father's self-respect.

When I went into this with Smith, I did not expect any help from anybody. Had MacPhail been in Brooklyn, had Rickey been in Brooklyn, I would have been backed up to the hilt—they would have demanded that I have a proper negotiation, even if it meant a hearing before Commissioner Ford Frick. But I was never O'Malley's man, could not have been, the way things had happened. Yet I felt I owed O'Malley the courtesy of reporting the exchange between the sponsor of the World Series, and his principal announcer—especially when his ball club was half of the Series.

I called Walter the next morning. As I started to tell him what had been said to me, and what I had said in reply, he broke in:

"That," said O'Malley, "is *your* problem. I'll nominate Scully to take your place."

As I heard Walter say "That is *your* problem," I said to myself, "From now on, Walter, the Dodgers are *your* problem." I was finished at Ebbets Field by the time I placed the telephone in its cradle.

It made a splash in the papers . . . Red Barber refusing the World Series . . . his protege, Vince Scully, taking his place. I had hired Scully to do some spots on the CBS Football Roundup in 1949—then that winter, when Ernie Harwell left Connie Desmond and me to join Russ Hodges at the Polo Grounds—I had gotten Mr. Rickey to take Scully on as the third man at Brooklyn. Before that Vince had not done an inning of a professional ball game. Connie and I trained him, loved him, teased him, and rejoiced in his remarkable development. Scully called me from his home in New Jersey, said Ed Wilhelm had offered him the job I had quit, but said he would not take the World Series until he talked with me . . . and, if I didn't want him to take the assignment, he wouldn't take it. Vince meant it.

I could have wept for sheer joy. I had not expected him to call me, to hold off Wilhelm.

"Vince," I said, "you didn't have a thing to do with my resigning the Series . . . this was something that's been growing and growing since 1939. When I quit, I quit. Somebody else has to do the job with Allen. I would rather have you get it than anybody else.

"In fact, my boy—you are welcome to my scorebook . . . my pencils . . . my egg timer. If you will let me, I'll come to the booth and give you a rubdown before you take the air."

"Thanks," Vince said. "I had to talk to you first."

I never had a son. And yet in a very real way, at a very particular time, I did have a son. Scully has stayed through the years as O'Malley's announcer, and all through the years

Scully has said openly that the two most important men in his life were his father and me.

The next day I was having lunchon at Louis & Armand's when a young dog robber working in the Maxon Agency came over to the table. I don't even remember his name. He got up across the room when he saw me enter and sit down. He swept over to where I sat, so rapidly he still had his napkin in his hand. In a voice filled with righteous anger, and with sufficient volume for everyone in the room to hear, he shouted as he waved his right index finger at me—

"Red . . . HOW could YOU do THIS to . . . *Craig Smith?*"

He turned and went back triumphantly to his table. He had done his duty to A. Craig Smith, Maxon Advertising, Madison Avenue, and certainly to God.

Always when the Dodgers played the Yankees, I got what tickets I needed—for Lylah and a few friends—from the Dodgers for Ebbets Field, and also tickets from their allotment of Yankee seats. I had arranged long ago with Harold Parrott, the road secretary, for the Brooklyn seats. Now for the first time I was going to use one for myself . . . was going to sit with Lylah . . . was going to watch it as a civilian, as just another spectator who paid for his ticket. But under no circumstances was I going to ask O'Malley or anyone else with the Dodgers for the pair of seats I needed for the Stadium. I wasn't going to ask the Dodgers for anything . . . ever again.

I went to the Yankees' office on Fifth Avenue and to Arthur Patterson, the publicity director. When we met, he was a first-string writer for the *New York Herald Tribune*. His by-line was Arthur Patterson, but most people called him Red because he was redheaded and had a temper that was red. He and MacPhail, another redhead, got into a brawl at Brooklyn when Larry was over there in 1942, and Patterson hit MacPhail in the stomach. That ended the fight. But when Larry came out of the Army after World War Two and started running the Yankees, the first thing he did was hire Patterson away from the *Tribune*.

I told Arthur I wanted to buy two seats for my personal use. He knew. Everybody in baseball knew I was off the Series broadcast. He also knew I had gotten my seats in the past out of the Dodger allotment. Now I was standing at his desk. He got up, said he would speak to George Weiss, the general manager—he was back in a flash with a pair of choice seats from Weiss's personal allotment. I handed him a check, and we walked to the elevator.

The elevator doors opened, and as I stepped on, I said: "Arthur . . . I own myself."

Before he could answer, the doors shut.

The first two games were at Yankee Stadium. Lylah and I sat together at a Series game for the first time. I was not working—for all I knew I was out of baseball for good. The next three games were at Brooklyn. Harry M. Stevens, Inc., was the caterer for both ball parks, and the four Stevens brothers entertained in a private room at each park for their guests—club officials, friends, well-known people. Snacks and drinks . . . on the Stevens'. Hal was the oldest brother and ran Ebbets Field. He had been most kind to me since I first came there in 1939. Before the fifth game, which was the third game at Brooklyn, Lylah and I were sitting in Hal Stevens' crowded kitchen at a table with Bob Carpenter—the owner of the Phillies, and his wife, and with Buzzi Bavasi, who had become O'Malley's right hand.

George Weiss and Dan Topping walked into the room. Topping stopped inside the door and leaned against the wall. Weiss came on straight to where I was sitting and asked me to come and speak to Topping. I got up and went to where Dan was waiting.

Weiss did the talking. Topping nodded in agreement as Weiss said:

"Patterson tells me you are free over here. Dan and I want to talk to you about coming to work at the Stadium . . . to do the pre- and post-game television shows. Can you come to my hotel tonight? The Commodore?"

I said that I was very interested, but, I had an engagement that evening out in Westchester County. We agreed to meet at Yankee Stadium before the game the next day . . . mid-morning.

Bob Carpenter knew something was going on. Buzzi knew very well what it was. He was my friend, he is still my friend, and he had a funny look on his face when I came back. As soon as we got out of the room, I told Lylah. She was pleased to think her husband might not remain unemployed.

HEARING

Crossing the river, moving from Ebbets Field to Yankee Stadium, set more things in motion than I had bargained for. At Brooklyn, I was the boss broadcaster, the principal announcer who gave the orders, assigned the innings, called the shots. At the Stadium, Mel Allen was the established Voice of the Yankees. He had earned his position. But—I was not to be his assistant. I came in as an associate—as Ed Murrow used to say of so many people on his staff, as a "colleague."

Television brought deep changes into our lives all over the country. It brought a drastic revision in my baseball broadcasting. When Weiss outlined the Yankee job and I accepted, before the sixth game of the 1953 World Series, I started out all over again—not completely all over again, but certainly into a new area, with new techniques, new demands, and new worries . . . one of which was the hearing in my left ear.

The four years at WRUF in Florida, the five at WLW-WSAI in Cincinnati, the fifteen at Brooklyn, the various stations and networks in New York, plus the job at CBS all had focused and centered on radio. After World War Two as television grew, I naturally learned with it, but radio was always dominant in my assignments and my thinking. Radio supplied the bulk of my income. I was in television from its first big-league game on, but I took television for granted.

Suddenly it was reversed. From now on at Yankee Stadium I would announce several innings per game on radio, yes, but I would also do two fifteen-minute television shows—one before each home game, one immediately afterward. I would run those two shows completely, both on and off the cameras. I would do the commercials, which meant rehearsals early in the day, or making them on film when the team was out of town. The days of casual personal dress were gone. Wardrobe was vital. Then, almost as an afterthought, I would announce on television several innings of the game itself.

Beginning in 1954, the daily schedule was: the pregame

show in a dugout, or wherever we wanted to locate it (bleach-ers, trainer's room, studio, umpire's dressing room, Weiss's office, press room) . . . go immediately to the play-by-play booth . . . do two and one-half innings on either radio or tele-vision, then switch to two and one-half innings on the other medium . . . leave after the seventh inning to go downstairs to the studio for the post-game show . . . watch the finish of the game on the monitor in the studio. My daily preparation for announcing the game was the same as always—the fewer innings actually broadcast in no way lessened the depth of the pregame preparation. On the other hand, the insistent de-mands of the camera increased the work. There was never a way to completely satisfy the camera's appetite. It was, and is, insatiable.

The last couple of years at Brooklyn I began to lose hearing in my left ear. My father, a locomotive engineer, had died deaf, so hearing was something I was alerted to, aware of, and fearful of. My wife began complaining that I did not always pay attention when she spoke, when actually I was simply not registering everything she said from my left side. I began com-plaining that she mumbled.

With radio reporting as my basic work, I didn't need balanced hearing, and the weakening in my left ear didn't bother me. It had bothered Lylah and a few others, but not me. I still enjoyed the theater, the symphony, the opera, cocktail parties. I had built a marvelous library of phono-graph records: opera, orchestra, John McCormack, Lawrence Tibbett, John Charles Thomas, Bing Crosby—from his earliest records on—big bands like Paul Whiteman and Jack Hylton, excerpts from Broadway shows. The world of sound was precious to me. Night after night I played the records by the hour.

We humans don't often make a big decision as suddenly as we think we do. The loss of hearing in the left ear was build-ing its problem inside me. Now that I had the Yankee job, I realized how much interviewing on camera and on mikes

I would be doing—two fifteen-minute shows a day . . . thirty minutes of public listening. That was a lot of television . . . and required a lot of listening.

I had a distorted ego—I felt that the audience would not accept me on camera wearing a hearing aid. But I had heard about an operation that restored hearing. It was called "fenestration" . . . putting a "window" in the ear. It was a serious operation, brain surgery, with a drastic, sea-sick-like period of recovery.

All by my little self . . . full of vanity, fear, and ignorance . . . I reasoned that because my hearing was going down, I needed to get the bad ear working normally again. Yet I could not afford to be seen with an ear-piece. I figured that I owed this new job and myself my very best. And, that you could believe whatever a doctor told you.

I soon found out there were two men in New York who had pioneered fenestration . . . believed in it, fought for it against medical resistance, went to great lengths to get cadavers to practice on. Both men were famous, one more than the other. I phoned half a dozen doctors I knew, asking which of the two men I should go to. It came out a toss-up. So— I picked one, and I liked him and what he told me. He told me what I wanted to hear.

He said I had a hardening in the ear, that I had a perfectly sound nerve and that I was an ideal candidate for fenestration, with a highly favorable percentage of success.

I asked him one question.

"Is there any chance of the operation doing any damage to the nerve, so *if* in the future I want to wear a hearing aid, it wouldn't do me any good?"

He said:

"Absolutely not."

We set a date for the operation. I remember what day we agreed upon. I told him I was preaching a noonday sermon at Trinity Church on January 13 . . . right in the neighborhood of his hospital . . . I would go from there to the hospital . . .

he would operate the next morning . . . and I would have six weeks to recover before reporting to the Yankees in St. Petersburg—this was before the move to Fort Lauderdale—to begin the new work in which hearing would be so vital.

They wheeled me into the operating room the morning of January 14, 1954, with a beginning hardness in my left ear and a perfect nerve. When they wheeled me out, I had no hearing in the ear. The nerve was destroyed. I didn't know it then. It took weeks. The doctor at first said many cases reacted late, and I held on to hope as long as I could.

I went to spring training on my new job with a new ball club in a new league with one-sided hearing . . . subject to dizzy spells as I stood or walked. My sense of balance was undone. The canals inside the ear that control stability had been disrupted. I learned later they had been punctured and drained. It was my annual custom not to drink whiskey during Lent—this is all, I am very sure, that saved me from being classified by my new associates as a drunk. At times I acted like one, rolling and swaying. I still have little confidence in my ability to retain my balance. I carefully stay away from the edge of platforms, bridges, porches, canyons—at times I start to walk through a door entrance and hit the side of it with my shoulder. It still makes me mad.

God gives us two ears for good reasons: to unscramble sounds until they are intelligible, for direction, for balance, for defintion. When you are reduced to one ear, you can't tell where a noise comes from, you can't unmix voices, you mishear sounds, and, thereby, you are never sure of exactly what you have heard—especially proper names. With one ear, you hear all right—you hear a roaring jumble of noise. Volume without definition.

It didn't make me sick. It made me ill. It nearly killed me. Casey Stengel was the manager of the Yankees, the man I had to work with more than any other at Yankee Stadium. Casey is hard enough to understand with two ears. Often I had to ask him to repeat himself. He didn't like to be slowed down.

It irritated him. But he knew I had a reason for asking, and he always repeated for me—always. He would go over it again, then say, "You got it?" And wink.

If Stengel had been rough with me that first spring, I think I would have had to quit. I was in a state of shock, going to a job of interviewing and reduced to one ear. I had never lost a big contest before in all my life. I was not used to losing, but I had lost this one, and what I had lost, I had lost forever. Forever.

I had been at Brooklyn so long, those fifteen years, had seen every one of the Dodgers come into the organization, seen them develop, knew them so well . . . had been in the National League so long . . . twenty years . . . that I never even thought about who any of the players were, where they came from, what they could do, how they pitched, how they looked. I knew the Dodgers like a father knows his family . . . names, birthdays, preferences, fears, wishes.

You can't announce a ball club properly until you know it in its multiple and detailed depth. I was a stranger to the Yankees, to the American League. After I had been standing around at St. Pete for a week, I went over to Stengel. He was sitting on the bench, shooting the breeze with some writers. I could only get about half of what they were saying. I waited for a pause, then said:

"Casey, when you get some time, I would appreciate it if you would run down your ball club for me . . . I need this before you start playing your exhibition games."

The Old Man knew what I was saying. He knew everything. That's why he is so great. He was a knowing man who thought with you . . . and ahead of you. Stengel took time to think what you did, what you said, why you said it, who you were, what you wanted. He knew I was a new broadcaster for the Yankees—and a new broadcaster *for him*. He knew I had to *know his* ball club—*should know his* ball club. He knew *he was the best man* alive to tell me about *his club*.

"Fellows," Stengel addressed the writers, "do you have anything else to take up before I settle down with Red?" They said they didn't. Then he turned to me, drew a roster from his hip pocket, and said, "Let's go over this here ball club of mine right now."

He spent a half hour, player by player. In thirty minutes, I *knew* the New York Yankees. I was around the Yankees for thirteen years, and not one thing Stengel told me ever came out wrong . . . not once was I ever surprised by different information about a player. No manager, no coach ever gave me the briefing he gave me. And without Stengelese.

I never in our years of association asked Stengel a question he didn't answer, and with grace, even though he might have been under heavy pressure. I never asked him to go on a microphone or before a camera that he didn't go.

Weiss and Topping and Stengel and the Yankees knew I had had an operation on my ear, but they didn't know the totality and permanence of the failure. That was not their business. It was mine. There was never any secrecy about the operation—the news services put out a story on it when I entered the hospital, saying it was a fenestration. The specialist who did it was very upset over the failure, and so was his friend with whom he had developed the technique. The adverse publicity disturbed them. The doctor who didn't operate on me later did a successful fenestration on Dan Daniel's wife. Dan was the veteran baseball writer for the *World Telegram,* and he covered the Yankees. This doctor told Dan he would like to see me. He wanted to check my ear to see if he couldn't do something to fix it . . . anything that would improve the public image of his fenestration procedure. He checked me for a long, long time . . . this test and that one. Finally, he said, "Your nerve is dead. . . . Thank you for coming."

Then the ear got infected, heavily infected. It ran pus. One of the things they did was inject me daily with massive doses of penicillin. My feet began to swell. During a game I started reacting to the penicillin. I finished the day at the Stadium, got home, and went into a violent reaction. They went to work on me with cortisone. Now I wear a tag around my neck saying *"No Penicillin."* But I was back at the Stadium the next day.

That first year at Yankee Stadium was an eternity. Friends said, "You look so strained on television." I *was* strained— straining to hear what the guest was saying. I was sick. All I wanted to do was find a hole, get into it, and close it behind me. I wanted the silence of solitude, not the yelling and commotion and confusion of Yankee Stadium.

The worst part was what I did to myself. I dwelt upon the failure of the operation, upon the loss of all hearing forever in the ear, upon the inability ever to use a hearing aid. I was so bitter about it, I went into an inner rage if anyone referred to my lack of hearing. I could not speak about it. I gave anyone who had to sit on my left side a cold, rude time. I refused to go to the theater, or to the Philharmonic, or to the Met. My wife made me go to some social affairs. I would not play a phonograph record—I knew all too well what I was no longer able to hear. I gave the bulk of my record library to a veterans' hospital. The only records we kept were kept by Lylah.

All I thought about was "what I had lost." That is enough poison to kill a man. I tried going to a psychiatrist—I was afraid the operation was a physical success, but somehow, maybe on account of my father's death in his deafness, I would not allow myself to hear. He said the debility was not psychological. Professional lip-reading lessons were suggested—but they were too painful for me. One specialist warned me that my speech pattern would soon become blurred . . . that I might have to give up the microphone. Because I no longer heard the way most people heard, he said, I would soon forget how to speak the way most people expected me to speak.

However, somehow, some way, when you are lost in the darkness at the bottom of the barrel, a clear ray of light breaks through . . . and by then you are ready to respond to it without further evasion. I had to turn myself around. Nobody could help me. I had made the medical rounds. I had to do it. And quick.

First, I made myself tell everybody I met that I was DEAF in my left ear—not hard of hearing, not just a hearing problem —but DEAF. When I began to say audibly to another human being, who heard me, what was then the most terrible word in the English language . . . the word DEAF . . . I began to heal. Everyone was relieved. Things became more normal again. If a person spoke, and I did not respond, the person touched me, I turned, the person repeated himself, and I answered. I began to hear again.

I made it standard practice to say to every ballplayer I interviewed, just before we went on the air, "Don't get on my left side or this will be the funniest interview you ever got into." The day Billy Jurges was made manager of the Boston Red Sox, his team was at the Stadium. Naturally, he was the pregame guest, in his dugout. I said to him at air time, "Billy, keep away from my left side." He said, "You keep away from my left side." And then I remembered; he had been hit with a pitch by Bucky Walters, back when he was playing for the Giants, and was deafened in that ear. We both laughed and did the interview the only way we could—nose to nose. For a long time around the Stadium that was called The Great Profile Interview.

But, I also had to get rid of the poison of self-pity. Instead of thinking of what *I had lost,* I made it my constant business to realize how much *I had left.* The more I worked at it, the more I realized how much *hearing* I had left. I returned to the concert halls, the theater, and to listening to records. I believe today I enjoy what I hear far more than what I heard when I had two ears working and took normal hearing for granted.

Certainly, the loss of hearing made me a better interviewer. I had no choice—I had to listen to every word of the guest, I had to watch his face, his eyes, his lips. I read lips now more than I know I do. I pay attention to people. I hear things now I never heard before. When you listen with one ear, you hear with a "third" ear—you hear even what people do not say, what they leave unsaid.

Things went very well with the Yankees those first years I was there—once I straightened myself and my hearing out. It was a joy to be around Stengel. Weiss was running the front office, and he left you to do your job—if you were doing it. If you didn't do it you went elsewhere. I never once heard from him during the season.

When I got to the Stadium, the Yankees were in the full flower of their greatness. From 1955 through 1964 they won nine pennants—that is, in those ten years they missed winning only once. In 1961, Roger Maris and Mickey Mantle put on their show, with Maris hitting his sixty-one home runs . . . and let me say for the record: no player was ever more co-operative with me than Maris was when he was under that terrible September pressure put on him by the writers, by Babe Ruth's record of sixty, and by opposing pitchers. Maris willingly came to my television shows every time I asked him, either before or after the game . . . and I asked him every time he hit another home run in those exciting, dramatic closing days. Maris got it bad after he broke Ruth's record— the very people who cheered him on were then shocked and wounded when he did it. So it goes.

If somebody had said in 1961 when the M&M boys, Mantle and Maris, were one-twoing the league, that this was the beginning of the end of the Yankees, you would have laughed. The big base hits were ringing, the crowds were spinning the turnstiles, another pennant was being won handily by Ralph Houk, and the Cincinnati Reds were quickly beaten in the World Series in five games.

But the Yankee organization, once the greatest in baseball, had begun to come apart, to suffer from attrition, to fade as money was steadily siphoned out by Dan Topping and Del Webb.

The trouble started in the fifties when the clubs began to compete expensively with each other with big bonuses paid to untried kids. Always before, when the Yankees wanted a player, they simply outbid everybody else. For the first time, the Yankees began nursing their money. Now Weiss was given a ceiling by Topping and Webb, and the ceiling was too low. The best young prospects were going to other teams . . . you don't see the effects of that sort of drying up until it is too late.

Stengel and Weiss were high-priced men. They went first. Other financial blows followed: the ground was sold to the Knights of Columbus . . . the Stadium itself was sold, and the man who got it was an alumnus of Rice University, and he gave it to his school . . . the franchise with the remaining players was sold in 1964 to the Columbia Broadcasting System.

The financial dying on the vine tightened up everything in the organization. Friendliness and openness gave way to guarded action and careful speech. People were afraid of their jobs, afraid to move. The scouts who had dug up the great players had passed on. The triple-decked stadium became a mausoleum.

Much of this decay got over into the broadcasting booth. Mel Allen began to force himself on the microphone, to try to talk a team into being something it was no longer able to be. Former ballplayers started invading the announcer's booth. The sponsor, Ballentine Beer, began it when they forced Weiss to fire Jim Woods to make a place for Phil Rizzuto. Next, Ballentine tried to get me to accept a sizeable cut in salary—in an already negotiated contract—to make payroll space for Jerry Coleman. When I refused, they waited a year and then hired Coleman anyway, which increased our announcing crew to four men.

When Houk became general manager, the interest by the sponsors in the pre- and post-game shows began to wane. Yet the Yankees wanted more for the rights, and WPIX kept hiking its ante for its television time. Weiss, when he was the general manager, kept the broadcast rights strictly under his and the Yankees' control. He worked on selling his radio and television. He didn't care how much trouble it was. Houk took no part in it, and Topping soon grew weary of the marts of trade. Dan was born rich, and he never had to be patient about anything involving money. He soon made a package deal with Ballentine, taking a lump sum and leaving it to Ballentine to sell off portions of the package as best they could, devil take the hindmost. As Topping told me with a grin, "I stuck Ballentine with it." But—the Yankees lost all control of the character of the package.

The first years I was at the Stadium, under Weiss, the pre- and post-game shows were fifteen minutes each, and had the solidity, dignity, and continuity of single sponsors—first, R. J. Reynolds Tobacco, then Bankers Trust, then the Ford Dealers of New York and Connecticut. Weiss left, Topping took over, Ballentine got the package, and with the connivance of WPIX, they sold spots to anybody who would buy them . . . there were spot commercials on film for the pre- and post-game shows, and there were "co-sponsors" for any fractions of the play-by-play anybody might purchase. It got so thin that the last two or three years I was there, they began cutting down the time and number of the before- and after-game shows until in 1966, they eliminated them altogether. Early that year during spring training, at a special meeting called to announce the new policy, I volunteered the opinion that this would deprive the Yankees of any personal warmth and appeal . . . that CBS and the Yankees with all their money ought to take seventy-five thousand dollars and buy the fifteen minutes from WPIX before the game—and without sponsors, if necessary, give the public fifteen minutes of warm humanness from chilly Yankee Stadium. I said that CBS threw fortunes away promoting lousy television shows, and who knew how much money the Yankees wasted on kid ballplayers who never made the grade. A cold silence suddenly offset the spring warmth in Fort Lauderdale. Houk's face got red; Bob Fishel, the public-relations man, looked hurt. The meeting broke up and nobody walked out of it with me.

The Mets, across the River, kept their pre- and post-game shows going . . . introducing this player and that to the audience. The Mets maintained human warmth by being genuinely human. There is no secret to having the public like you—you give the public more in the field of entertainment than it thinks you are taking away from it. As long as you try to sell baseball as a *game,* you must preserve the *illusion* that it is a *game,* and not the *capital-gains business* it has become.

The Yankees—let me hasten to say—were very considerate of me, personally for a long, long time. They knew I was battling the loss of hearing in my left ear when I came to the Stadium. In 1960, two-thirds of my stomach was cut out, and I lost considerable weight. I looked thinner and was gaunt on camera until I could regain the weight—it took two years, but that was all right with Topping. I never had any trouble with Topping. Driving to spring training camp in 1964, I had a heart attack in Emporia, Virginia. I blew spring training, but I was determined to make it to the mike on Opening Day at the Stadium, and I did. Then in June, I got a blood clot in my left leg, it let loose three times, and I was back in the hospital; I missed two weeks of actual work, and another two weeks while the team was out of town. But that was all right with Topping, too.

If the Yankees had said after that season of 1964, "Red, look —you are going uphill, old boy. You've been great for us. We love you. We love you so much we don't want to risk you climbing the grandstands anymore, doing all that work, absorbing all that pressure. You've had a fenestration, a heart attack, a blood clot that burst, a gastrectomy. This job you've got is murder . . . it's a man-killer. You ought to go on down to Florida and sit in the sun. Let a younger fellow take your place." If in September of 1964 they had said this, I could not have found much fault with them and with their decision.

But as that season drew to a close, Topping and Houk had different notions. The Yankees, because of rain early in the season, had three double-headers coming up in Cleveland . . . six games in three consecutive nights. That is quite a load for anyone to carry. But I was determined to demonstrate that I was healthy again and fully able to do anything a broadcaster would be called upon to do. I hated being sick, being asked how I felt every time I went into the ball park . . . and I knew if I hoped to stay on with the Yankees, I had better pull off a tour de force. I wasn't scheduled to make the trip to Cleveland, but I appraised those six games in three nights, knew if I could bowl through them, that ought to set any doubts to rest. It was easy to go to Cleveland. I merely asked Rizzuto if I could go in his place, and Phil, who always had his eyes on the golf course, didn't hesitate.

So it was quickly set for me to make the trip. I felt great— vigorous, rested. I had outlived the post-gastrectomy problems, was over the fear of another heart attack. I was taking dead aim on doing my work for years to come. I was itching to get to Cleveland, grab the mike, face the camera, shoot the moon. I was ready.

Topping abruptly sent for me. He and Houk were in his office. It was an off day for the ball club. We were flying to Cleveland the next morning. We didn't waste much time in season's greetings. Topping never minced words. He asked: "How do you feel about next year?"

I knew he hadn't called me to tell me I was not in his picture for next year. That would have waited until the winter. Also, Dan wouldn't have bothered to tell me I was through . . . he had boys on his payroll to do things like that. Topping went on:

"How are you getting along with Ballentine?"

That did it. I had been boiling inside for two years about Ballentine trying to cut my salary, trying to make me afraid of my job so I would take a one-third reduction of pay in exchange for the security of a two-year contract. I said, and I will delete the profanity I used:

"I want no part of Ballentine . . . ever. In fact, I might as well tell you I am going to apply for the job with the new club in Atlanta next year . . . and if I get it, you know what you can do with Ballentine."

Topping looked at Houk. Houk looked at Topping. Topping said to Houk:

"I guess we'll have to tell him."

Houk nodded. The room was very quiet.

"I didn't want to have to bring this out, right now," Topping said, "but I had Mel in here this morning and told him he is through . . . that I was tired of his popping off . . . that if we win the pennant, I have already nominated Rizzuto to the Commissioner to announce the World Series as our representative."

I said, "I'm sorry to hear this." I was. I knew what the Yankee job meant to Mel Allen, and I knew what the broadcast of the Series meant to him. His job was his life . . . the wife and children he never had. It was that much to the man.

Topping might as well not have heard me.

"This is not to get out," he said. "I told Mel he can finish the season and make his own announcement, any way he wants to make it, when he wants to make it. I have to tell you now, because I must know your plans for next year. I want you here. With Mel gone, we need you here. And you won't have to have anything to do with Ballentine. I'll take care of that."

Houk gave me the big smile . . . the long, slow, full one.

"Red," Ralph said, "you know you're our man. They may not move that club into Atlanta next year. This is the big job for you . . . right here. With Mel gone, you can do pretty much what you please."

I didn't have to take any time to figure out my answer. I said, "Dan, I never have thought the broadcasts over here were balanced right. I believe the new announcer hired to replace Mel should be a professional announcer . . . not another ballplayer. He should be a youngster like Vince Scully was when we brought him to Brooklyn. And that one pro should always be paired with a ballplayer, but the pro should run it, calling in the player only when he thinks the player has something cogent to say . . . no more aimless Amos 'n Andy stuff on the air."

They both nodded. Topping fiddled with a cigarette; Houk had a chew of tobacco working.

"I ran it as Brooklyn," I went on, "and I've never tried to

run it here—it was always Mel's show not mine. I was brought over here to take charge of the pre- and post-game shows . . . and I think they have been well done."

Houk said, "Red—I know—you handled yourself very well with me and with all the players. Everybody likes to go one with you."

I had not realized until right then how much I had missed being in the command position, the position I'd had at Cincinnati, at Brooklyn, and at CBS.

I resumed, "I can smooth out the announcing booth if I am given the authority to do it. If I am given the position as senior announcer, who can order Rizzuto to go into the dugouts and do his preparation, for one example . . . if I have the say over who is to do what innings . . . if I am allowed to find a young announcer who is eager, willing to listen—I am very interested in staying."

Topping asked, "Where will you find that announcer?"

"There is a guy over at Armed Forces Radio who knows every sports announcer in the United States. You know him— Gordon Bridge [now with the Hughes Sports Network]. He takes the work of all the sports broadcasters and uses it or doesn't use it for Armed Forces broadcasts overseas. I've worked with him on nine or ten World Series broadcasts to the troops abroad . . . he'll give me all the names I need to know. I'll bring them back to you, and we can go from there."

Topping thought about it a moment.

"Find out from Bridge what young announcers he thinks are worth a chance. There's no hurry. Do it after the World Series." Then he said, "What about your traveling with the club?"

"Dan," I replied, "when you and Weiss offered me this job, you said I didn't have to travel . . . and I said I didn't mind traveling . . . but we agreed I would go on the road when you needed me. From time to time you have wanted me to travel, and I have traveled. One afternoon at one o'clock I was sitting over in the apartment and I got a call to be in Minnesota for the game that night . . . and I made it . . . walked into the booth as they played the national anthem. I jumped out to Los Angeles without warning and did a double-header when Mel got sick. Right?"

He said, "I remember. But what about next year?"

"I don't have to travel all the games, and neither does anybody else with a four-man crew. But for next year, I will promise two things: I will guarantee to travel more than fifty percent of the games, and I will see that the job is taken care of, and not slighted."

He smiled. "That's more than I hoped for. Anything else?"

"Yes," I said. "I want a raise."

"How about five thousand?" he said.

"Fine," I said. We shook hands and I left. That put me at fifty thousand dollars for the next year, a round figure that tasted good. The opportunity to direct the broadcasting booth at Yankee Stadium also appealed to me very much. Until the next night.

Each of us on Earth is so desperately selfish. I was wrapped up in the discussion in Topping's office . . . my mind was already auditioning for the right young announcer . . . another Vince Scully. I got on the phone with Gordon Bridge, told him what I wanted, and he agreed to do it. It's always been this way with me—let somebody give me a job to do, place a bet on me, and it's heady wine.

Mel Allen had developed a habit of walking into the play-by-play booth at the last minute. I mean the very last minute. At the Stadium, his brother Larry would have his scorecard in order, waiting for him. On the road, Mel often penciled in the batting orders while announcing the first inning. I never asked him why he cut it so close, but I sensed he felt it gave him "an entrance." Mel would just suddenly appear out of nowhere. His chair would be empty . . . then he was in it . . . "Hello everybody . . . this is Mel Allen . . ."

I got shook up that first night in Cleveland. I stopped thinking about myself abruptly. When I got to the booth about fifteen minutes before air time, Mel was already there. He was sitting in his place. He was staring across the ball field. He didn't speak. I don't think he knew I had come in. I don't think he knew where he was. He was numb. He has protruding dark eyes. They were bulging out so far they looked like Concord grapes. He was the saddest-looking man I have ever seen. He was in a nightmare. His look was not frantic, not wild—just sad, numb, deserted. He just couldn't believe it. He was desolate, stricken.

And he didn't know I knew. We had six games to do together in three nights.... God.

When air time came, I touched him on the shoulder, shook him slightly. He looked at me, blinked, turned to the mike, and said, "Hello everybody . . . this is Mel Allen. . . ."

How he did his work, I don't know. Doing mine was hard enough. When Mel got back to New York, he went wild. Word had gotten out that Rizzuto would be on the Series. Bob Fishel told me he dreaded each day . . . because Mel was on the phone with either Topping or him—all the time. Mel could not believe he wouldn't be on the Series, could not accept he wasn't the Voice of the Yankees, until he wasn't. He did some work for the Milwaukee Braves the next year, and he thought he'd get the big job when the Braves went to Atlanta, but he didn't. He got nothing. He did television one season for Cleveland . . . commuted from New York, tried to take root in Cleveland, but couldn't. He is now off the air except for spots.

While Rizzuto was broadcasting that 1964 Series in Mel's place, I was announcing in the New York studios of Armed Forces Radio with Jerry Coleman and Gordon Bridge. On the field, it was Yogi Berra and the Yankees against Johnny Keane and the Cardinals. Harry Caray, as the St. Louis voice, was one of the Series announcers, and another one was Joe Garagiola, a former St. Louis ballplayer.

Armed Forces Radio has the right to broadcast any program it wants without asking permission . . . but the military will not permit use of any commercials. In the New York studio, we had a television set turned on to the games, with the volume turned off. On the loudspeakers in the studio, we had the radio from the ball park turned on—we had to synchronize with that. To avoid commercials, we in the studio began the broadcast fifteen minutes before the game, giving the weather, crowd, batting orders, umpires, pitching and hitting records. Gordon Bridge was the producer, and he had a ten-second lag on tape for protection. If an announcer at the game threw in an ad-lib commercial, Gordon cut it out before the lag went past. This also meant we had working room of ten seconds— when we saw on the television that they were ready in the park to sing the anthem, we had the leeway to bring it in direct and not be late. (Most of my radio exposures on a mike were a matter of "Say it now—say it right—because you can't take it back." And to have this safety valve of ten seconds! WOW! That was eating high up on the hog.) Anyhow . . . Gordon and I most years, sometimes Jerry, even Rizzuto got in with us once or twice . . . we'd do the opening quarter hour, and hold it until the exact second to introduce the first play-by-play man at the ball park. As soon as he finished a half-inning, we cut in from the studios. We'd "expert it," recap it, feature it until just time to hand it back to the announcer at the field for the next half-inning. So it went. After the final out, we'd take the air and finish it. Counting up the thirteen Series I did domestically, plus those overseas for AFRS, they total some twenty-five. That's enough for one country boy . . . And you know something? The listeners to Armed Forces got the full broadcasts, all the details and no commercials. I did five USO tours, and everywhere I went overseas people talked about those World Series—some of our servicemen had to get up at three or four o'clock in the morning over in the Far East to hear them . . . difference in time . . . but they heard them. I got nothing in pay from AFRS for working on their broadcasts, except satisfaction. You know something? That's about the only thing the government doesn't tax.

As we sat in that New York studio, listening to and working

that 1964 Series, we began to get embarrassed, and then we got angry. Garagiola kept interrupting Rizzuto on the air, cutting in on him, taking the mike away from him. It was as though Rizzuto wasn't good enough to detail a routine play—Garagiola had to explain it or make a wisecrack. Then we got doubly mad because Rizzuto sat there and took it like a sweet, little lamb. Rizzuto just let Garagiola cut in on him—and when Garagiola had the play-by-play, our little Phil let Old Joe run with it all he pleased.

I said, "Listen to Garagiola cutting in on Phil." Coleman said he thought it was terrible. Bridge said, "Joe does it all the time to everybody he works with . . . had trouble with Harry Caray in St. Louis about it . . . Caray stopped him . . . they don't like each other."

During the Series, Gordon told me he had the list of sports announcers ready whenever I wanted it . . . said he would sit down with me when I was ready, and would discuss the work of the men, as he knew it, and also would tell me what he knew about them as human beings. I said I'd call him.

I never asked him for the list. The way it turned out, I had no use for it. The day after the Cardinals won the Series, Berra got fired, and Keane quit at St. Louis. A few days later, Bob Fishel called me and said, "I wanted you to know before you read it in the papers . . . we have hired Perry Smith, who has been the number-two man in sports at NBC, to be vice president of the Yankees in charge of radio and television . . . Perry will assign the announcers their work . . . will supervise them . . . and he will sell the sponsors for radio and television . . . Topping and Houk are very happy . . . I just wanted you to know about it. . . ."

The coming of Perry Smith was a warning bell. A few weeks later, Perry introduced Joe Garagiola at a press party as the new Yankee announcer, the fourth, and that was another alert bell. I heard both of them.

When the 1965 season began, there were other alarm bells going off in all directions, which I heard, but didn't want to hear. I was being used less and less on the between-inning commercials . . . I did fewer and fewer before-game shows . . . I was not given the attention Garagiola was. He and Smith had been buddies at NBC . . . Now Smith had brought him in . . . put his marbles on Joe.

Johnny Keane was hired to inherit the impending storm at the Stadium. I had great respect for John as a manager, as a man, as a friend. When the Yankees crumbled a year later, losing sixteen of their first twenty games, Keane was made the scapegoat, was fired. I was a Keane man, on and off the air. Also, I never hesitated to speak well of Casey Stengel and of George Weiss. I did not do it deliberately, but by doing it, I got numbered among those who had best be forgotten. It wasn't "nice" anymore to talk favorably about Casey or Weiss or even MacPhail. In fact, I got the word several times that Joe Cronin, president of the American League, listening in at his home in Boston, didn't like my occasional references to Bill Klem and his greatness as an umpire. Klem, you see, had umpired in the National League.

Oh, yes, there were bells going off. CBS now had the Yankees, and Topping was working for them, trying to hold on for himself, and also trying to hold a job for his son. A friend at CBS told me not to turn my back on Mike Burke—that he had the fastest knife on or off the CBS television screen. In 1965, Perry Smith publicly—at a table in the pressroom with writers, announcers, various television people listening—told me I was talking too much on the broadcasts, that he had letters to that effect, and so had Topping. When I went to see Houk about it—Ralph was still general manager—he was profanely not interested.

Every so often in 1966 there were blurbs in the columns that the Yankee announcing staff would be reduced in number . . . that Barber and/or Jerry Coleman were slated to feel the axe. Perry Smith was blank-faced noncommittal. After Keane was fired and Houk became field manager again, Topping sent a mimeographed sheet to the ball park to all the announcers saying we were "horrid" . . . and to get "with it."

I never felt better than I did during those last two years at the Stadium. Never had even a cotton-picking head cold. I told Jerry Coleman at Fort Lauderdale during spring training of 1965 that the Yankees as they were then constituted were a bad ball club . . . that they would not come close to winning . . . and that he and I would have to be broadcasters in the real sense of the word . . . we would have to dig for new material . . . we could no longer just ride with a team that won and won. I went to work to do deeper research, to get more into the broadcasts than just balls and strikes. This was what Perry was talking about when he publicly laced me down.

Always I had responded to the challenge of announcing a losing team. I bore down in Cincinnati and rejoiced as the Reds went up and up from the cellar. Twice I had had to work at Brooklyn with teams that were being rebuilt. Rebuilding was my dish. When you rebuild, you work. I was ready for this type of job.

So—I heard all the warnings . . . Smith, Garagiola, Houk, Topping, Burke, Ballentine, the newspapers. I knew. But I let my ego—my vanity and pride—call the shots.

Also, I added up: this would make thirty-three straight years of big-league baseball for me . . . I wanted at least two more to make a round figure of thirty-five . . . to keep my cycles in fives . . . five at Cincinnati, fifteen at Brooklyn, and I wanted fifteen at the Stadium. That would then make me sixty years old, four times fifteen. I had not said to myself I would then quit . . . but I firmly wanted at least two more years. Isn't it silly to get hung up on a numbers kick?

Lylah and I bought a house in Key Biscayne in 1965, and that was to be our home. We had had enough of living in New York, especially in the winter—and with the development and use of tape for everything, except play-by-play, there was no longer any professional reason to remain in New York during the off season. In the summer of 1966, I lived at the Hilton Hotel in New York—kept the same small suite there whether the team was at home or out of town. Lylah went to Europe in early July, and I traveled steadily with the Yankees. I not

only had nothing to stay for in New York but I was also showing how much work, how much interest, how much value I
was contributing. I was nailing down my future with the
Yankees, nailing it down in my own way—a way that had
carried me from Florida to Ohio to Brooklyn to CBS to the
Stadium. I was, in essence, showing the Yankees, New York,
everybody, what a polished and resourceful broadcaster I was.
I was demonstrating what thirty-three years of hard experience
meant when the chips, as well as the ball club, were down. I
knew I was challenged, and I wanted to let everybody know
who was the broadcaster and who were the ballplayers in the
broadcasting booth. I don't believe I ever did better work, more
balanced work, more deft, sure, sharp broadcasting. I have
always been hard to please about my work. I was pleased with
it in 1966.

Late in the season, on the Yankees' last trip to Baltimore,
Larry MacPhail invited Bobby Richardson and me to spend
the day at his home—before a night game. He drove in, picked
us up, showed us his stables and his brood mares, gave us
lunch, and after lunch, Jeanie, his daughter, showed Bobby the
rest of the "farm." I told Larry how things were going with
me and the Yankees. He listened very thoughtfully. I told him
I wanted to stay there at least another two years, but that I
couldn't feel the pulse of the situation except for what I read
in the papers, that Topping was in a corner with his personal
survival problems, that Smith was elusive and stayed clear of
me, always sat at another table in the pressroom. Larry said he
was going to call Bill, his youngest son, who was now Director
of Sports at CBS . . . had followed me into the job. And Larry
said to me, "Here is the phone number of Joe Iglehart. He lives
down here in Baltimore and is home now for this series. Call
him early in the morning and talk this over with him. Joe can
do more about this than anybody but Paley himself. Call him
early tomorrow. He gets up early."

Iglehart had been a big stockholder in both the Orioles and
CBS. When CBS bought the Yankees, Iglehart had to choose

between selling his Baltimore stock or his CBS stock. He stayed with CBS. So he had baseball savvy, was on the CBS Board of Directors, and MacPhail fingered him as the guy for me to talk with.

I called Iglehart early the next morning. He said he was coming to the game that night with some of his family. Could I arrange to sit in his box with him the first few innings? I said I could. He was very receptive to my story . . . promised to straighten out all questions very, very soon. I told him I had to get this situation cleared up, or else I wanted to shoot for another job, maybe at Atlanta. He said to forget about announcing anywhere next year but for the Yankees. He told me I had nothing to worry about. I told this to MacPhail later that night. He said, "Good."

The next week, CBS picked up its purchase option on Topping's last ten percent of the Yankees. CBS now owned the ball club one hundred percent. Topping was finished. He called a press conference at the Stadium, said he was through, but hoped CBS would retain young Dan on the payroll. Then he stepped back, and Mike Burke stepped in, the new president of the CBS Yankees. As I sat there listening to Topping and Burke, and in spite of having been warned about Burke, I felt smug. I had won this thing. I'd come to feel that Topping was not' my strongest supporter, and he was gone. Burke was CBS, but I counted up the nine good years I'd had at CBS, I remembered how Bill Paley himself had given me the initial interview, how Frank Stanton had thanked me for thinking of the company first when I said he needed a full-time Director of Sports, I was basically a broadcaster and not an office man, how Joe Iglehart had been settling things behind the scenes, and that Larry MacPhail had talked to his son Bill. I added up that Perry Smith and Joe Garagiola had come from arch rival NBC. Finally, I told myself, "CBS is radio and television— they appreciate a broadcaster who is a broadcaster." It is a very foolish thing to allow yourself to think what you want yourself to think . . . it can be very costly.

The Yankees had two weeks to go in the saddest season in their history. They were to play the White Sox, then the Red Sox, close the Stadium, go to Washington, then to Chicago, and then try to forget it all. The White Sox were in for just one game—Tuesday. It rained and there was a fog and more rain and a wet, wet field. The game was called off. The next day it was again called off.

Thursday morning, with the White Sox still in town and the game set for that afternoon, I read in *The New York Times* that the day before at Wrigley Field in Chicago the Cubs had played to their smallest crowd of the year, and it was also the smallest crowd of the season in the National League. The *Times* story placed the attendance paragraph ahead of how the game itself was won and lost. That was the story— the smallest crowd of the season.

When I drove from the Hilton Hotel to the Stadium later that morning, it was still raining lightly. It was misty, over-cast, grim. As I drove along, I had the car radio tuned to WCBS. I kept expecting every minute the announcement that the game was called off. When I walked into the park, the word was, "We're playing."

The field was a muddy mess. The stands were ringing wet. The fog and the light rain cut the visibility down to almost nothing. It was a depressing place. But the rain quit at noon, and it just stayed foggy and misty and ghoulish inside the old triple-decked monster. Yankee Stadium has had crowds of nearly eighty-two thousand, and it is one place when it is filled and the sun is shining and the flags and bunting are draped around the mezzanine . . . and it is another place when it is empty and wet and shrouded in gloom.

I went into the White Sox clubhouse to see my old friend Eddie Stanky, the White Sox manager. He wasn't there. I had arranged not to go to Chicago for the final games of the season, so I wanted to wish him a pleasant winter. In baseball, there are two times you permit yourself some show of genuine sentiment: in the fall when you say good-bye, not knowing if you'll meet again the next season; and in the spring when you do meet again. Then, you either wish a man a good winter and health for his family, or else you ask how was the winter and how was his family. The rest of the time is cutthroat. Whoever said baseball was a game never earned his living playing it. Red Ruffing told me once he "Wouldn't give his mother a good pitch to hit," and as he walked away, his catcher Bill Dickey said, "And she better be ready to hit the dirt, too."

Stanky was standing behind third base, about the only piece of dry ground in the Bronx. I started toward him, picking my way through the mud. He saw me and came toward me. We stood there, wished each other the pleasant winter, and then we started looking at the empty stands. He grinned and said: "They can't cheat us today . . . I can count the fans myself from right here." There were not fifty people in the stands then.

There was no pregame show on television that day. I drew the assignment of starting play-by-play on the television side. I was to stay there for two and one-half innings, later do two and one-half on radio, then sign the radio side off. We came on the air with the first pitch of the game, so it took the first half-inning to fill in the batting orders and the pitchers' records.

Long before I signed on, I knew what the story would be: this was the smallest crowd, by far, in the entire history of the massive ball park built by Babe Ruth, Ed Barrow, and Colonel Jake Ruppert. The story in the *Times* that morning had alerted me, the remark by Stanky had zeroed it in. Any reporter would know what the story was, and it was a big story. I knew all the newspaper reporters would center on it. I knew what the New York *Daily News* would do—they'd cover the whole back page of the paper with pictures of the yawning emptiness of Yankee Stadium. And the *News* did, with Mike Burke sitting alone in the stands, on his first day as the Yankee president.

In television, you have cameras scattered in different positions in the stands. I think we had five cameras working that day. In a studio under the stands, the heart of the telecast is located—the director sits watching a monitor for each camera, plus the master, or the on-the-air monitor. Next to the director is the "switcher." The director calls the number of the camera whose picture he wants, the switcher punches a button and that camera's picture goes on the air faster than you can blink your eyes. On the other side of the director is the sound engineer. Throughout the game, all five cameras keep photographing. The director sees the game entirely through the various cameras. He has an assistant who sits alongside the announcer in the broadcasting booth, who sees the game and can telephone data to the director or get answers from the studio. The cameras and the announcer's booth are connected by two-way telephones—communication is instant. The men wear headsets and everybody hears whatever is said on this closed circuit. Except the announcer—he communicates only through the assistant director. The announcer has an on-the-air monitor in front of him, so he knows what the audience is seeing, and he can synchronize his words with the picture.

We took the air, and the first half of the first inning was played. During the following commercial, I turned to Jimmy Hunter, the A.D. in the announcer's booth, and asked him to ask Jack Murphy, the regular director of WPIX for a picture of the empty stands when we came back on the air. (A thoughtful, professional announcer does not try to lead his director by saying over the air what particular picture he wants —he asks for the picture off-mike, waits for it to appear on the monitor, then says what he wants to say about the shot.) It didn't take a smart fellow to know a pan of those empty stands would have high drama. I saw Mike Burke sitting by himself, a lost soul, and I intended to say this was exactly the fitting way it ought to be for Mike Burke and CBS—starting at the very bottom, nowhere to go but up. I was going to say that Burke couldn't have asked for a better beginning for himself.

The bottom of the inning began, and no picture of the empty stands. I leaned over to Hunter and again asked for the picture of the stands. I heard Jimmy ask for it. Then he got up, walked to the end of the booth to another telephone. He had left to talk out of my earshot, this I understood. Something was going on.

Jimmy came back and whispered to me, "No shot of the stands." I said, "Tell Murphy I *want* the shot." Jimmy said, "It isn't Murphy—it's Don Carney . . . Murphy is off today." I said, "Tell Carney I *want* the shot." Jimmy said, "Carney says to tell you you can't have the shot." All of this exchange was off the mike, between pitches. I said, "Who told Carney to tell me I can't have the shot?" I knew somebody had had to tell Carney—both Carney and Hunter were very cooperative men, men I'd worked with for years, and we always worked well together. Carney wouldn't have told me I could not have a shot I asked for so strongly. Hunter said without hesitation, "Perry says you can't have the shot." Perry Smith, the vice president of radio and television for the Yankees, was in the control room. Whom he had consulted, I don't know, but he had consulted with someone—Perry graduated from Annapolis, he was all-Navy, he went by the book and by delegated authority.

That settled that. With Smith standing over Carney's shoulder, there would be no way to get a camera shot of the empty stands. *Then,* like the drawing together of a curtain, the cameras cropped down on their pictures—only the infield and outfield were shown the rest of the game. No foul balls that went into the stands were followed in. Not a single picture was taken showing the stands for that entire game. When I saw the cropping down of the pictures, I knew. The public was not to be allowed to see what was inside Yankee Stadium that day, even though it was the big story of the day, of the month, maybe of the year: the turning point in the Yankees' history.

I sat there . . . announcing by reflex responses. My mind

was evaluating the situation. I thought back to that old man with the white hair, Judge K. M. Landis, and I heard him say, "Report everything you see." I thought about MacPhail saying, "And if my ball club needs to be burned—then, by God, burn it." I thought about Rickey saying, "You are closer to your work than any man alive . . . you do it." I thought about when Ed Murrow called the tune on Senator Joe McCarthy, when nobody else—in or out of government—would report who McCarthy really was. I had to ask myself once again who I was . . . what my business was. And I heard my father saying, "Don't ever let a man make you afraid of your job . . . make you believe the job you have is the only job you'll ever have."

I knew I could not get the television picture, but I also knew they could not cut off the microphone fast enough to prevent me saying what I thought I should say . . . should say as a reporter . . . should say to the audience that trusted me . . . and should say before the newspapers said it.

I leaned into the mike and said, "I don't know what the paid attendance is today—but whatever it is, it is the smallest crowd in the history of Yankee Stadium . . . and this smallest crowd is the story, not the ball game." I didn't rub it in. I let it go at that. I had said it, reported it. When I got on the radio side, it was time for the actual attendance figures to come to hand—after all, the Yankees didn't dare withhold the official count from the writers . . . and when I gave the number of the paid . . . four hundred thirteen . . . I said again that it had to be the smallest crowd ever for the Stadium. The Red Sox were on a bus coming in from the airport, heard what I said on radio, and before the game the next day, several of them laughed and said, "We yelled on the bus . . . Old Red will sure catch hell for saying that." I didn't, except the silence after the game was complete. Perry had left the park by the time I got downstairs.

I felt very satisfied about being a reporter. I had it in my mind that CBS would want me to be a broadcaster . . . a reporter . . . and would be upset over Perry Smith's edict of eating news. I even thought, "This ought to nail down who the broadcaster is around here."

Saturday morning I got to thinking: I was leaving New York on Tuesday morning for the three games in Washington and then for home. Monday was open. Why didn't I see Burke before I left and get the next year, or the next two years, settled? I called his office, and his secretary took my message. She called back shortly to say he was swamped all day Saturday. She knew that I was on the Sunday game at the Stadium, but what about breakfast on Monday? And would I pick a place at my hotel?

I said it would be fine, just fine. Would Mr. Burke call me in my room when he got into the lobby, and then I'd say where we would eat. I had a kitchenette in my little suite, and I planned for us to have breakfast there, looking out at Central Park from my room on the forty-third floor. I make good coffee and toast, and I went forth and selected an excellent melon. We would be free to talk. We would begin our working partnership.

Sunday evening I went to bed fairly early, at peace in my mind. I was looking forward to breakfast, to our meeting. Tomorrow morning would be Burke's sixth day as Yankee president, and I thought I had some things to say that would be helpful . . . things from MacPhail and Rickey and Weiss and thirty-three years of being in the big league business.

About ten-thirty that Sunday night Perry Smith called—he said Burke had asked him to tell me to meet him at the Edwardian Room at the Plaza Hotel at eight-thirty. Then he hung up. All night I tried to figure it out—until the phone call I didn't know Perry knew anything about my meeting with Burke.

Breakfast didn't take too long. On the way out of my room I saw a book, *Best Sports Stories 1966,* for which I had been one of the three judges. Remembering that Burke had once told me he had a young son, I took the book along. He was already seated at his table by a window on Fifty-ninth Street. As I sat down, the waiter poured me a cup of coffee. I said: "This is a book for your boy—it has some great writing in it. In fact, Michael, I am amazed at how much good writing is done in the noise and confusion of the press box."

He broke in.

"There is no reason for us to be talking this way. We have decided not to seek to renew your contract."

My breakfast was half a cup of coffee . . . black.

There was never any doubt about my immediate procedure. I had not forgotten Mel Allen and the way he was fired. I was not going to let the Yankees call the tune for me any longer. They had made their move. The next one was mine. After I phoned Lylah in Key Biscayne—and she was great—I sent word for Jack O'Brian and Val Adams to call me at my hotel. O'Brian, who called back first, was writing for the *World Journal Tribune*. When the paper hit the streets early that afternoon, the story made page one. Adams was with the *Times,* so he had all day to call, and he did call. I stayed in that room all day and all night answering the phone. I wanted to talk to everybody. It was a full day.

Burke told the press that the decision to dismiss me was made two weeks before—that Topping was supposed to do it, but hadn't. Yes—the same Topping who had fired Stengel, Weiss, Berra, Allen, Keane. . . .

In our brief breakfast meeting, Burke had said he'd learned that I had told people that "When I know I am making my last broadcast it is going to be a beaut" . . . that I would rip everybody and everything. He said I didn't need to go to Washington for those three games. He implied strongly that he would be greatly relieved if I didn't go to Washington and get on the Yankee air anymore.

I said, "Yes, I said that in jest. But," and I never spoke more coldly, "do you think I am going to tarnish a thirty-three year career of clean, good work by saying something messy in one broadcast? No—you needn't worry about what

I'll say in Washington. I insist on finishing my work . . . on doing those three games. I have a contract for those three games."

I went to Washington, but I didn't get on the air again for the Yankees. All three games were rained out, so I got in my little car and drove to Key Biscayne, where Lylah was standing on the front porch, waiting for me. The hunter was home from the hills.

I have been told, however, that the Yankees ordered the radio station to make a complete tape of all my broadcasts in Washington. Nobody has ever asked me what I was going to say, had there been a game. But I was not going to say one word about being fired. Nothing. I was just going to do play-by-play as though nothing had happened, and when it was time on the third and final game for me to hand the mike to someone else, I was going to say six more words—"This is Red Barber saying good-bye." That was all.

SIX:

THE BUSINESS OF BROADCASTING

SIX SERVING-MEN

For many years I kept on my desk a stanza by Rudyard Kipling—it's from "The Elephant Child":

> I keep six honest serving-men
> (They taught me all I knew):
> Their names are What and Why and When
> And How and Where and Who.

These six are, of course, the essentials of reporting. For the sports announcer they are so basic as almost to be taken for granted. Without trying to top Kipling, let me name an additional six serving-men for the radio-television sports broadcaster to call upon in his play-by-play profession. They are preparation, evaluation, concentration, curiosity, impartiality, and, if such can be achieved, imperturbability.

Preparation

Preparation, like creation, never stops. Announcing sports is a business that should be approached as a business. It is not romantic or glamorous or gee-whiz-kid or my-Cubs or my-Yankees or old school-tie. It is work. At times millions of people are hearing this work. On the field other men are doing their work. Their families depend on them. How these men are estimated as players by the audience comes, to a great degree, from the broadcaster. The broadcaster is an influential man . . . more than he sometimes realizes.

The preparation begins in school with our magnificent language. The King James Bible is unsurpassed for beauty of language and for concise use of words. Winston Churchill wrote the best pithy-salty-useful-action-English I know . . . especially in his history of World War Two.

The young announcer today has available to him a considerable library of sports books—some of them informational, some of them pictorial, some of them pot-boilers. These books should be read for professional background and for depth and insight. It is recommended collecting the more useful of these books—not necessarily to read each through but, as it comes to hand, to skim it in order to know what is in it against the time it may be needed. An educated man is one who knows where to find information.

Every year each sport issues books of records, dates, biographies, and other pertinent statistics. In baseball there are several: *The Baseball Register, The National League Green Book, The American League Red Book,* and *The Little Red Book.* These record books must be kept at hand for every broadcast. One never knows when exact information will be required—and with statistics, the announcer should not rely on his memory. He should take the few seconds needed to look in the book. The audience will wait for the information from the book. But this same audience, while willing to be patient for the correct information, will never forget your mistake if you guess wrong. This world has a lasting memory for mistakes. And let me add that an announcer doesn't have to be in the almighty, split-second hurry his ego persuades him to be. . . . *Look in the book.*

Each day's preparation starts with the morning newspaper . . . read from the front page on through, including, of course, the sports section. An announcer should know more than just who won what games the night before.

Over the years I have tried very hard to make mental notes as I read the paper, I would pause at a particular story, remind myself I might wish to use it that afternoon, and then resume reading. This habit—with practice—will produce surprisingly rich returns. It's using your mind, and one's mind won't work any harder than one makes it work.

The announcer should start for the ball park with plenty of time to get there, even if he has a flat tire or the bridge is up or an accident has stopped all traffic. One cannot get into a lather for fear of being late and then arrive in a proper emotional state to do one's work. To enter a broadcasting booth out of breath, unprepared, and without having had a bite to eat is insulting to all of the fates.

But it is wasteful to get to the park too early, when nothing is going on and the players are not even on the field. To come out too early and sit around in the empty stands dulls one's keenness, dampens the spirits.

I have found that two hours before a baseball game starts is just the right time for the announcer to reach the park. The players on the home team are coming from the clubhouse into their dugout. The home-team manager is there and has the time to be available. You check the home dugout for a half hour or so, until the visiting team takes the field for practice. You move across to the visitors' dugout. Then, right on schedule, you go to the pressroom for a light meal . . . a snack. One cannot announce on a full stomach . . . or an empty one.

When you are in the dugouts, your job is to find out who

is playing, position by position—who is hurt—whose wife had a baby during the night—who will pitch tomorrow, et cetera, et cetera. You are in the dugouts to listen to the managers . . . to listen to the players . . . to listen to the writers as they interview the managers . . . you are there to listen. Your job of talking comes later—up in the booth.

After you've eaten, you move easily toward the booth, arriving just about a half hour before air time. You put out your scorebook, record books, four or five sharp pencils, egg timer (I'll explain that one in a moment), and the commercials. You have left yourself time to put everything in order.

There is absolutely nothing so important as daily, thorough, hard-boiled preparation. When the game begins and your preparation is complete, you are ready, *and you know it*. You have an inner confidence that you can do the work that is set before you. This confidence is based upon the certain knowledge that you know all that you should know about the two teams.

For example, a manager may be playing a different second baseman today than he did yesterday. Discovering this in the dugout, you have the right to—you must—ask the manager "why." Most times he'll tell you, and it's routine information . . . maybe he's resting the man . . . maybe there's a pulled muscle . . . maybe a batting slump. Sometimes the manager— Ralph Houk of the Yankees would do this often—will say, "Well, I'll tell you, but you can't use it." My answer was, "Don't tell me if I can't use it." And I would walk away. There is certain information I don't think an announcer should have in his head . . . and for an obvious reason . . . what you don't know you can't say.

Each day is a new day, requiring fresh preparation. Each game is a new game. Everything is new every day but the exactitudes of work.

About that egg timer. I have in mind a cheap fifty- to sixty-cent egg timer you can get in any hardware store. The sand in it runs through in about three minutes. Keep two or three in your briefcase. They break. Every game is played by the score. The audience is lost without the score. So—give the score, invert your egg timer, and go on about your business. When you see the sand has run down again, give the score, invert the timer, and go on about your business . . . and with this inexpensive device, you have one less worry: *Remembering to announce the score.*

One last item, a vital one. Never arrive at the broadcasting booth without stopping en route at the men's room. Whether you feel you need to stop there or not . . . stop there. It might be a long ball game, and you just might not be able to get away from the microphone. The rising of the inner tide is not conducive to broadcasting serenity.

Evaluation

The announcer has printed the names of the ballplayers in his scorebook, checked his commercial cues and copy, arranged his stock of record books, loosened his tie and collar, given the engineer a voice level, discussed whatever anybody who works on the broadcast wishes to discuss. He now has five to ten minutes to sit quietly and bring today's game into a working focus. This is the last calm before the competitive storm. The fans are getting seated. Only the groundkeepers are busy, smoothing off the infield . . . rechalking the foul lines.

Now is when the announcer decides "what they're playing for." Is first place at stake? Is a pitcher going for his twentieth win? Is a winning streak up for grabs? Is a player trying to hit his sixty-first home run? Is a rookie making his first appearance? What do you tell the audience that will focus its interest on today's ball game?

When the announcer signs-on, he uses his opening remarks the way headlines are used in a newspaper, to call attention to certain stories. This is the pregame evaluation. As the game progresses, it is up to the announcer to be alert for new situations and new personalities that require changing the evaluation. Records are always being approached, tied, and broken. The announcer should be abreast of each challenge as it develops.

Concentration

The game lasts from two to three hours or even longer . . . the announcer says what is to be said . . . and any one word, or group of two or three words, can be a public error or public embarrassment. There is no eraser on a microphone . . . no rewrite man on the news desk.

He never knows what will happen. The baseball moves unpredictably. Further, the players do odd things, things totally unexpected. Something suddenly occurs in the grandstands. Or the scoreboard operator can make a mistake and post the wrong set of figures.

The television announcer must keep an eye on the monitor —its picture is the same one seen by the audience—in order that his words match the picture. As the game goes on, the figures entered into the scorebook accumulate—always they must be checked and rechecked to keep them correct—so many runs, so many hits, so many errors, so many walks, so many strikeouts. The egg timer must be watched—give the score every three minutes, somebody may have just tuned in.

People are around you, working people—the engineer, cameramen, statistician, associate announcers, a representative from the advertising agency. Noise is around you. The distractions are multiple.

Only a disciplined concentration can carry you through, can see that the job gets done. This professional concentration starts with the recognition that the announcer comes to the ball park, to the broadcasting booth, only to work. His job is exclusively to work. In the morning, the announcer must dispose of his other obligations—financial, domestic, physical, emotional. If there is sickness in his house, he must arrange for any necessary care or assistance, so that he can leave for his work—or else stay home. If he himself is ill, he must decide whether he is well enough to keep his mind on his work—or stay home. You can't come into the booth with your mind on yourself or another place, and then concentrate.

It is hard, sometimes, to concentrate . . . to shut out your private life when you walk into the broadcasting booth. I know. And I didn't always do it.

One afternoon I went to the dentist and had more of a session than I'd anticipated. My mouth was very sore—teeth, gums, all of it. There was a night game at Brooklyn, and I went to the ball park; but I was giving in to the biggest sin a man can indulge in, according to what my dad used to tell me . . . "Son, the worst thing a man can do is feel sorry for himself."

I felt very sorry for myself, and all I wanted was to get the game over and get home and go to bed. Philadelphia was playing at Brooklyn, and Freddy Fitzsimmons was managing the Phils. He had a new third baseman with him, just purchased from Columbus, Ohio—Johnny Antonelli.

I got to the park, checked Leo Durocher and the Dodgers, and went over to see Fitzsimmons. He gave me his batting order, with his new man in it. I'd never seen him. I asked where he was, and Fred said he was at the plate right then. I studied him, eye-photographed him as a right-handed, brunet, thick-chested fellow. I went to the booth, feeling very sorry for Old Red.

I closed my mind, my ears, my eyes, I didn't hear the public-address announcer give the lineups. Why should I? I had gotten them myself, and my mouth hurt. I looked quickly when Antonelli came to the plate—yes, that was he . . . right-handed batter—thick-chested. I didn't check his number. After the game I got home, went to bed, and that was that.

The next morning I read the paper, and there in *The New York Times* was the account of the ball game, but with Andy Seminick at third base, not Antonelli. As soon as I got to the park I looked up Fitzsimmons. He said, "That was a funny thing last night. You hadn't more than left the dugout when

Antonelli stepped on a ball and sprained his ankle. I had to play Seminick."

I confessed it promptly on the air, that I had had the wrong man playing the entire ball game the night before . . . I've never again given way to feeling quite so sorry for myself.

Every mistake I've made on the air came from breaking my concentration upon my work.

From the time you get the signal "you're on the air" you must hold your mind strictly on the job. You must not permit distractions to break your concentration. Pay no attention to the people who move around behind you. Allow no one to talk to you—if they must communicate with you, have them write you a note. Then you can read it between plays, or at a convenient pause.

The professional announcer talks with his eyes. He has schooled his mind to stay at attention during the game. He is unaware of "style"—he hasn't time to sustain artificial speech or vocal tempo. He loses himself in the balls and strikes, the hits and runs and errors, the safe and the out, the score and the inning, the depth of the defense, the type of pitches being thrown. His eyes see the runner take his lead, and his words tell it . . . his eyes see the fly ball, and his words tell of the catch.

Curiosity

The announcer should not care how a game comes out, but he must be interested—curious—as to how it will go. He must be interested from the very first pitch on. He wants to see it happen, see why it happens, tell how it happens. He wants to report it, every detail. He wants to do this particular piece of work very much.

There is a three-letter word that should be pasted on the microphone instead of the call letters of the station or of the network. The word is "Why," one of Kipling's original serving-men.

For every move on the field, there is a reason, a why it was attempted, a why it failed, a why it worked. The manager sends in a new player—why? The bullpen gets up—why?

The infield is played in—why? Time is called—why? A pitcher is doing well and is suddenly removed—why? The manager steps to the front of his dugout and moves his outfield around—why?

The listener wants to know why without thinking why. The announcer should find out why, or know why.

Realistic humility works. When a why situation arises, one that is not apparent, the announcer should routinely tell the audience he doesn't know why, but he'll find out, and when he does know why, he'll broadcast it. The associate announcer, or the statistician, should then get on the proper inside-the-park telephone and find out why. The broadcasting booth should be the headquarters of a broadcast team that works together to get the work done . . . to find the whys.

No matter the years of announcing, on the very last inning of the final game, there will still be a why that requires the satisfaction of an answer.

Don't guess why—ask.

Impartiality

Human beings take sides. You are for or you are against. In a contest the aim is to win, not lose, not tie. Since early times a man who didn't take sides was regarded as weak, afraid to make up his mind, fearful his choice would cause him difficulty. It is important that a player have people behind him, who wish him success. It is vital that a team have rooters, urging it on.

When I was in charge of sports at CBS, following Ted Husing, and a sports event was being considered for broadcast on the network, I used a rule-of-thumb appraisal—"Who cares who wins it?" If not many people cared, not many people would tune it in. Why broadcast something without an audience?

The announcer makes his living because of a large number of people who care who wins and who loses. But what is the relationship of the announcer to the unseen multitude—some of it very partisan?

The listener wants to know, deeper inside himself than he consciously thinks, what is going on. He does not want to know what the announcer wants to see happen, but what he actually sees. He wants to know a line drive is a line drive, no matter who hit it. The listener needs the constant assurance that he is getting an accurate report of the event.

To care, to root, to anguish, to rejoice—these are the rights of the fan. They are not the rights of the professional announcer, any more than they are of the umpire who rules safe or out . . . ball or strike.

I got along well with the Brooklyn fans, with the Giant fans, with the Yankee fans. Tom Meany once wrote something about me, which I think I treasure above everything that has been put in print about my work. Meany once wrote that a taxi driver in Brooklyn complained, "That Barber—he's too fair."

Two teams play a game. Every man on each team is trying to make his living, earn his rating, sustain his ego—to say nothing of sustaining his family. From the radio booth it looks easier than it is to hit a curve ball, to stand firm against a real fast ball, to go against the wall for a long fly.

To be fair to all the players, to be able to report them for what they do, I always believed it a mistake to be personally close to any of them. I felt I should be on good, friendly, working terms with them all—speak to them all, be interested in them and their work, but no more interested in one of them than in another.

I never visited in a ballplayer's house, nor had a ballplayer come to my house. I was very careful never to ask a favor of a player. My wife sat in the stands close to where the players' wives sat—she was happy to have short visits with them—but she sat with her own friends, or she sat alone.

I never bet on a sporting event—not even for a Coca Cola. Gambling is the worst enemy of sports, bar none. But, and this is where the Coca Cola comes in, the second you bet anything, even a soft drink, you have bet your judgment, you have bet your ego, you have put blinders to some degree on your emotional vision . . . you have impaired your reporting.

Starting back in 1930, I have refused to make predictions, especially on football games. When you pick this team to win over that team, and do it publicly, you have again dimmed your ability to see clearly—especially if you are going to do play-by-play . . . be a reporter.

If you are going to be a feature, studio announcer trying to sell prediction programs . . . I have no advice.

Imperturbability

This is a favorite word of mine. Of course a human being cannot be imperturbable. He can appear to be, but he isn't. He can strive to be, and he can come closer and closer. As a boy I read how General Jackson got his nickname in the Civil War. The battle was raging around him as he sat his horse. The bullets and the shells were flying. Men were charging and some were falling. It was hot, and the battle was so poised, it could go either way. A soldier saw the general and cried aloud, "Look at him—he's standing like a stonewall."

Jackson was watching, and when the time came for him to give his orders, he was ready to give them—and he did. His coolness inspired his men to win the battle. Somehow I've tried to remember Stonewall Jackson when a big ball game got to a pinnacle moment. When the stakes are big, when the climax is exciting, or the turn of events is stunning with its surprise—like Bobby Thomson hitting that home run off Ralph Branca in that play-off game in 1951 at the Polo Grounds—that is when the listener, who can't see for himself, needs so desperately to know, and to know with detailed exactitude, what is going on. Then the man at the microphone needs to report, needs to announce the ball, needs not to be swayed as the crowd in the park is swayed.

I guess imperturbability is too much to ask of an announcer —but it isn't too much to ask him to try for it.

To end this section as I began it, let me refer again to Kipling—"To keep your head when all about you are losing theirs."

BROADCASTING FOOTBALL

The broadcasting of major league baseball is at once more exacting and yet less difficult than announcing college or professional football.

The real test of a professional sports announcer is a baseball season—which begins in spring training around the first of March and goes onward, day after day, night after night, until around October. In a baseball game, each tiny detail is readily apparent, pitch by pitch—and the fans know their game. The baseball fan is himself the constant challenge. However, because of the continuity of the games in their long daily schedule, and because of the openness of play, baseball is an easier business—provided the announcer knows his business, and prepares thoroughly before each game.

Football is organized confusion. Not even the coaches know much about what is happening until they study the films after the game is played—and restudy them—and break them down into slow motion. It doesn't make any difference how many years you announce football, it doesn't get any easier, as baseball does. The basic problem of football is identifying the players . . . naming them correctly.

There should be no mechanical difficulty for the football announcer if he can count as high as fifty. The field is twice that long, but it is divided in half—a team either plays in its own fifty-yard territory, or goes into the opposition's fifty yards. There cannot be more than four downs, ten yards to gain in a sequence of these four downs. The penalties go from five yards to fifteen, or at most, half the distance from the spot of the foul to the goal line. There must be eleven men on each team. The score is counted by two for a safety, three for a field goal, six for a touchdown, and after the TD either one point for the kicked extra point or two if the ball is either run or passed into the end zone.

The problem of describing types of offensive or defensive formations is so much easier and simpler than most of the mike-men of today make it sound. The former coaches and the former players who've muscled in have brought a pseudo-professional jargon that makes them sound as if they're speaking from Olympus. Most of the radio-television football language today is vocal misdirection. It is used to cover up a definite lack of working English, and is a deliberate attempt to make the "experts" sound far more expert than they are.

But the new microphone "former player expert" gets away with whatever he says. The audience doesn't know what he is talking about, the television picture doesn't show the defenses —and on radio he can be as home free as Bill Stern once was in creating lateral passes.

If you are a young professional announcer who is starting out, let me make this one point: Let the experts go their way, which they will anyhow, as they are riding on reputations made outside the broadcasting booth. The young announcer must make his reputation inside the booth. In essence, learn your trade, be yourself, and don't try to "play the other fellows' game."

Football preparation begins with the study of the rosters of the two teams—the memorizing of the jersey numbers— primarily those of the ends and backs, because they will be where the ball is—plus an analysis of the season's statistics. From the statistics sheet comes such information as who passes, who receives, who carries the ball the most, who returns the punts, who punts, who kicks off, and so on, and indicates which player's numbers to concentrate on. No man can memorize two full squads in one week.

The science of football coaching has been developed concurrently with the motion pictures. Only with the pictures, which the coach could run and rerun and even stop completely, could he and his staff know what each player was doing. Only with the pictures could the defenses be studied and analyzed.

The heart of the football announcer's preparation is the use of these same motion pictures. I never needed more than a look at the films of the last game the team played. When you see the pictures on the screen, you see the players as they move, as they are, as they will look to you during the game. The pictures are in small scale which is a plus—most broadcast booths are so high above the field, and so far back atop the stands that the players during the game are seen on the same small scale.

Today, schools freely swap their game films—in fact, they often send film to each other in the summer to allow for more thorough study. It has now settled down to a big business, big money, big stakes. Years ago, the announcer had to contact both schools, as each school kept close guard on its motion pictures. Nowadays, you merely report to the home school—all your preparation materials for both teams will be there.

Today, the announcer is most welcome and is expected, and his needs are well anticipated. In 1935, I went to Indiana two days ahead of the Ohio State game—it was to be played at Indiana. The celebrated Bo McMillan was then the coach of the Hoosiers. He barred me from his practices, refused to show me film, he even refused to talk to me . . . he contended I was an Ohio State scout. I think in his heart he knew better—maybe—but that was the way the game was played in those days. McMillan put on a good two-day show for his local press anyhow . . . and lost the game.

Naturally, you listen to the coaches as they discuss their players. You note items of personal interest. You fix the "specialists" in your mind—the kickers, the receivers, the extra-point men—you concentrate on their numbers. As you watch the films, you observe if anyone is left-handed or left-footed.

What you want from each coach is his evaluation of the strengths of the two teams—is one basically a running team with only a fair passing attack? Is one a wide-open, free-wheeling squad? Is one more powerful on defense? Who is hurt and definitely out of the game? Is there such a stand-out star you must give him special attention, whether or not he has a good day?

I have written so far about college teams, which are by far more difficult to prepare for and to announce than are professional teams. The pros are very well-established, easy to identify, and each man in the pros is well-known. He has a history.

You must have two spotters for a college game, one for each team. It is advisable to have two spotters for a pro game, but you can do the pro game all by yourself. In the years when Connie Desmond and I announced the New York Giants' games Sunday after Sunday, we had one man, Harold Holtz, who always spotted the opposing team—and we never had need to use a spotter for New York.

The football assignment that never gets any easier is the one in college where you are doing *two* new teams *each* Saturday. (At least, this is the way it was when the radio networks were in flower.) This not only means the study and the memorization of two new squads each week, it also means the forgetting of all you learned and committed to memory the week before. In other words, when you see number twenty-seven today, you had better say that particular player's name—not the boy who wore the same number a week ago. . . . One needs a quick memory—and an efficient memory eraser.

Spotters' boards, game statistics, scores of other games, weather factors, binoculars, half-time coverage, band pickups—all of these are working details that each announcer will handle in his own fashion. Each announcer swears he has the best system of spotting charts, the very best . . . if his system functions well for him, then it is the best.

However, I would like to summarize the coverage today, and make a few points based upon being a viewer-listener as well as a play-by-play announcer going back to the University of Florida games in 1930. And what I set down now stems mainly from being helpless on the looking side of the television picture or on the hearing side of the radio set.

The business has so drastically changed, it has in fact become such a high-priced, complicated business, there will never be another McNamee or Husing or Munday. Today, there are too many interruptions—commercials, plugs, and promotional announcements—for the announcer to have time to be a personality. Also, the backup announcer, the former star player or the former coach, is breathing down the play-by-play announcer's neck while waiting to grab the microphone.

In the last several seasons, I've concluded that there was, at times, much more of a contest in the announcer's booth between the two announcers than there was on the field itself.

However, the only way there can be any sense or balance for the listener-viewer is for the play-by-play man to be the boss. He must lead the way. He must set . . . he must control . . . the pattern. The "expert" should not come on mike after every play. He should come on only when there is a genuine need for him to comment. The way it is today, football announcing sounds like an unrehearsed Punch and Judy Show, or like Amos 'n Andy ad libbing. Curt Gowdy and Paul Christman, before Christman quit the team, were by far the outstanding pair on television football—Gowdy ran the show and Christman made it his business to fit into the show.

The fellow looking in can see the obvious for himself. It irritates him like fleas on a dog to have two faceless voices accentuating the simple positive. For the radio listener, a little quiet is needed here and there to let him mentally visualize the game. For either radio or television, the guy on the receiving end doesn't want the "experts" *guessing* what is coming next—he wants to know only what happens, when it happens . . . and if it has some bearing, then why it happened.

In essence, the two-man team of nonstop broadcasting has shut out the imagination of the audience, has taken away any possible participation from the listener. The force-feeding of inane details quickly becomes unpalatable.

The great danger of football broadcasting, especially in television, is that of mechanical boredom. The play-by-play man should be freed to paint the picture in a series of headlines. The "expert" should study the defensive play, for example, and from time to time present an Eric Severeid commentary . . . remember—Eric, as good as he is on the Walter Cronkite CBS News, only speaks once in a half-hour program, and then only very briefly.

VOCAL CORDS

Mel Allen and I did the play-by-play of the 1942 World Series. In the fifth game, Whitey Kurowski of St. Louis hit a home run into the stands at Yankee Stadium that decided the game and ended the Series for that year. It was a big hit. I had the mike when Whitey lofted it toward left field, and my voice rose and went into the stands with the ball . . . "It's a home run!"

Several weeks afterward, the advertising manager for the Gillette Safety Razor Co., Craig Smith, told me of an irate letter he got from a listener in St. Louis. Gillette sponsored the broadcast. The fan wrote: "It was obvious to the listeners in the Midwest that Red Barber, an eastern announcer, was deeply upset when the Cardinals went ahead on Kurowski's home run, you could hear it in his voice."

Smith gave me this letter to needle me. He should have known better. My throat was in such bad shape that I'd asked him just the day before that game to take me off the broadcast.

But the fan was right in what he heard—something had happened to my voice. He heard a pair of vocal cords crack—and an announcer's heart break at the same time. The heartbreak was for the guy whose meal ticket was those same busted vocal chords.

Mel Allen was genuinely sympathetic. And he found out what a hazard it is to make a public living with just a set of vocal cords—he found it out twenty years later on the World Series when he had to give up the mike, his voice completely gone.

This thing in 1942 that nearly put me out of the radio business for keeps was the only time I ever had serious throat trouble. I learned something from it, and I've tried to pass it on since then to fellow announcers with throat trouble.

The Brooklyn Dodgers had won a bitter pennant race with St. Louis in 1941. The Dodgers were the favorites of the whole country. That was baseball excitement as high as it could get.

In 1942, it looked like Brooklyn again, until the last month. The Dodgers played good ball under Leo Durocher, but the young Cardinals under Billy Southworth caught fire, and here they came down the stretch . . . the two teams . . . neck and neck.

St. Louis caught Brooklyn, then got ahead. The Dodgers won their last eight games, but failed to gain an inch. Every pitch, every inning, every game those last two weeks was vitally critical. The Brooklyn fans were roaring day and night; the St. Louis fans were loudly confident.

Late that summer WHN, the radio station that carried the Dodger games, conceived and pioneered the War Bond Radio-Telephone sale. It went over with a bang, a big bang. The Treasury Department in Washington wanted to know how we did it. I was tapped to go down and spend the day in Washington talking about the WHN technique and pattern. The only off-day of that pennant stretch I spent in Washington, talking all day long to first one official, then another. After all, a war was going on.

My throat was going bad, and I was puzzled about it, but I did nothing. I didn't know a throat doctor, and in my youthfulness, I figured that tomorrow I'd wake up and it would be all right again. But that one day of steady talking in Washington did it. I came home hoarse and straining. I knew I should rest, but those daily Brooklyn games were too big . . . or so I thought.

I thought I was too important to stay off the air a few days. I thought if I rested people would say "I couldn't take it," especially with the Dodgers falling behind the Cardinals. I thought the throat would get better . . . I don't know what all I thought, but I found out later I hadn't thought it right.

So I stayed on, inning after inning, the Dodgers straining and losing, right through the last game of the season. There were two off days before the Series began in St. Louis on Wednesday. I was sure those two days of rest would fix me up.

But the voice was bad in St. Louis—still bad when we got

back to New York. I sucked lemons, gargled everything on the market, melted a thousand lozenges in my mouth. Before the third game, I went to see the Cardinals' trainer, Doc Weaver, and he gave me a massage treatment and put an ice bag on my throat for half an hour . . . but nothing helped.

I was now very deep into the cycle of weak vocal cords—the harder I tried to speak, the weaker they got, the more frantic I got, and the harder I tried . . . and around and around and around. The night before the fifth game, I was humbled enough to ask Craig Smith to take me off the Series broadcast. He wouldn't. I rode to the Stadium for the fifth game (which proved the final one, thanks in large measure to Kurowski's home run) with Mel Allen in his car. He was sorry for me, but there wasn't much for him to say, and by then I couldn't say much in return.

The weather for that game was gray, overcast, foggy. It was gloomy inside the triple-decked Stadium up in the Bronx. My throat hurt, my heart hurt. I could barely croak, each word coming slowly, painfully, grindingly.

I went through the pregame routine of preparation: checked the two batting orders, asked who would be in the bullpens, and as in a nightmare, I went up to the broadcasting booth. How I managed to announce, word after word, I'll never know. I kept thinking, kept knowing, each word would be the last one I would be able to say. . . . Broadcasting is a joy when you face the mike, let your eyes do the work for you, and your words pour forth without your even thinking of them. Once you have to measure your every word, your ad-lib flow breaks down, but when you also dread every next word, you are doomed.

Whitey Kurowski swung and met the ball. Into the mists of the distant left-field stands went the little white dot. Somehow my words went with it. Somehow I finished the game and left the Stadium. But I was finished.

That weekend I was scheduled to do a football game at Princeton for Les Quailey. There was no chance. I asked my wife to telephone him, and he understood. When I had forced those vocal cords to say, "HOME RUN," I cracked them. I didn't know then what I'd done, but afterward when I tried to talk, nothing but awful sounds came out.

I stayed home a couple of days, heartsick, afraid. I didn't know a doctor I could trust. I was in trouble, serious trouble, and I didn't know how to get out of it. My radio career was done. I'd come so far and had so far to go, but I wasn't going to go any further. The end of the line.

Slowly the mental wheels began to turn. I knew I needed the best specialist I could get. But who was he? And where? And who could tell me his name?

Suddenly I thought, "Where are the most valuable vocal cords in the world?"

And the answer came, "At *The Met*."

I didn't know Edward Johnson, general manager of the Metropolitan Opera Company, but when he arrived at his office the next morning, I was waiting. He saw me promptly. When I came into his office, he was at his desk, his silver hair gleaming. His face was clean and kind. There must have been two hundred pictures of great singers all around the room.

"Mr. Johnson," I croaked, "I'm in trouble."

"Yes," he said, "I can hear it."

"Mr. Johnson, my vocal cords are just as valuable to me as any opera singer's are to him . . . I don't know a doctor."

That's all I said until I managed later to say "Thanks—and good-bye."

He looked at me steadily for a moment. Then he began, "You know The Met isn't in the business of recommending physicians . . . we can't be."

My face must have dropped a foot. He reached into a desk drawer, got out a small pad, and started to write. I just sat there, empty. He smiled, and said:

"Here are two names I've written . . . it just happens both of them are doctors . . . both have done excellent work here.

I am not recommending either one of them, but if you happen to go to the first name I've written, or the second, you might get some help."

My wife was waiting outside, and we went straight to Dr. William F. Mayer-Herrmann. Did you ever see that huge oil painting in the Museum of Modern Art in New York of a doctor in his white coat with a light reflector on his forehead? That is the doctor. It was painted in Vienna before he had to leave, just ahead of Hitler.

He was a big man, a fat man. He was an excellent throat specialist. He took care of most of the big voices. He was also a kind man.

He examined me, sent for my wife, and told me the best news and prescribed the best medicine I ever got:

"You will talk again . . . it will take time . . . you have cracked your vocal cords and they have blood in them . . . but you'll talk again . . . but you must do exactly what I tell you to do."

He ordered me not to say a word for seven days and nights . . . complete silence, complete rest. I was to keep a pad and pencil and write what I had to say. It was funny at times, as a lot of strangers took me for deaf and dumb and would write back to me or do charades.

The completely silent week passed. Then Dr. Mayer-Herrmann told me to speak, and I spoke . . . not the full, strong sound again, but a good sound . . . it was months before real strength came back.

He used some medication and a few localized heat treatments. But most important he used psychology, and he prescribed rest—complete silence, complete rest, coupled with a quiet mind. When he first said that I would be all right again, I was halfway healed. Fear is a terrible poison, especially for human vocal cords.

This good man died suddenly. Dr. Stuart Craig was next recommended. We became fast friends. He carried me through any further trouble, and his main strength was the same as

Dr. Mayer-Herrmann's—psychology. Stuart always told me I'd be able to do what I had to do next . . . World Series, football, day-to-day usage . . . confidence is basic medicine.

Dr. Craig has a blue-stocking list of patients. You'd go to his office and see Governor Averill Harriman, Ethel Merman, Mary Martin.

Jackie Gleason was headlining at the Palace, and his voice was going down fast. It looked like he was going to have to quit . . . not finish the engagement. The harder Jackie tried to speak the less voice he had.

Gleason's agent called my agent, Bill McCaffrey, and asked for a doctor. Bill called Mary Martin, and she said Stuart Craig. I said Craig. McCaffrey called Dr. Craig and asked him to go to the Palace and see Gleason between shows.

Jackie is a big man, and he throws his weight around. He is the boss. He has to be the boss no matter who else is in the group. And Jackie was in a foul mood when Dr. Craig entered his dressing room.

Dr. Craig is small in stature. He has penetrating brown eyes and white hair. He wears loafers for shoes, and when he walked in with his black bag, he looked like a little, old man . . . and there towered the raging, frightened Gleason.

Maybe you saw the *Look* article on Jackie, with pictures, about the time he played the Palace . . . maybe you recall seeing a photo of Jackie with his mouth wide open and a doctor swabbing his throat. You only saw the back of the doctor . . . that was Dr. Craig at work.

McCaffrey told me later what Gleason's agent told him:

"Dr. Craig said, 'Sit down, Jackie,' and the way he said it, Jackie sat down. The little, old man examined him, talked to him, stayed with him, ordered him around, and got him through the week . . . in fact, his voice improved as he worked."

McCaffrey said Dr. Craig "fixed" Jackie . . . put those brown eyes on him . . . hypnotized him.

Late in the summer of 1963, Mel Allen's voice started coming apart at Yankee Stadium. His voice was breaking up, and the vicious cycle of fear-pressure-weakness-ego had him in its grip. He was getting into deeper trouble with each passing day. His doctor tried to get him to rest, but Mel wouldn't. I tried to talk to him, but I suppose because I was a fellow-announcer for the Yankees I was suspect.

He wouldn't lay off and take a complete rest, physical and mental. I guess he couldn't. Joe Ripley, of the advertising agency, advised and begged him to rest every day and several times absolutely made him get off the mike for the rest of that one game—then—Mel would sit in the back of the booth and jabber at the engineers and cameramen, at anybody. He wouldn't stop talking. He was wild.

My wife and I parked at the Stadium before the first game of the World Series, and standing right there in the parking lot was Allen, surrounded by a group of fans, arguing and talking baseball. I looked at Lylah, and she looked at me, and we went on.

It was a shattering thing when Mel was taken off the air in the closing innings of the broadcast of that same World Series—and Vince Scully had to come back and take his place.

Let me sum up with this advice for anyone in broadcasting. Don't hurt your vocal cords. Never raise your voice. Never yell. When you are broadcasting, talk in a natural range, well under your full strength. When the crowd yells, shut up . . . let the roar of the crowd go into the microphone . . . and when it subsides, then, and only then, resume speaking. You can't talk over the roar of a crowd, but by trying to do it, you can hurt your voice.

The two best friends a voice can have are rest and peace of mind. If you have a doubleheader the next day, get a long night's sleep. When your throat starts kicking up (and if you get into announcing or singing, some day your throat is going to start kicking up), take all the rest your doctor tells you to take . . . and then add two more days on your own.

Don't let yourself get laryngitis. At the first sign of throat weakness, instead of trying to push your voice, ease it off, speak softer, lower, and as soon as possible, stop speaking. Silence.

Dr. Craig pointed out once that the telephone is one of the worst enemies of vocal cords. Stay off the phone when you are having throat trouble . . . you might not realize it, but there is always a nervous strain about talking on the phone.

Cigarette smoking? Any doctor will tell you that any kind of smoke is an irritant. I smoked for years, and now I haven't smoked for years. When I smoked, I had extra congestion in my throat, nose, and chest. Now that I don't smoke, I've never had clearer cords.

The fewer medications you put into your nose and throat the better you'll be. Most medicated lozenges add extra irritation just at the time your throat needs to be soothed. The only lozenge Dr. Craig let me use was Allenbury's—which is flavored glycerine . . . no medication, just a lubricant. Soothing.

The best gargle is the one your great-grandmother used— hot salt water. It's cheap and handy and doesn't come from the drug store, so it's not popular anymore. I've never seen a hot salt water gargle advertised on television, so what chance has it today? But it's still the best one.

Don't drink milk for two hours before you go on a microphone. Milk is a coagulant. Chocolate is, too. So is gravy. Drink a cup of hot tea with a squeeze of lemon before you go to the booth. When you are on the air, drink only plain water that is not too cold.

A lot of vocal-cord trouble begins with a head cold. I spent a fortune trying to find something that would cure, or at least shorten, a head cold. A friend of mine did come up with one surefire prescription—"a pair of clean sheets." Rest.

So—Dr. Red Barber prescribes for the common cold: some books you've wanted to read, some liquids to drink, somebody to wait on you, a radio or television, no telephone, and, a pair of clean sheets.

The world will wait for you, my dear important young friend. But you can't get a new pair of vocal cords from Sears Roebuck.

INTERVIEWING

There is no way a man can work in the field of sports reporting without mastering to some degree the art of interviewing. When you go into the baseball dugout to ask the manager what is his batting order, what is the news of the day with the ball club, why he did a certain thing in yesterday's game, that is interviewing. You must get the manager to talk.

When you are preparing for a football game you must get the coach to talk. If you wish to get information from a player, you must get the player to talk. The more you think of it, the fundamental of all sports reporting is interviewing. Red Smith, my nomination for the very best sports columnist, says the basic thing of writing a column, day in and day out, is summed up in two words: "Be there." Naturally, you must go to the events. But when you get there, then in some form or fashion, you must interview. You see the actual event for yourself . . . yes . . . but before the event, and certainly after the event, there are things to know, and to know them, you must get somebody to tell you. This is interviewing.

Good listening is good interviewing. A good reputation for writing or broadcasting the truth is also a big help. Good manners are valuable. It is an asset when a manager is glad to see you come into his dugout—he moves over and invites you to sit beside him, he is ready to be interviewed. For hard news, you will often have to conduct an interview of an important person over the telephone . . . and then *who* you are, *how* you report, makes or breaks your interview.

These days my television interviewing is not as intensive as it once was. However, I am doing more interviewing for radio than I ever did . . . some live but more and more on tape for future broadcasts. Now that I am writing a weekly column, the technique of interviewing is even more important to me. I just don't go anywhere without a portable, battery-operated tape recorder. You never know who you'll meet.

In 1962, I was doing a great deal of live, on-the-air television interviewing at Yankee Stadium. Dick Tobin at *Saturday*

Review asked me to do a piece for him on the subject, and here are some thoughts from it:

> . . . What you *don't* ask is more important than what you *do*. Ask a loaded question, a touchy question, and your interview is in serious trouble. . . .
>
> I want the player or the manager or the coach to be himself. Should a player just have taken infield practice, I encourage him to keep his towel and rub the sweat away as the interview progresses. I like the players to hold something in their hands—caps, gloves, or, for pitchers, the ball itself. I don't want them to be conscious of the camera. I don't look at the camera, I look at them. Then they look back at me. A human being likes to stick his toe into water that isn't cold. I always start with a pleasantry. Maybe the guest was written up in a column that day. I either refer to it or, better still, show it to him on camera. Perhaps he recently pitched a whale of a game. Maybe he is leading the league in hitting, or in home runs. He may have broken up the game the night before. Any player in the big leagues has positive facets, or he wouldn't be there. My job is to single out one or two.
>
> I not only want the guest to be at home, to know he is not going to be asked a wrong question, but also to *talk*—about himself, his team, the pennant race, how lively the ball is, how tough it is to earn a living as a pitcher . . . whether baseball is a good business for a young man, what managing is, how you throw a knuckleball.
>
> I will have several questions in my mind. I believe it is far better to have no notes, no papers in my hand. After we have "how-de-dood," just the same as if I'd met the fellow on the street, we get into the first topic. Then, as he talks, I listen to

him, listen to what he is saying. That is why I have him there, for him to talk. As he talks he may well branch off into another area that is much more interesting than what I had thought about. So I go along with him. *Any* person can talk about what he knows, and about what he is interested in. I asked Willie Mays one night on an NBC interview that used to follow the fights if he spent much time in the batting cage. I asked him this as the first question, just to start things smoothly. All players, even pitchers, love to hit. They won't give their mothers a swing in batting practice. I counted on Mays smiling and allowing as how he certainly did, and that this would break the ice and get us going. Instead he replied to the effect that he hit well, so he didn't fool around the batting cage much, but spent his time working on what he didn't do "good." Well, we went on from there, for suddenly he had put his finger on one reason he is a star—he works on what, as he put it, "I don't do good." Let me say that I don't know today what Willie doesn't do very well, but that remark opened up a fine interview.

Today we have varied camera techniques, we have videotape, we have hand mikes and chest mikes, we have dugouts and we have studios, we have still pictures and motion pictures. But the fundamental ingredient is the guest *talking*. He is the show, and the interviewer must never forget it. Techniques are routine. Certain rules of thumb pertain: never ask a pitcher who is starting the game to be your guest that day; one, he is warming up and should be left alone, and two, you don't want it on his mind or yours that he has a TV routine after the game. And further, suppose he gets knocked out in the third inning? Don't ask managers, unless you know them very, very well—to go on after a game—something drastic may happen in the ninth inning. Ask them for before the game, when they don't know how the day will turn out. The manager is always a pre-game optimist. Don't have a player on when he should be taking infield or outfield—instead, visit with a pitcher who is not to start, or a coach, until the regular can come in on his accustomed schedule. This is merely respect for, or concern for, a working man's problems. . . .

The case of the young player you know little or nothing about is not too tough. Find out on the air what you do not know and wish to know— where he's from, how he got started in baseball, where he has played. Listen to him as he talks and you'll know whether to go on further with him, or thank him and turn to the next guest. In the case of the player you know who simply can't talk too freely, put him on with a player he likes so he doesn't have to carry the full load.

Once a person has agreed to be interviewed, the rest of the job belongs to the interviewer—his the researching, his the generating of confidence that all will go well and smoothly, his the listening to his guest, his the leading of the way, his the concern for his guest. . . . *Agape.*

SCORING

There is no way to write a complete book on the techniques of broadcasting, any more than there is a way to detail all the assignments a newspaper writer has to perform. To a beginner there must seem so many things to learn, most of them small things, and yet every one of them is important.

Learning how to do the mechanical routines of broadcasting comes to you as you work in the booth, and soon becomes habit. One learns from doing, and also by observing professionals at their work.

You cannot announce baseball, you cannot write baseball, you cannot report baseball in any fashion unless you score it. Human memory is fallible. The announcer must not attempt to rely upon his memory whenever he can have a written record. Memory is like love—sometimes wonderful, often dangerous.

Nor do I believe a fan can fully enjoy the game he sees unless he scores it in some fashion. The only time my wife doesn't score is when we sit together, and she gets me to score for both of us. Burt Shotton, when he managed the Brooklyn Dodgers, always kept score in the dugout for himself. Mrs. Johnny Keane scored every game her husband managed, and thus she was always ready with the complete record whenever John wanted it.

So here is a chapter on scoring. It is so basic, so easy. It is a plus for those who only see a game on television. Anyone who ever scores just one game will keep score from then on.

Baseball scoring is merely baseball shorthand. There is no law anywhere that says you must score this way, or you must score that way. The main thing is to be able to read what you have put together—read it the next minute, the next day, the next month, even years later.

Scoring should be utter simplicity. The game is going on, the scorer must wait until the play is completed, then quickly write down the play and be ready to observe the next one.

Should scoring be so complicated that it interferes with the game, then your system is wrong from every standpoint.

There are nine positions on the field. Most writers and broadcasters number these positions starting with the pitcher, then the catcher, the first baseman, and so on, putting the shortstop after the third baseman, then left, center, and finally right field:

Pitcher	1
Catcher	2
First	3
Second	4
Third	5
Short	6
Left	7
Center	8
Right	9

The major reason for using this set of numbers applies only to the working press and radio-television—we in the business need from time to time to look into each other's scorebook . . . you have had to leave for an inning, and you must get a fill-in. A glance, and you read it . . . for you fans who resent being regimented, please feel free to use any numbering your little heart dictates. When I came up to Cincinnati, there was an established writer, a crackajack, named Tom Swope, who was so perverse he deliberately scored in something I think was Ohio River Sanskrit in order that not even his wife could read his book . . . much less a radio fellow.

I streamlined my scoring because my bookkeeping time as a play-by-play announcer was so short. I eliminated even a dash between numbers, such as an out from second to first 4 3 rather than the neater appearing 4–3.

As you will see, I use one dash – for a single, and I score the field the single went to. A single to left would be –7. Two dashes for a double ⁼7, three for a triple ≡7, and four for a home run ≣7.

For an error I use the letter E with the fielder's number ... an error by the shortstop is E6.

K is the accepted symbol for a strikeout. I add a small c if the third strike is called (K^c).

W is the code for a walk. The (W) is ringed if the walk is intentional. B is for a balk. WP stands for a wild pitch. PB for a passed ball. SB for a stolen base. HP for a batter hit by a pitch. SH for a sacrifice. FC for fielder's choice. FO— which is a type of fielder's choice—for a force-out. TI means taking an extra base on the outfielder's throw-in. When a batter fouls out, I mark the number, plus the letter, so that a foul to third would be 5F. L means the batter hit a line drive. RBI a run batted in. AB at bat.

SFO means sacrifice force-out, the batter tried to sacrifice, but instead forced out the man he was trying to advance. This is scoring in sharp detail, but why else score?

I ring the inning number (7) at the top of the column if a run or runs score in that half-inning. Should a threat occur, I pencil an X by the inning number ... a double-barreled threat, but no runs, then I use two Xs. Also, and this is vital, I write on the edge of the score sheet, either at the top of the inning or on the side of the sheet, any notations I think should be recorded.

I designed the score sheet I used as a play-by-play announcer. I have no patent on it, and anyone is free to copy it. I incorporated the pitcher's balance at the bottom of the sheet, which is vital in my work ... you use tallies as each hit, run, walk, wild pitch, strike out occurs ... so whenever you look at it, it is up to date.

Further, on this sheet you have a three-way check system of hits and runs ... one, at the end of the inning, two, over at the right-hand set of totals, and three, in the pitcher's balance box. You should check all three ways frequently, and if you find your figures are off, this should alert you to search for the discrepancy.

What does the ER stand for in the pitcher's balance?

Earned runs—very vital to a pitcher, and to his wife and children. An earned run, as you know, is a run the pitcher is technically responsible for.

What do you do when extra innings come along? Use a fresh score sheet, and merely pencil in a 1 before the already printed number of the innings . . . thus inning 1 on the new sheet becomes inning 11.

The WP penciled alongside a pitcher's name means Winning Pitcher . . . the LP alongside means the saddest words of tongue or pen for a man who makes his living trying to throw baseballs past hitters . . . Losing Pitcher.

You can have score sheets printed. Or you can draw them up yourself. Or you can buy a scorebook in a sporting-goods store. Or you can forget the whole thing, unless you are going to broadcast a ball game—then you have no choice.

I have found that common, everyday wooden pencils are the best. I use number two pencils, and I have a half-dozen freshly sharpened ones at hand for each game. You haven't time to sharpen a pencil when it breaks, or dulls, or falls on the floor under your chair. And you can erase a pencil mark— which is why pen and ink do not work. You are bound to make some mistakes that need erasing.

But let's say you are not going to make any mistakes. Let's say you are going to be so good you won't have to erase anything. I still wouldn't advise a pen. The official scorer may change his mind an inning later and rule what once was a hit, is now an error. It's not your mistake, but an eraser is plainly indicated.

Shakespeare said, "The play's the thing." That's right, the play is the thing. But just what was the play? Who made it? In what inning did it happen? That's when "Scoring is the thing."

The Mets, in only their eighth year of life, became the bull-of-the-woods the afternoon of October 16, 1969 . . . at Shea Stadium, in a little town called New York. That afternoon The Amazing Mets on the soil of Long Island defeated the tough Baltimore Orioles 5 to 3, to win the fourth game of the five they played in the World Series. Some fifty-seven thousand people saw it from the grand stands, and heavens knows how many million saw it on television. I was looking at the tube, and of course, I was scoring. Here are my score sheets. If I want to keep the two sheets and look at them ten years from now, twenty years from now, I can see then how the Mets and the Orioles played that fateful game on that hysterical October afternoon, just east of the East River . . . the river MacPhail didn't wish to get blasted into. (And wasn't.)

Now that you have glanced over my shoulder, let's take them up in a little more detail. Everything pertinent that happened in that game is noted on those two sheets . . . the date, the place, the game number, the weather, the crowd, the umpires, that Pearl Bailey sang the national anthem, that Joe DiMaggio threw out the first ball, that after the game Don Clendenon of the Mets was voted the Outstanding Player of the Series by the press.

The Orioles went down in order their first at bats. The Mets had a threat going in their half: Agee was walked by McNally, stole second base (the throw was dropped) as Harrelson took a third strike, and went to third as Jones lifted a fly to right. McNally, with first and second bases open and a hot hitter, Clendenon, at bat, pitched carefully and walked him . . . he meant to walk him rather than give him a good pitch to hit. Had McNally given Clendenon a deliberate base-on-balls the W would be ringed Ⓦ. McNally then pitched to Swoboda, with two men on, and got out of the threat by striking him out.

Baltimore broke loose against Koosman in the third inning. Belanger singled to right, and pitcher McNally hit a home run to left, two runs were in. Frank Robinson, with two out, hit his home run over the fence in left center . . . Baltimore caused no further trouble, as a glace at the score sheet for the Orioles shows . . . and shows very starkly. Koosman settled right down, and he was the master the rest of the afternoon.

In the top of the sixth, there is this ring ○ at the top of

WORLD SERIES #5
THURS-OCT 16-1969
SHEA STADIUM, N.Y.

Clear -Cool- Windy 1ST to 3rd   O ROBINSON-WEAVER
CLAIMED HIT BY PITCH
9 DIMURO NO

ANTHEM-PEARL BAILEY   FIRST BALL-JOE DI MAGGIO

ORIOLES 1-3	Pos	1	2	3	4	5	6	7	8	9	10	AB	R	H	RBI	E
BUFORD	7	63		63		9			8							
BLAIR	8	8	K			8		63							
F. ROBINSON	9	9	78°			Kᶜ			W ⁴⁄₀			1	1	1		
SALMON 739 POWELL	3ᵗ	7	K		-7			FO				1		1	
B. ROBINSON	5	63		8	7			9				1			
JOHNSON	4	-7³⁴	13			9ᶠ	7					1			
ETCHEBARREN	2	FO	43		K										
BELANGER	6		-9°	9		63					1	1			
WATT 178 McNALLY	1		7°	K			3				1	1	11	1	
Totals			1 3/3			1					3	5		2	

Pitcher	Ing	R	ER	Hits	BB	WP	HB	SO	Pitcher	Ing	R	ER	Hits	BB	WP	HB	SO
KOOSMAN 17-9	1-0	111	111	ЖН	1			ЖН									

x 57,000   SB THROW DROPPED @ 2nd

UMPIRES-DIMURO-WEYER-SOAR-SECONY
LF NAPP - RF CRAWFORD
HP SHOE POLISH DIMURO
WATTS FAILED TO COVER

CLENDENON VOTED OUTSTANDING PLAYER OF SERIES

METS 3-1	Pos	1	2	3	4	5	6	7	8	9	10	AB	R	H	RBI	E
AGEE	1	W SB 9 K	8		B-J		9						1			
HARRELSON	6	Kᶜ	K		8		5L									
JONES	7	9	3			HP°		8°			11	1			
CLENDENON	3	W		Kᶜ	UD #3 7°³		53				1	1	11		
SWOBODA	9	K		M ᵗ₆	4		E1-E3 7°				1	11	1		
CHARLES	5		53	2F	53		7								
GROTE	2		8	FO	67		E3-E1								
WEIS	4		6L		53		7°	Kᶜ			1	1	1		
KOOSMAN	1			=5	K		K					1			
Totals				1		2	1	2/2			5	7		0	

Pitcher	Ing	R	ER	Hits	BB	WP	HB	SO	Pitcher	Ing	R	ER	Hits	BB	WP	HB	SO
McNALLY	0-1	7	111	111	ЖН	11			ЖН								
WATT	5-2	1	11	1	11				1								

Ⓛ

the box for Frank Robinson—and also penciled above the inning are the words, "O Robinson-Weaver claimed hit by pitch DiMuro no." Robinson claimed he was struck by an inside pitch and should be awarded first base. Plate umpire DiMuro said the ball had hit the bat first, and that it was only a foul strike, and the batter was not entitled to first base. Manager Weaver came out and argued. The argument went on for some length, but the Orioles lost it. Then Robinson went to the dugout, went out of sight under the stands, and the game was held up several minutes waiting for him to come back. Finally, he angrily returned and resumed batting, and was called out on strikes. (Robinson is still convinced the umpire was wrong, but the record shows and will always show that Robinson struck out.)

A quick look at the Mets' sheet shows they didn't give McNally any trouble until the last of that turbulent sixth inning. Plate umpire DiMuro had himself an inning. The HP by Jones's name in the sixth has a note above the inning, "Shoe polish DiMuro." Jones skipped rope on a low pitch around his feet, and DiMuro said it was a ball. Jones claimed it had hit him on the foot, and that he was entitled to first base. DiMuro said no. The ball was retrieved and taken to Manager Gil Hodges of the Mets, who brought it to the plate and showed DiMuro a black spot on the ball, which the Mets claimed was shoe polish, and, therefore, the ball must have hit Jones on his foot, gotten smudged with shoe polish . . . and in the face of this evidence, the plate umpire changed his decision and awarded the batter first base. (This made four plate umpiring decisions the Orioles lost in the last two games.) Now—Jones was put on first base, and look at your score sheet . . . look at it. Clendenon hit a home run, and in a trice, what was 3–0 Baltimore was suddenly 3–2 Baltimore, and it was another ball of wax . . . a one-run game, a wild crowd, all the adrenalin the Amazing Mets needed to charge on and on and on. In the seventh, Weis homered and the matter was 3–3.

Watts relieved McNally and faced Jones to start the last of

the eighth. Note: penciled in above McNally is "Watts 1 7 8"—meaning 1 he is the pitcher, 7 is the batter he will face first in 8, the inning he begins pitching. Watts, in taking over a tied game, became the pitcher of record . . . to win it or lose it. He quickly lost it. And there it is for all to be looked at: Jones, a double to center . . . Swoboda, a double to left, which scored Jones with the actual winning run. The roof fell in when Grote was safe on an error at first (note above the inning, "Watts failed to cover") and went to second on Watts's error on the throw from the first baseman. These two errors let Swoboda score an extra and final run.

These score sheets of that game have a meaning to anybody who cares to look at them, study them, use them to stimulate the imagination of the event and of its component plays and personnel. The working broadcaster is scoring as the game is played; he must constantly refer, batter by batter, inning by inning, to whatever has gone before. And the broadcaster must be correct. Must be.

Memory cannot be relied upon, day after day, game after game, batter after batter. I remember a play, a person, an outstanding game in its overall impact—but not anything like the mass of details the score sheets preserve. Major league managers have great recall. Some of them have close to total recall. Casey Stengel remembers what time it was in Kankakee, Illinois, when he hit a 3–2 pitch off Sam Jones in 1897 . . . and which side of pitcher Jones's nose had a small, dark mole . . . and Stengel knows it was a mole and not a wart . . . and he can reel off the batting order of both those teams for that Tuesday afternoon . . . and he knows it was Tuesday because of all the things he remembers that happened on Monday.

But for broadcasters who don't have that amount of total recall, I do recommend keeping a scorebook . . . and keeping it very carefully.

I remember a triple play once that happened when that arch-conservative Deacon Bill McKechnie was managing Cincinnati. It was a spring game against Boston. The Reds had men at first and at third . . . nobody out. McKechnie himself was coaching at third base, and what happened nearly killed him—exhibition game or not. He watched it happen . . . and he couldn't prevent it.

The batter grounded to third, the runner at third started home and the throw to the plate was well ahead of him. He was caught in a run-up. He ran back and forth, many players handled the ball, and finally he was tagged out.

The runner at first had by now somehow gotten hung up between second and third, so the Braves started running him down, with many more throws involving many more players. Finally, they tagged him out.

The batter was now seen to be stranded halfway between first and second, so they went to work on him. Finally, he was tagged out. Triple play. And the scoring looked something like this:

TP 5 2 6 2 5 1 7 4 7 8 5 4 6 4 3 4 9 6 3 X

All nine men on the defensive team handled the ball at least once—the *only* time I recall seeing an entire ball club involved in one sequence.

Happy scoring, amigos.

SEVEN:
FOCUS 3

It was all evolving into a new life. I had not the sense to quit the Yankee job. It paid fifty thousand dollars a season. I thought the job was important, that I was therefore important, and I wanted two more years. Burke and the Yankees had not meant to do so, but they had done me the greatest service possible. They were better friends to me than I was to myself.

How long, how many years, does it take to learn to tell a ball from a strike, especially when the plate umpire announces the difference? You get locked into a pattern—you resemble nothing so much as a squirrel in a revolving-wheel cage—you go on from spring training to World Series to spring training. You stop thinking. You don't realize you have stopped thinking—you are too vain about getting to the ball park two hours before each game, of going to clubhouse and dugout and broadcasting booth, and then saying to yourself you are never late for an assignment . . . that you are always prepared for it. You allow yourself to think people need you, depend upon you. You think you are the best in your business and therefore you are surrounded by understanding respect. You lose your creative individuality because you are going through the same paces, doing over and over again what you do by habit. There is no new work to be done, but you don't know it. There is security inside a cocoon, but there is also darkness.

Listen—

When Michael Burke said coolly, "We have decided not to seek to renew your contract," he gave me back my life. He gave me a new taste for life, he lifted my horizons, he gave me my home, and he gave me a return to pure broadcasting with more appreciation of the words from which we fashion our human communication.

Listen—

Instead of two more years of following a ball club from coast to coast . . . hotels, night planes, busses, snacks, loneliness . . . there is now the world of the printed page: the weekly column in the *Miami Herald,* syndicated by Columbia Features . . . articles for *Reader's Digest* . . . a book called *Walk In The Spirit,* which is a distillation of some wonderful men and what they believed . . . this book, *The Broadcasters,* about some other men and their profession, some of whom achieved greatness, many of whom have been forgotten . . . and there are other books coming.

Listen—

March 4, 1930 . . . my first job in broadcasting . . . a small university station called WRUF. As I sit here today, that station is still broadcasting, and on March 4, 1970—for the fifteenth time—one of the student broadcasters was given one hundred dollars and an engraved silver bowl in my name. The man who gave me that first job, Major Garland W. Powell, helped me set up the award in 1955, a few years before he died. Here is part of the letter that I sent him that first year:

> . . . I do appreciate your willingness to establish a committee at both WRUF and the University, to

designate for me an annual recipient, commencing March 4, 1955 to receive the Red Barber award. This award will be for $100.00 each year as long as I am able to continue it.

This award is to fall should WRUF discontinue to use student broadcasters. It is up to you and your associates to form whatever type of committee you desire. My wish is that each *March 4* a student announcer at WRUF be chosen for the award on the basis of *Industry, Improvement, Initiative, and Integrity*. The award is *not* to be given on the basis of natural talent, unless the student announcer has so used his natural talents as to qualify.

Some people are born with excellent voices. Some are born wtih fine appearances. Some seem to be born with an indefinable sense of timing. Some seem to be born with photographic vision. However, I believe that nothing takes the place of intensive preparation. . . . I believe every successful sports broadcast is at least 75% preparation . . . and therefore I ask your committee to regard the candidates on the basis of their Industry.

Further, a person should not stay in the broadcasting business unless he continues to improve, and so I ask the consideration of Improvement.

Third, the successful broadcaster must be daring, he must not be bound completely in the chains of tradition. He must be creative and be willing to attempt new techniques and so develop his individual style, and this is why I include Initiative.

Fourth, a broadcaster cannot succeed and endure for any length of time unless he is a servant of Truth as best he sees it, and is not swayed by the people around him from the truth. And so I further request the yardstick of Integrity.

To sum up, if a young broadcaster has a reasonable natural talent and is willing to pay the price of hard work, continues to show improvement, is daring, and is a servant of the Truth, I predict a sound career for him.

I keenly remember and warmly appreciate the opportunity that you personally gave to me back in 1930, twenty-five years ago, and the opportunity presented by WRUF and by the University itself. I hope in this small way I may be able to show my appreciation and encourage some youngster who is just starting out. . . .

Sincerely,
Red
One of your boys

P.S.   One further request for your committee. Once a student announcer has won the award I prefer that he be ineligible for another one.

P.S.II This is not limited to sports broadcasters—it is to include *all* student broadcasters—

Listen—

Winston Churchill always referred to himself "As a child of Parliament." I am a child of radio. I'm not mad at television—you work in television to make money. But radio is my leather. It is still the greatest communication medium for getting the word of one man to another in the quickest time and from the most inaccessible place. A television camera conked out on the moon—not radio.

Listen—

I started in radio. I have never been away from radio. I am now again in radio, where broadcasting is a joy. In 1968, WGBS put a broadcast line into my house, into the room I use for an office. That room has my working books in it . . . it has a desk, storage files . . . it has my typewriter . . . it has an amplifier . . . it has two microphones in it. One mike I use three times a day. The other is an old carbon mike that was at WRUF when I started there in 1930. The station then had just two of these mikes. I have one, the University museum has the other.

Listen—

I do a ninety-second highlighting of sports news five mornings a week at seven-ten . . . another such feature at eight-ten. Then for those five days I do a five-minute feature—anything I wish to do—at five-ten in the afternoon. That is a total of fifteen broadcasts a week. I get up at five-thirty in the morning, feed two cats, get the paper, check the station for later news, get up to the minute again, turn to the typewriter, time the material, and edit it down to fit. The material is mine to select —the words are mine to choose, to arrange—the ideas must be mine. There is no advertising agency to please. No sponsor to battle or to ask which cap I may wear.

Listen—

I am back in the fundamental work of radio. I am communicating with other human beings. It happens as fast as I speak.

Other DA CAPO titles of interest